Cecil Tudor Davis

The Monumental Brasses of Gloucestershire

Cecil Tudor Davis

The Monumental Brasses of Gloucestershire

ISBN/EAN: 9783743394223

Manufactured in Europe, USA, Canada, Australia, Japa

Cover: Foto ©ninafisch / pixelio.de

Manufactured and distributed by brebook publishing software (www.brebook.com)

Cecil Tudor Davis

The Monumental Brasses of Gloucestershire

THE MONUMENTAL BRASSES
OF
GLOUCESTERSHIRE.

BY
CECIL T. DAVIS,

Member of the Bristol and Gloucestershire Archæological Society.

London:
PHILLIMORE & Co., 36, ESSEX STREET, STRAND,
1899.

IN
MEMORY
OF
MY FATHER,
5th NOVEMBER, 1807.

PREFACE.

Scattered over the county of Gloucester, sometimes in out-of-the-way places, are still to be found a goodly number of those very interesting memorials called Monumental Brasses. These brasses are worthy of more than a passing notice, they furnish us with information most valuable to the historian, both general and local, and give many details of much importance to the herald, genealogist and antiquary. To the general reader they are equally interesting, since they are richly suggestive, and full of the touching pathos of the past. They clearly mark the successive steps of our nation's progress—they tell of those stern and terrible times of strife and glory through which England has passed — they bear silent witness to those grand and far-reaching changes which have made our country what it is—and they give an insight into the currents of thought and feeling which deeply moved our forefathers.

Gloucestershire contains more than eighty of these incised memorials, embracing a period of several centuries. In one place we have the valorous knight clad in glittering coat of steel—in another a tonsured ecclesiastic in vestments rich and elaborate—then the gentlewoman in the costume peculiar to her time—but whether knight, or priest, or lady fair, each is of importance in giving with remarkable fidelity a life-like picture of the military, sacerdotal, and domestic life of bygone times.

One cannot but deeply regret that these unobtrusive memorials have suffered much mutilation and spoliation at the hands of the thief and the religious fanatic, as well as from the culpable neglect of their lawful custodians. Many brasses, whose matrices alone are left to record the melancholy fact, are utterly lost and doubtless many more have perished of whose existence not a trace remains. One would fain hope that every particle still left us will be jealously guarded and saved from further harm by those to whom the care of them is entrusted. As works of art, many being of the finest execution and of great merit, they are deserving of careful preservation. They form an attractive class of engraved portraitures in metal. Among them will be found the quaint, the picturesque, the bold, the simple, the graceful and the magnificent; even to the casual observer they are each and all of them attractive.

Trusting to awaken interest in, and to draw attention to, these long neglected memorials, descriptions are now given of those Brasses in this county, on which are engraven figures of men and women and children. Mere inscriptions, and even those accompanied by coats of arms, have been omitted. I shall always be glad to hear of any discoveries of brasses or matrices which may be made in the county.

Much might be said of the fascination that a study of these memorials induces. One is brought, as it were, into contact with the ages in which the persons commemorated played their respective parts in the great drama of life.

The series is a thoroughly representative one, deeply interesting and instructive. The examples too are varied. We have the knightly effigy of the doughty warrior as well as that of the peaceful citizen; the stoled priest in vestments rich, the uplifted chalice; as also " ye ladye faire " arrayed in the quaint though costly dresses of the olden time; the wealthy woolstapler, ancestor of a noble house; the grave judge in his official robes, and even the miner in his work-a-day homely garb, carrying his mattock—all are included.

I beg to thank many friends—some alas! are no more—for much valuable help most ungrudgingly given, and especially I wish to offer my acknowledgments to the clergy without whose kind permission I should have been unable to obtain the many rubbings needed to render this series of Gloucestershire Brasses complete.

It gives me much pleasure to express the great indebtedness I owe to the Rev. C. G. R. Birch, LL.M., for the excellent metrical translations of the quaint Latin inscriptions, and to Mr. H. E. Jackson for the great care he has devoted to the illustrations.

The Rev. W. E. Hadow, M.A., Vicar of South Cerney, described the Monumental Brasses at Cirencester in a paper which appeared in the Transactions of the Bristol and Gloucestershire Archæological Society for 1877. By his kind permission some of his descriptions have been reprinted. I also acknowledge my indebtedness to the late Sir Wollaston Franks, F.S.A., and Sir John Maclean, F.S.A., also to the Rev. W. Bazeley, M.A., Rev. J. M. Hall, M.A., the late Rev. T. P. Wadley, M.A., Messrs. C. R. B. Barrett, M.A., the late J. H. Cooke, F.S.A., E. H. W. Dunkin, R. L. Leighton, F. W. Newton, the late J. D. T. Niblett, F.S.A., Mill Stephenson, F.S.A. T. Wareing, and A. E. Hudd, F.S.A.

The index has been made by Mr. F. W. Short, Hon. Secretary of the Monumental Brass Society, and it greatly enhances any value there may be in the work.

At the spring meeting of the Bristol and Gloucestershire Archæological Society, in April, 1882, I read a paper on the Brasses of Gloucestershire; a promise was then made of collecting the rubbings of the Monumental Brasses in the county, and describing them in detail. These accounts were commenced in the issue of the *Gloucester Journal* in May, 1882, and were finished in April, 1890. Some of the descriptions were reprinted in local newspapers, as the *Evesham Journal and Four Shires Advertiser*, and the *Stroud Journal*.

The following pages are the descriptions mentioned above, they having been carefully re-read before being printed in book form. They have appeared as a separately paged supplement of *Gloucestershire Notes and Queries*. The first instalment appeared in the issue dated January, 1894, and the last in 1899.

The following arrangement has as far as practicable been observed in the several descriptions of the Brasses.—(1) An abstract of the record of the brass from the " Manual of

Monumental Brasses," by the Rev. H. Haines, M.A., Part II. ed. 1861. (2) The position of the brass in the Church. (3) Its size. (4) A description of the figure, etc. (5) Inscription. (6) Heraldry. (7) The titles of works in which engravings of the brass are extant. (8) What portions, if any, of the brass are lost. (9) A brief memoir when possible of the person commemorated. The Brasses are described as far as possible, in chronological order, following the dates given by the Rev. H. Haines.

CECIL T. DAVIS.

Public Library,
  Wandsworth, S.W.

CONTENTS.

	PAGE
PREFACE	i
LIST OF BRASSES ...	xiii
LIST OF ILLUSTRATIONS	xvii
DESCRIPTIONS OF THE BRASSES	1
SUMMARY	200
LOST BRASSES	206
MODERN BRASSES ...	221
CORRIGENDA ET ADDENDA	222
INDEX ...	225

LIST OF BRASSES.

1	c1370	WINTERBOURNE. A lady of the Bradestone family ...	1
2	1392	WOTTON-UNDER-EDGE. Thomas, 4th Lord Berkeley, and wife Margaret	2
3	1396	BRISTOL, TEMPLE CHURCH. Civilian, half effigy ...	9
4	1400	DEERHURST. Sir John Cassy and wife Alice ...	10
5	c1400	CIRENCESTER. Wine Merchant (?) and wife Margaret	16
6	c1400	NORTHLEACH. Wool Merchant and wife	19
7	1401	CHIPPING CAMPDEN. William Grevel and wife Marion	21
8	1401	DYRHAM. Sir Morys Russel and wife Isabel ...	25
9	1411	BRISTOL, TRINITY. John Barstaple.	28
10	c1411	BRISTOL, TRINITY. Isabella, wife of last	28
11	c1430	QUINTON. Joan, wife of Sir William Clopton ...	30
12	1438	CIRENCESTER. [Richard] Dixton.	33
13	1439	BRISTOL, ST. MARY REDCLIFF. Sir John Juyn ...	37
14	1440	CIRENCESTER. Robert Page and wife Margaret ...	39
15	1442	CIRENCESTER. Reginald Spycer and four wives, Margaret, Juliana, Margaret, and Joan	42
16	c1445	NEWLAND. Man in armour and wife; crest, representing a "free miner"	44
17	1447	NORTHLEACH. Thomas Fortey, imperfect, William Scors, and their wife Agnes	48
18	1450	CHIPPING CAMPDEN. William Welley and wife Alice	51
19	c1450	LECHLADE. [John Townsend] and wife	52
20	1458	NORTHLEACH. [John Fortey]	54
21	c1460	BRISTOL, TEMPLE CHURCH. A Priest, on reverse a lady	58
22	1461	BRISTOL, ST. PETER. Robert Lond, chaplain ...	58
23	1461	RODMARTON. John Edward	60
24	1462	CIRENCESTER. William Prelatte and two wives, Agnes and Joan	62
25	1467	CHIPPING CAMPDEN. John Lethenard and wife Joan	66
26	c1470	CIRENCESTER. William Notyngham and wife Christina	68
27	1475	BRISTOL, ST. MARY REDCLIFF. Philip Mede, Esq., and two wives	69

LIST OF BRASSES.

28	1478	BRISTOL, ST. JOHN. Thomas Rowley and wife Margaret	73
29	1478	CIRENCESTER. Ralph Parsons, priest	75
30	c1480	BRISTOL, ST. MARY REDCLIFF. John Jay and wife Joan	76
31	c1480	CIRENCESTER. A priest	81
32	c1480	CIRENCESTER. Civilian and wife	81
33	1484	CHIPPING CAMPDEN. William Gybbys and three wives, Alice, Margaret, Marion	82
34	c1485	MICHELDEAN. Margery and Alice, wives of Thomas Baynham	83
35	c1485	NORTHLEACH. Woolman and wife	87
36	c1490	NORTHLEACH. [John Taylour] and wife Joan	89
37	1493	TORMARTON. John Ceysyll	91
38	1497	CIRENCESTER. John Benet and wife Agnes	94
39	1497	SEVENHAMPTON. John Camber	95
40	1500	FAIRFORD. John Tame and wife Alice	98
41	c1500	CIRENCESTER. Civilian, head restored	103
42	c1500	MINCHINHAMPTON. Civilian and wife	103
43	1501	NORTHLEACH. Robert Serche and wife Anne	105
44	1505	OLVESTON. Morys Denys and son Sir Walter Denys	106
45	c1510	LECHLADE. [John Twinyhow]	109
46	c1510	MINCHINHAMPTON. John Hampton and wife Elyn in shrouds. Their daughter, Dame Alice, in the dress of a nun	110
47	1513	CHELTENHAM. [Sir Wm. Greville] and wife	113
48	1515	BISLEY. Katherine, wife of Thomas Sewell	115
49	1518	EASTINGTON. Elizabeth Knevet	117
50	1519	GLOUCESTER, ST. MICHAEL. Alys and Agnes, wives of William Henshawe	119
51	1519	MINCHINHAMPTON. Edward Halyday and wife Margery	122
52	c1520	DEERHURST. A lady	124
53	c1520	DOWDESWELL. A priest	124
54	1521	KEMPSFORD. Walter Hichman and wife Cristyan	126
55	1522	BRISTOL, ST. MARY REDCLIFF. John Brook and wife Joan	127
56	1523	NEWENT. Roger Porter, Esq.	129
57	1525	DEERHURST. Elizabeth, wife of Walter Rowdon	131
58	1526	BERKELEY. [William Freme]	132
59	1526	NORTHLEACH. Thomas Bushe and wife Joan	135
60	c1530	CIRENCESTER. Two ladies	138
61	c1530	NORTHLEACH. William Lawnder, priest	139
62	1534	FAIRFORD. Sir Edmond Tame and two wives, Elizabeth and Agnes	141

63	1534	FAIRFORD. Same as last	144
63A	1540	GLOUCESTER, ST. JOHN. John Semys and two wives	149
64	1544	GLOUCESTER, ST. MARY CRYPT. John Cooke and wife Joan	154
65	1546	WESTON-UPON-AVON. Sir John Greville	158
66	1559	WESTON-UPON-AVON. Sir Edward Greville ...	162
67	1560	WHITTINGTON. Richard Coton and wife Margaret ...	163
68	1570	BRISTOL GRAMMAR SCHOOL. Nicholas Thorne and two wives, Mary and Bridget	165
69	1571	THORNBURY. Avice, wife of Thomas Tyndall ...	169
70	1583	CLIFFORD CHAMBERS. Hercules Raynsford and wife Elizabeth	172
71	1586	BRISTOL, ST. WERBURGH. William Gyttyns and wife Mary	176
72	1587	CIRENCESTER. Philip Marner	177
73	1590	WESTON-SUB-EDGE. William Hodges	179
74	1590	YATE. Alexander Staples and two wives, Avis and Elizabeth	180
75	c1598	LECKHAMPTON. William Norwoodd and wife Elizabeth	181
76	1601	CLIFFORD CHAMBERS. Elizabeth, wife of Edward Marrowe	185
77	1605	WORMINGTON. Anne, wife of John Savage ...	187
78	1609	ABBENHALL. Richard Pyrke and wife Joan ...	190
79	1614	TODENHAM. William Molton and wife Millicent ...	192
80	c1620	MINETY [Nicholas Poulett] and wife Mary ...	194
81	1626	CIRENCESTER. John Gunter and wife Alice ...	195
82	1636	BRISTOL, ST. JAMES. Henry Gibbes and wife Ann...	197

List of Illustrations.

1	1392	Wotton-under-Edge.	Collar of Mermaids	...	2
2	1392	,, ,, ,,	Gauntlets ...	...	3
3	1392	,, ,, ,,	Sword Belt ...	...	3
4	1392	,, ,, ,,	Sollerets and Lion	...	4
5	1392	,, ,, ,,	Dog ...	...	5
6	1400	Deerhurst.	Head ...	...	11
7	1400	,,	Lion ...	...	12
8	1400	,,	Dog "Terri" ...	...	13
9	1400	,,	St. John the Baptist	...	13
10	1400	,,	St. Anne and the Virgin Mary		14
11	1400	,,	Honeysuckle ...	...	15
12	1400	,,	Arms of Cassy ...	...	15
13	c1400	Cirencester.	Wine Cask ...	...	17
14	c1400	,,	Shield ...	...	17
15	c1400	Northleach.	Girdle ...	...	19
16	c1400	,,	Anelace ...	...	19
17	c1400	,,	Woolpack ...	...	20
18	c1400	,,	Dog ...	...	20
19	1401	Chipping Campden.	Merchant's Mark ...	...	22
20	1401	,, ,,	Arms of Grevel ...	...	23
21	1401	Dyrham.	Sollerets and Lion	...	26
22	1401	,,	Dog ...	...	26
23	1401	,,	Shields ...	...	27
24	1411	Bristol, Trinity Chapel.	Feet ...	...	28
25	1411	,, ,, ,,	Groundwork ...	...	29
26	1411	,, ,, ,,	Merchant's Mark ...	...	29
27	1411	,, ,, ,,	Inscription ...	...	29
28	1411	,, ,, ,,	Shield ...	...	30
29	c1430	Quinton.	"Pear" ...	...	31
30	c1430	,,	Shield ...	...	32
31	c1430	,,	Shield ...	...	32
32	c1430	,,	Shield ...	...	32
33	1438	Cirencester.	Dog ...	...	35

34	1438	CIRENCESTER. Pommel of Sword	...	...	36
35	1439	BRISTOL, ST. MARY REDCLIFF. Break	...	...	38
36	1439	,, ,, ,, Shields	...	..	38
37	1440	CIRENCESTER. Pendant	...	...	41
38	1440	,, Woolsack	...	...	41
39	1440	,, Son	...	...	41
40	1440	,, Daughter	...	...	41
41	1440	,, Merchant's Mark	...	...	41
42	1442	,, Reginald Spycer and four Wives		...	43
43	1442	,, Merchant's Mark	...	...	44
44	c1445	NEWLAND. Head and Helmet	...	...	45
45	c1445	,, Inscription	...	...	46
46	c1445	,, Crest	...	..	47
47	1447	NORTHLEACH. Feet of William Scors	...	...	49
48	1447	,, Inscription	...	...	50
49	1447	,, Date	...	...	50
50	c1450	LECHLADE. Feet	...	...	53
51	1458	NORTHLEACH Feet	...	...	55
52	1458	,, Detail and Canopy	...	...	56
53	1458	,, Merchant's Mark	...	...	56
54	c1460	BRISTOL, TEMPLE CHURCH. Lady	...	...	59
55	c1460	,, ,, ,, Priest	...	..	59
56	1461	RODMARTON. Head	...	...	61
57					
58	1462	CIRENCESTER. Defence of Arm	...	...	63
59	1462	,, Feet	...	...	65
60	1467	CHIPPING CAMPDEN. John Lethenard and Wife Joan	...	67
61	1475	BRISTOL, ST. MARY REDCLIFF. Philip Mede and his two Wives		...	70
62	1478	,, ST. JOHN. Purse and Beads	...	...	73
63	1478	,, ,, Merchant's Mark	...	...	74
64	1478	,, ,, Shield	...	...	74
65	c1480	,, ST. MARY REDCLIFF. Purse and Beads	...	76
66	c1480	,, ,, ,, Daughter	...	...	77
67	c1480	,, ,, ,, Rose	...	...	77
68	c1480	,, ,, ,, Shield	...	...	77
69	c1480	,, ,, ,, Merchant's Mark	...	77
70	c1480	CIRENCESTER. Priest	...	..	80
71	c1485	MICHELDEAN. Margaret Baynham	...	...	84
72	c1485	NORTHLEACH. Feet of Husband	...	...	87
73	c1485	,, Daughters	...	...	88
74	c1485	,, Merchant's Mark	...	..	88

75	c1490	NORTHLEACH.	Sheep on Woolpack	...	90
76	c1490	,,	End of Inscription	...	90
77	1493	TORMARTON.	Feet ...	...	91
78	1493	,,	Inscription	...	93
79	1497	CIRENCESTER.	Merchant's Mark	...	95
80	1500	FAIRFORD.	Lance Rest	...	99
81	1500	,,	Sabbatons	...	99
82	1500	,,	Shield	...	101
83	1500	,,	Shield	...	102
84	1500	,,	Shield	...	102
75	1501	NORTHLEACH.	Scroll	...	105
76	1501	,,	Monogram	...	106
77	1505	OLVESTON	Morys Denys	...	107
78	1505	,,	Shield	...	108
79	1505	,,	Shield	...	108
80	1505	,,	Shield	...	109
81	1505	,,	Shield	...	109
82	c1510	LECHLADE.	Merchant's Mark	...	110
83	c1510	MINCHINHAMPTON.	John Hampton	...	111
84	c1510	,,	Eldest Son ...	...	112
85	c1510	,,	Alice Hampton	...	112
86	1518	EASTINGTON.	Shield ...	...	117
87	1518	,,	Elizabeth Knevet	...	118
88	1518	,,	Shield ...	...	119
89	1518	,,	Shield ...	...	118
90	1519	MINCHINHAMPTON.	Merchant's Mark	...	123
91	c1520	DEERHURST.	Pendant ...	...	124
92	c1520	DOWDESWELL.	Morse	...	125
93	1521	KEMPSFORD.	Merchant's Mark	...	126
94	1523	NEWENT.	Shield ...	...	129
95	1532	QUEDGELEY.	Shield ...		130
96	1526	BERKELEY.	Heart ...		133
97	1526	NORTHLEACH.	Feet ...	...	135
98	1526	,,	Feet ...	...	136
99	1526	,,	Merchant's Mark	...	136
100	1526	,,	Canopy ...	...	137
101	c1530	,,	At End of Inscription	...	140
102	c1530	,,	"Holy Trinity"	...	141
103	1534	FAIRFORD.	Sir Edmond Tame	...	142
104	1534	,,	Inscription ...	...	143
105	1534	,,	End of Inscription	...	144
106	1534	,,	"Holy Trinity"	...	145

107	1534	FAIRFORD.	Shield	146
108	1534	,,	Shield	146
109	1540	GLOUCESTER, ST. JOHN BAPTIST.	John Semys ...	150
110	1540	,, ,, ,, ,,	Margaret Semys ...	151
111	1544	GLOUCESTER, ST. MARY DE CRYPT.	John & Joan Cooke	154
112	1544	,, ,, ,, ,,	Canopy ...	155
113	1544	,, ,, ,, ,,	Canopy ...	157
114	1546	WESTON-UPON-AVON.	Sir John Greville	159
115	1559	,, ,, ,,	Sir Edward Greville	162
116	1560	WHITTINGTON.	Child	165
127	c1570	BRISTOL.	Mary Thorne	166
128	1571	THORNBURY.	Avice Tyndall	170
129	1583	CLIFFORD CHAMBERS.	Feet	173
130	1583	,,	Arms	174
131	1586	BRISTOL.	Circular Plate	176
132	1587	CIRENCESTER.	Philip Marner	178
133	1590	YATE.	Child	180
134	c1598	LECKHAMPTON.	Shield	182
135		,,	Seal and Autograph of William Norwood. 21 Jac. I. ...	184
136	1601	CLIFFORD CHAMBERS.	Elizabeth Marrowe ...	186
137	1601	,,	Shield	187
138	1605	WORMINGTON	Anne Savage	188
139	1605	,,	Shields	189
140	1609	ABBENHALL.	Thomas and Robert Pyrke	191
141	1604	TODENHAM.	Shield	193
142	1620	MINETY.	Crests	195
143	1624	CIRENCESTER.	Alice Gunter	196
144	1624	KINTBURY, BERKS.	Shield	196
145	1636	BRISTOL, ST. JAMES.	Henry Gibbes	198
146	c1460	CIRENCESTER.	Lily Pot	207
147	c1500	,,	Civilian and Wife	209
148		,,	Vase	211
149	c1511	CUBBERLEY.	Shield	212
150	1500	NORTHLEACH.	Children	216
151	1400	DEERHURST.	Shield	222
152	1526	BERKELEY.	Head	223

NOTE.—All the illustrations are reduced to quarter of the original rubbings, with the exception of Figs. 131, 133, 134, which are half scale.

GLOUCESTERSHIRE
MONUMENTAL BRASSES.

I.—Winterbourne.

A lady, *circa* 1370, canopy and marginal inscription lost.—*Haines*.

Position.—On the floor at the east end of the North Aisle.

Size.—6ft. × 2 ft.; figure only, 4 ft. 5 in. × 1 ft. 1 in.

Description.—This is the oldest brass now existing in Gloucestershire, though indents still remain of earlier ones. The lady wears the veil head-dress which was the prevailing fashion of the period. It consists of a cap which closely fits the head and hides the forehead, reaching down in a horizontal line to the eyebrows, and falling vertically at each side, encloses the face in somewhat of an oblong frame. Over this is thrown a veil or kerchief falling down on the back and over the shoulders. Her cote-hardie or gown, which is without buttons—is peculiar in having pocket-holes in front and through these is seen the cincture of the kirtle which was worn beneath—it fits closely to the body and arms, it is cut square and low at the neck and the sleeves extend nearly to the wrist. The kirtle has long sleeves closely buttoned, reaching nearly to the knuckles. The feet are represented small and she wears shoes with pointed toes. The hands are folded in the attitude of prayer.

Inscription—Lost, not given in any of the county histories.

Heraldry—" The Bradestones of Winterbourn bore for their arms,—Argent, on a canton gules a rose or, barbed proper."—*Rudder*, p. 834.

Illustration.—*Boutell's Series.*

Portions lost.—The inscription, canopy, two shields at the top and a portion of the right hand corner of her skirt.

Biographical Account.—Haines suggests " Perhaps Agnes, wife of Sir Thomas de Bradestone, 1369-70, or Blanch, widow of Robert Bradestone, 1391-2."

II.—Wotton-under-Edge.

Thomas, fourth Lord Berkeley, 1417, and wife Margaret, daughter and heiress of Gerard Warren, Lord Lisle, 1392, large, inscription lost. Altar Tomb, North Aisle. *Haines*.

Position.—The above are placed on a raised altar-shaped tomb of Purbeck marble as recorded by Haines.

Size.—6 ft. x 5 ft.

Description.—On his head Lord Berkeley wears a pointed bascinet, or conical helmet of steel, to which the camail is attached by means of a cord passing through a groove formed by two raised rims with separate enriched plates placed over the holes of the bascinet. This groove is round the lower end of the bascinet, and carried up by the sides of the face, the rings to which the cord is fastened are shown at the top. The indent of a heaume, or tilting helmet, shows the former support of the head. The beard is covered by the camail, but the moustache is visible. The shoulders are protected by the camail, or tippet of chain mail, and over it is thrown a collar of mermaids, a cognisance of the

Berkeleys; no other instance of such a collar is recorded. The mail is represented as made of over-lapping rings, or of rings set edgeways. Mail is also used at the gussets to allow the arms and feet to be used freely. A portion of the hawberk hangs beneath the escalloped edge of the tight-fitting jupon or jerkin. The arms are protected by brassarts of plate, of which the fastenings can be seen, with coudières or elbow-pieces and épaulières or shoulder-pieces. On his hands are leather gauntlets with an ornamental border at the wrists; the knuckles are protected by three rows of gadlings or knobs, which were occasionally used for offence. To keep the jupon in its place there is no baldrick, but an ornamental belt, sometimes termed the belt of knighthood, passes round the hip, the end, passing under the belt, hangs down nearly to the knee of the left leg. The vacant space at the end was most probably filled by a jewel either real or imitative. Unfortunately the sword which hung by his side is gone, but a portion of the guard is left, and the point of the chape may be seen near the left foot. The cuisses are made of plate, the knees are guarded by genouillières, and pointed sollerets protect the feet. Rowel spurs were generally used at the end of the fourteenth century, but the rowels of his spurs have disappeared, though the footstraps are left. His feet are resting on a lion, facing the spectator.

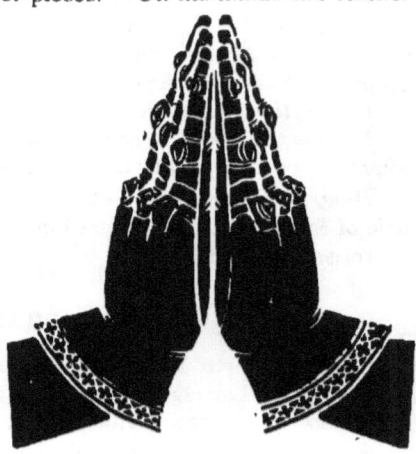

The brass of Lady Berkeley is remarkable for her head-dress. The hair is worn over the forehead only, and brushed back to show the ears, which are not disfigured by earings; it is confined in gold or silver net-work, called crestine or crespine,

ornamented with jewels at the intersections, a small kerchief is also pinned at the top of the head and depends behind, it is to be seen at the top of her head and behind her ears, drooping in graceful folds nearly to her shoulders; across her forehead stretches a jewelled fillet. Yet all the ornamental work to be seen round her head is not to be confounded with her head dress, for her head is resting on a piece of cloth adorned with sprays stretched diagonally on an embroidered cushion, with tassels at the four corners. Her mantle is long and fastened in front of her shoulders by a cord which passes through two metal loops with studs in front, termed fermailes, placed on each side of the mantle, and usually adorned with jewels; this cord passes through a slide, also made of cord, and terminates below the waist in two tassels. Beneath is a tight-fitting gown, but whether sleeveless or short sleeved it is impossible to determine as the mantle hides it, it is cut low at the neck. Under this emerge the close sleeves of her kirtle buttoned underneath. Her mantle and gown cover her feet, at which lies a lap-dog wearing a collar of bells.

The dog represented at the feet of the wife is doubtless of the same kind as "smale houndes" which were the favourites of the gentle Prioresse—

" Of smale hounds hadde she, that she fedde
With rosted flesh and milk, and wastel brede;
But sore wept she if one of hem were dead,
Or if men smote with a yerde smart."—*Chaucer.*

In the *Ménagier de Paris* written *circa* 1393, the lady of the household is particularly recommended to think of the "chamber beasts," such as little dogs.

They are both represented full face, with their hands folded in the attitude of prayer, Lady Berkeley lying at her husband's right hand.

Inscription.—Lost, even Smyth who gives the epitaphs of other members of the family fails to record this one.

Heraldry.—Smyth gives illustrations of the following three seals:—

1. When he attained full age, a chevron and ten crosses,

about two inches in diameter, without supporters or crest, circumscribed "*Sigillum Thomæ de Berkelee.*"

2. In the middle part of his life, as above, supported by two mermaids without crest, circumscribed "*Sigillum Thomæ dni de Berkeley.*"

3. In the latter part of his life, a chevron and ten crosses cornerwise, with mermaids as supporters, and "a helmet for crest, the circumscription as last."

In the British Museum are two examples of his seal, which are thus described in the Catalogue of Seals:—

4. "On a tree-stump set on a mount of herbage, a shield of arms, couché, a chevron between ten crosses crosslet, six in chief four in base, *Berkeley*. Crest on a helmet and mantling, a mitre stringed and garnished, charged with cross crosslets derived from the arms. Supporters two mermaids. Background replenished with small sprigs of foliage. Within a carved gothic quatrefoil of elegant design, ornamented with small ball flowers along the inner edge. Legend between the lobes of the quatrefoil—[*Sigi*]*ll' thome dni de berkley.* The letters *ho* of *thome*, and *be* of *berkley* are conjoined."

5 "A shield of arms *Berkeley*, suspended by a strap from a forked tree on a mount. Supporters; two mermaids. Within a carved gothic quatrefoil panel or quadrilobe ornamented along the inner edge with small quatrefoils. *Sigillu' :* [*tho*]*me : dni : de : berkele :*"

Illustrations.—Illustrations of this brass will be found in *Fosbrooke's Gloucestershire,* vol. I., p. 477 ; *Hollis's Monumental Effigies,* pt. IV., pl. 10 ; *Boutell's Monumental Brasses,* p. 57 (Collar of Mermaids) p. 135 ; *Haines,* vol. I. p., cxlviii. (Head of Lady Berkeley); *Cooke's History of Berkeley,* p. 31 ; *Art Journal,* vi, p. 34 ; *Planché's Cyclopædia of Costume,* p. 129, (Collar, Mermaid) ; *Bigland's Gloucestershire.*

Portions lost.—The inscription, heaume, sword, dagger, rowels of spurs, and shields, if any.

Biographical Account.—Though this Lord Berkeley is termed *fourth* lord, he was really the *tenth.*

In Smyth's "Lives of the Berkeleys" the second volume commences with "The life of Thomas lord Berkeley the fourth of that name." Thirty-eight pages are devoted to him and from them the following information is taken.

He was born at Berkeley Castle on January 4th, 26 Edw. III., 1352. In 41 Edw. III. it was agreed between his father Maurice lord Berkeley, and Gerrard Warren lord de Lisle, that Thomas should marry Margaret, daughter of the said Gerrard, her portion being 1,100 marks. "And that the said Margaret, by reason of her tender age (then being about seaven) should for fower years remaine with her father, and this Thomas de Berkeley with his father." "But the sickness of the lord Maurice Berkeley increasing, notwithstanding the former agreement of fower years stay: they were by his request maryed at the said lord Lisle his house at Wengrave, in Buckinghamshire, in November next following." He was 15 years of age when his father Maurice died on June 8th, 42 Edw. III. The king appoints his father-in-law, Warren de Insula, his guardian, who so well looked after the property that when Thomas came of age he was well off. At this time he was knighted "and forthwith passeth to the warrs of France." In 5 Ric. II. his wife and her father come to Berkeley; and Thomas gives his father-in-law free permission to live at Berkeley and to enjoy the fishing and hunting pertaining to the Castle: "the good old lord de Insula, the 28th of June next after these sweet and sociable agreements, in 6 Ric. II. dyeth." In 1 and 2 Ric. II "this lord was imployed both by sea and land in the warrs that then were hott both against Ffrance and Spaine." In 4 Ric. II. he was fighting in Britany, in 8 and 9 Ric. II he accompanied the king against the Scots, and the next year the king came to Berkeley Castle. In 16 Ric. II. "this lord went beyond seas into Ffrance and other Countryes." "This was no martiall expedition but occasioned as it may seeme upon greefe conceived by the death of his wife, or to avoid the danger of Court stormes which then began to bluster with an hollow wind." In 1399 a meeting of nobles took place at Berkeley, and Thomas declared "hee made himself a spetiall witnes at Flint Castle of king Richard's promise to renounce the Crowne." He testified it in the king's presence in the Tower of London; and on the meeting of the three estates in Parliament, a bishop, abbot, earl, baron, and knight being the representatives chosen to pronounce his majesty's deposition, he was the baron appointed for that purpose. In 5 Hen. IV. he was made admiral of the king's fleet, from the mouth of the Thames to the west and south, and sworn of the king's privy council in open Parliament. He (Walf, *eodem anno*) burnt fifteen sail of French ships in Milford Haven, part of the fleet sent to the assistance of Owen Glendower, and took fourteen more, on board of which were the seneschal of France, and eight officers of note, whom he made prisoners. In 6 and 7 Hen. IV. he was chief commander in the Welsh wars, and engineer at the sieges of Lampadervar, in Pembrokeshire. He was at the battle of Agincourt in 1415, and Drayton mentions

"Berkeley and Burnell two brave English lords."

He was also fond of sporting, and preserved foxes and game largely. He greatly increased his estate by purchasing manors, advowsons, etc., and other property from time to time. Pope Urban VI., in 1380, "by his Episcopall bull," gave him leave to choose his own confessor. "In short, he was not only a great soldier, but was distinguished as a lover of learning. John Trevisa, the famous vicar of Berkeley, celebrated by Bale for his learning and eloquence, translated the Old and New Testaments into English at the request of this lord Berkeley." He made his will 2nd February, 1415, (3 Hen. V) and amongst his numerous bequests appears, " to the Church of Berkeley, one green pair of vestments, with all their furnyture; and to the Church where his body should bee buryed his best paire of vestments, with all their furniture, £20 money, and one guilt crosse, with all the relikes inclosed in the same, with all his best cruets, and also one white pair of vestments with all their furniture, and also the best paire of his black vestments, and his best missale, with a good chalice; and to the Chaple within Berkeley Castle, one paire of satten vestments, one missale, two chalices, and one paire of cruets." Unfortunately he made no testamentary disposition of his property, which became the source of lawsuits between the descendants of his nephew James, who succeeded him, and the descendants of his daughter.

"Upon the 13th of July in the fifth year of that victorious king Henry the fifth, Anno. 1417, the glasse of this lord Thomas runneth out, at Wotton-under-edge, hee then of the age of 64 yeares six monthes and eight days, whereof hee had sate lord 49 yeares one month and 5 dayes; and lived a widdower the last twenty six years thereof, or neer thereabouts; and lyeth buried in the parish Church of Wotton under-Edge with the translated bones of the lady Margaret his wife resting by him, under a faire tombe there.

> Nos quos certus amor primis conjunxit ab annis
> Iunxit idem tumulus, junxit idemque polus.
> In youth our parents joyn'd our hands, our selves, our hearts,
> This tombe our bodyes hath, th' heavens our better parts.

It has been already stated that he married Margaret, sole daughter and heiress of Gerard Warren lord Lisle (de Insula) by Alice, daughter of Henry lord Tyes. Her brother Gerard married Anne, daughter of Monsieur Michael de la Pole, but dying without issue, Margaret became the heiress of her father. On his death, when she was twenty-two years of age, the two baronies of Lisle and Tyes came to the Berkeley family, and her husband's estate was doubled. Smyth describes her as a " very mild and devout lady." " This lady Margaret died at Wotton-under-Edge, the twentieth of March, about the fifteenth year of Richard the second, then about thirty years of age; having been maryed at seaven; and lyeth buried in the parish Church of Wotton under a faire tombe by the side of her husband, whither her bones were translated: The greefe of whose death soe fastened upon the affections of her lord and husband, that hee never after affected mariage, although hee was at her death but thirty eight years of age, and of an able constitution, and then without issue male to uphold his name and barony." They had only one child, a daughter named Elizabeth, who married Richard Beauchamp, son and heir of Thomas, earl of Warwick and left issue, three daughters (1) Margaret, who became the second wife of John Talbot, first earl of Shrewsbury; (2) Ellenor, was first married to Thomas lord Roos of Hamelake, and secondly to Edmond Beaufort, Duke of Somerset; (3) Elizabeth, was married to George Neville, lord Latimer, a younger son of Ralph Neville, earl of Westmoreland.

III—Bristol—Temple Church.

A civilian [1396] half effigy, four latin verses. North aisle.—*Haines.*

Position.—The brass is now on the chancel floor, but originally it was in the Weaver's Chapel.

Size.—22½ in. x 19 in.

Description.—His hair is cut short, and he is represented as clean-shaven. He wears simply a hood and a tunic, which is the usual costume of demi-figures of this period. His tunic has close fitting sleeves with ornamented cuffs: buttoned gauntlets extend half-way up his hand. He is shown full face with hands folded in the attitude of prayer.

Inscription.—This is below the figure:—

Es testis xpe: qd' non iacet hic lapis iste
Corpus vt ornet': set spe vt memoret
Hinc tu qui transis: magnus medius puer an sis
Pro me funde preces: dabit' michi sic venie spes

which is thus translated in "*Notes on the Ecclesiastical and Monumental Architecture and Sculpture of the Middle Ages in Bristol,*" by George Pryce, 1850:—"Thou art a witness, O Christ! that this stone is not intended to ornament the body, but to commemorate the spirit, into which thou hast passed, great Mediatory Son: pour out thy prayers for me and thus give me pardoning hope." In "*Bristol, Past and Present,*" it is thus rendered:—"Thou art witness O Christ, that this stone is not here laid to adorn the body, but that the soul may be remembered. You who pass by, whether old, middle aged or youth, make supplication for me that I may attain hope of pardon."

Haines records that these verses, with slight variations, were oftentimes introduced into inscriptions.

Illustration.—In Pryce's "*Notes,*" a poorly executed sketch of this brass is given on p. 118, fig. 9.

Portions Lost.—The inscription round the margin.

Biographical Account.—As the marginal inscription is lost, it is not known who is commemorated by it. In "*Notes on Monumental Brasses in Gloucestershire,*" Sir A. W. Franks, F.R.S., F.S.A., says it is "of a wool merchant, for which this part of England has been so long famous."—*Proc. Soc. Antiq.,* 2 s. vol. vii., p. 409.

The Rev. T. P. Wadley, M.A., kindly supplies the following names of Bristol worthies, buried in the Temple Church there:—William Hervy, 1394; William Temple, 1393; Alexander Moys, 1395; Peter Atte Barugh, 1396.

IV.—Deerhurst.

Sir John Cassy, 1400, and wife Alice, canopy with SS. Anne and John Baptist (the latter lately stolen) and marginal inscription. North Aisle.—*Haines.*

Position.—On the floor at the east end of the North Aisle.

Size.—7ft. 5in. × 3ft. 1in.

Description.—This brass affords a very fine illustration of the costume worn at this period by Judges, Barons of the Exchequer, and other law officers. He wears a close fitting coif, or skull-cap, which was worn by judges to conceal the tonsure, for they were occasionally priests as well : this cap has an embroidered band crossing from the forehead to the back of the head (6). Serjeant Pulling, in "*The Order of the Coif*," says, that the original coif was a close fitting white cap of lawn or silk; but this gradually disappeared until nothing remains but a curious circular patch visible upon the crown of a serjeant's wig. The hair is cut short, and is seen on the forehead and brushed back behind the ears ; he is clean shaven. Around his neck he wears a tippet. The mantle is lined with minever or vaire, buttoned on the right shoulder, where three of the buttons are visible, and gathered over the left arm, from which it hangs in graceful folds. Beneath is a long robe extending to the ankles, with close sleeves reaching to the wrists, where they are turned back so as to form narrow cuffs ; beneath these, sleeves of an underdress appear, closely buttoned, and extending nearly to the knuckles. His feet are encased in embossed shoes with pointed toes, and they rest upon a lion.* (7)

Fig. 6. Head, 1400. Deerhurst.

---

* " It is assumed that the dog and lion of such frequent recurrence at the feet are so placed as respectively emblems of fidelity and courage. But we cannot reason this in respect to the little lap-dogs at the feet of ladies as they are so manifestly introduced as the pets or companions incidental to rank. The lion was of old a symbol of rank and power, the embodiment of material force. It is not confined to the effigies of knights and nobles, but the *judge* is also so distinguished, he being a delegate of royal power."—*Waller's Mon. Br. p. viii.*

12   Gloucestershire Notes and Queries.

Fig. 7. Lady, 1400. Deerhurst

Lady Cassy wears the reticulated head-dress; this consists of a close cap of network, brought round the face so as to resemble a horse-shoe, which, reaching partway down the ears, confined the hair from off the face, but allowed it to fall down on the shoulders, and there apparently the ends of the hair are kept in place by network, similar to that on her head. Along the forehead is seen the edge of a small plaited cap, also called a "fret."

"A fret of gold she had next her hair."
CHAUCER.—*Legend of a Good Woman.*

It was probable that false hair or something else was used for padding this kind of head-dress. The reticulated head-dress first appeared on our monumental effigies about the middle of the fourteenth century, and was, doubtless, introduced into England from the Continent, (where it was in earlier use), by Philippa of Hainault, Queen of Edward, III, who died August 5th, 1369. Her gown has narrow sleeves, and is buttoned up to the neck, and gathered in closely round the throat, four buttons are seen: it is not confined at the waist by a girdle. The ends of the sleeves are turned back so as to form cuffs, which are deeper than her husband's, revealing the fur lining: and round the neck she wears a frill. Proceeding from beneath the sleeves of the gown are other sleeves, closely buttoned, and ending in funnel-shaped cuffs. The pointed toes of her embroidered shoes are seen resting upon a greyhound, which wears a collar of bells, and evidently a favourite, for under it is engraved its name, "*Terri*." † (8)

Fig. 8. Dog *Terri*, 1400. Deerhurst.

The figures are under a double canopy with pointed and cusped heads springing from foliated corbels; the crocketted ogee gables are terminated by foliated finials, each tympanum is filled in with a circular panel containing a conventional rose. On either side and between the canopies rise panelled pinnacles set on diagonally, and terminating in crocketted finials. The outer pinnacles are continued down on either side till they meet the diapered band at the base, and upon which the figures stand. The centre pinnacle is terminated at the springing by a foliated pendant. The husband is not represented straight under the centre of the canopy above his head, but the wife is. Between the gables and central pinnacle were two plates of brass containing effigies of saints. Unfortunately the plate containing St. John the Baptist has disappeared, but I am able to give an illustration (9) from a rubbing of this brass, kindly given me by the late Mr. J. D. T. Niblett, F.S.A. It represented St. John Baptist, his head surrounded by a nimbus; his hair and beard are long. He is dressed in a hairy garment, girt about the loins with a girdle, tied in front and the ends

Fig 9. St. John the Baptist, 1400. Deerhurst.

† On a brass formerly at Ingham, Norfolk, the pet dog's name was *Jakke*.

hanging down. His feet are bare. He is holding a book fastened by a long clasp, and on which is the sacred lamb, to which he is pointing with his left hand. Behind the lamb is a cross with a streamer flying from the shaft, and on the streamer is a cross. The corbel on which St. John stands is ornamented with trefoils.

Fig. 10. St. Anne & Virgin Mary. 1400, Deerhurst.

The other plate (10) represents St. Anne instructing the Virgin Mary; St. Anne is wearing the ordinary costume of widows, consisting of the veil head-dress, barbe and long robes. The Virgin Mary has her hair long, and her head surrounded by a nimbus. A cape is over her shoulders, and she is clad in a dress which fits the arms and body tightly and is laced up the front from the skirt. The Virgin Mary is holding a book in her left hand and apparently writing from the dictation of St. Anne, who is pointing to the book with her right hand, whilst her left hand is resting on the Virgin Mary's right shoulder. An illustration of the same subject appears in the *Art Journal*, 1851, taken from the chapel of Henry VII., in Westminster Abbey. It is termed "a good example of the peculiar taste of the fifteenth century."

Both are lying full faced, with hands folded as if praying, Lady Cassy being at her husband's right hand

Inscription.—Round the verge is the following inscription commencing over Lady Cassy's head :—

Hic iacet Johes Caffy miles et quondam capitalis Baro S'cc'ij Dni Regis qui obijt xxiij° die Maij Anno d'ni M° CCCC° Et Alicia vxor eius quor' a'i'ab3 p'picietur deus.

Which may be thus translated :—

"Here lies John Cassy, knight and formerly chief Baron of the Exchequer of our lord the King, who died on the 23rd day of May, A.D. 1400. And Alice, his wife, on whose souls may God have pity."

The intervals between the words are filled with scrolls, leaves, and flowers, *e.g.*, between "Hic" and "iacet" is a biped fabulous monster, between "vxor" and "eius" is a spray of honeysuckle. (11)

Heraldry.—In each angle was a shield, but the ones above and below the lady are gone. Over the knight is—" . . . a chevron between three hawks' heads erased,

Fig. 11. Honeysuckle. 1400, Deerhurst.

Cassy," (12) and below " . . . three lions passant in pale . . ." In the *Gentleman's Magazine* for February, 1840, the latter shield is stated to bear the three lions of England, the writer having probably been mislead by Gough or by the plate in Lysons' 'Gloucestershire Antiquities,' and Mr. Foss has fallen into the same error."—*Waller's Mon. Br.*

Fig. 12. Arms of Cassy. 1400, Deerhurst.

Rudder thus describes the shields—Argent, a chevron between three eagles' heads erased gules for Cassy, and three lioncels passant guardant, the arms of England. Mr. Dan. H. Haigh blazons the second shield—three leopards, passant guardant, but the lions or lioncels are not passant guardant. Possibly the second shield is for the Gloucestershire family, *e.g.*, Giffard,—gules, three lions, passant in pale, argent. On the brass to Richard Cassey, priest (1427) at Tredington, Worcestershire, the former coat appears twice.

Illustrations.—*Lysons' Gloucestershire Antiquities*, plate XVII., *Waller*, plate XV. and in *Haines's Introduction*, p. clxviii (Lady Cassy only).

Portions Lost.—Two shields, one above and the other below Lady Cassy, and the plate on which was engraved St. John Baptist. (9)

Biographical Account.—"The name of this judge first occurs among the council in Richard Bellewe's Reports in the time of Richard II. He came of an old Gloucestershire family, whose possession of the manor of Compton, on the little river Coln in that county gave it the name of Cassy Compton (*Rudder's Gloucestershire*). Sir John was appointed chief baron of the exchequer 12 Richard II. 1389; letters of privy seal for that office being ordered by the council on the 13th November when payment was directed to be made to him for the time he was in Wales (*Nicholas's Ordinances of the Privy Council*). He received a new patent upon the accession of Henry IV. in 1399, but died in the following year."—*Waller's Monumental Brasses.*

"For more than 300 years the Cassy family appear to have held the same estate (Wightfield) in the parish. The moated house on that estate is a very interesting one, and still bears on its front the Cassy crest." *Butterworth's Notes on the Priory and Church of Deerhurst.*

In 2 Richard II. one Ruyhale and Otho, late clerks of the peace, certified falsely into the Chancery a record concerning this Lord Thomas (*i.e.* Thomas, tenth, Lord Berkeley) and the King, supposed to be taken before Judge Cassy and his fellow Justices of the Peace; for which unjust fact this lord complaynes, and upon hearing thereof Ruyhale is fined 100 marks; and Otho five marks, which either of them do pay, and so obtained their pardon. *Pat.* 18, *Ric.* II., p. 1, m. 26.

A release, dated Saturday, the feast of St. Swithin, 7 Henry IV., mentions William Cassy, son and heir of John Cassy, of Wightfield, Knight.

V.—Cirencester.

A wine merchant (?) and wife Margaret, *circâ* 1400, under canopy, large, much worn. Nave.—*Haines.*

Position.—On a ledger stone in Lady Chapel.

Size.—8ft. 4in. × 3ft. 5in.

The following particulars respecting this brass are taken from the valuable and exhaustive paper *On the Monumental Brasses of Cirencester*, by the Rev. W. E. Hadow, M.A., Vicar of South Cerney; read at the Cirencester meeting of the Bristol and Gloucestershire Archæological Society. The paper is published in the Transactions of that year, and Mr. Hadow has kindly granted permission to make use of this important monograph.

Description.—"But in the same Chapel (Lady Chapel) there is a very fine specimen, at least sixty years earlier than Nottingham's; it lies near the north wall of the chapel, and is greatly mutilated; it represents a merchant and his wife, with a fine double canopy, the underpart of which shows the groining of the arch, while cusps terminate in trefoils, characteristics which mark this brass as dating between 1320-60 (temp. Edward II. and Edward III.) The male figure, which has lost the head, is clad in a gown with flowing sleeves, and bound round the waist with a girdle falling in front of the figure: on the end of the girdle the letter T is found worked as a monogram; the feet are in pointed shoes, resting on a wine cask *(13) and above the canopy, over the male

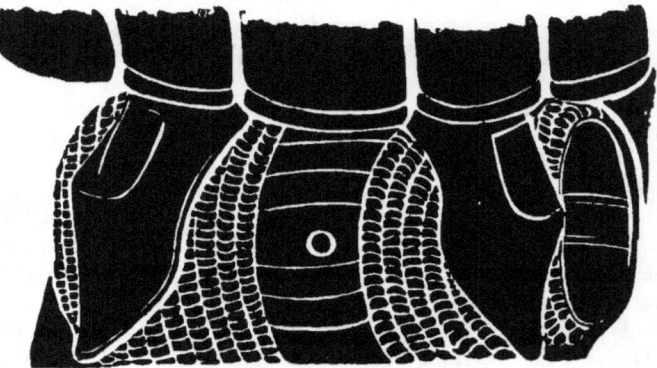

Fig. 13. Wine Cask. C 1400, Cirencester.

figure, is a shield (14) bearing an almost obliterated escutcheon of arms, somewhat resembling the old arms of the city of Bristol; so possibly this merchant may have had some connection with that place. There is also another escutcheon with the following:—Jhc haue mercy on us. The female figure has almost entirely disappeared, but the lower part still remains, showing the bottom of a long-flowing kirtle, buttoned to the feet, which, like her husband's rest on a wine cask. The inscription, only a fragment of which remains, is remarkable for being alternately in raised and sunken letters, and is the only specimen** of the two sorts of lettering occurring

Fig. 14. Shield. C 1400. Cirencester.

---

* The feet of Simon Seman, Vinter, and Alderman of London (1433) at Barton-on-Humber, Lincolnshire, rest on wine barrels.

** Inscriptions in raised and sunken letters also occur at Balsham, Cambs. Dr. John Blodwell, 1462; at Biggleswade, Beds. John Rudyn, 1481; and others.

in the same inscription that I am acquainted with."—*Trans. Bris. and Gl. Arch. Soc.: Vol. ii., p. 152.*

The canopy is double with pointed and cusped heads, and crocketted ogee gables, terminating with foliated finials. The arch is groined. Each tympanum is filled in with a circular panel with an ornamental centre. The spandrels are filled with sprays. On either side and between the canopies are panelled pinnacles set on edgeways and terminated with crocketted finials; the outer pinnacles are continued down on either side, forming a border, but the centre one is terminated in a foliated pendant.

The husband is represented in the attitude of devotion, the wife is on the husband's left hand.

Inscription.—The portion of the inscription which remains (two-fifths of the whole) is much worn, but the following words may be deciphered :—

> . . . Margeria coniux sua femina
> . . opes reperat gaudia quod subeat
> . . . mihi . . . tempore . . . (scroll work)
> . . . cunctis meritis illis sit uita perhennis

Unfortunately this inscription has not been preserved in any of the county histories.

Heraldry.—As mentioned above, the shield is not easy to decipher.

Illustration.—I am not aware that this brass has formed the illustration of any work.

Portions lost.—Head of husband, upper half of wife, more than half of the inscription, several crockets,, one of the finials, two of the pinnacles, and two shields at the top of the brass.

Biographical Account.— Rev. T. P. Wadley, M.A., Naunton Rectory, kindly suggests that perhaps the brass was erected to " Thomas Beaupyne, whose will was made in 1403. and proved or administered to, in 1404. He desired to be buried in the Abbey of Cirencester, in the chapel of Sir Henry Mourton, and left the residue of his effects to *Margaret*, his wife. He had been a burgess of Bristol."

The Rev. E. A. Fuller, M.A., supposes that he was a "Gotorest," there being wine-merchants of that name who lived at Bristol, and were connected with this town.

VI.—Northleach.

A wool-merchant and wife, *circâ* 1400, large, once in north aisle, relaid in nave.—*Haines*.

Position.—On the floor in the centre of nave.

Size.—Husband 4ft. 9in. × 1ft. 4in.; wife 4ft. 7in. × 1ft 3in.

Description.—The hair of the husband is short and brushed back from the temples.

"His heer was by his eres rounde i-shorn,
His top was docked lyk a preest biforn."

He has moustaches and a forked beard. He wears a tight-fitting tunic reaching to the ankles; from the waist it is fastened by buttons, of which nine are visible, the others being concealed by the hanging portion of the girdle. The sleeves of this tunic are close-fitting, and from beneath them emerge the tighter sleeves of an under-dress with many buttons, fifteen showing on the right wrist and thirteen on the left.

The tunic is confined at the waist by a girdle (15) of leather adorned with rosettes, and passing through a square buckle the end is passed under the 'girdle hanging down in front, and terminated by a metal pendant, on which is engraved the letter ℭ, probably one of his initials. Suspended from the girdle by a thong on his left side is the anelace or dagger. (16) The top of the

Fig. 15. Girdle. C 1400, Northleach.

Fig. 16. Anelace. C 1400, Northleach

scabbard is ornamented with four Gothic canopies, and two on the chape. Over all is a mantle, fastened by three large buttons on the right shoulder, which, gathered over the left arm, hangs gracefully. Round his neck he wears a hood of which two buttons are fastened and three unfastened. The shoes are pointed and fastened across the instep by a plain buckle. By his standing on a woolpack it is surmised that he was a wool-merchant. (17)

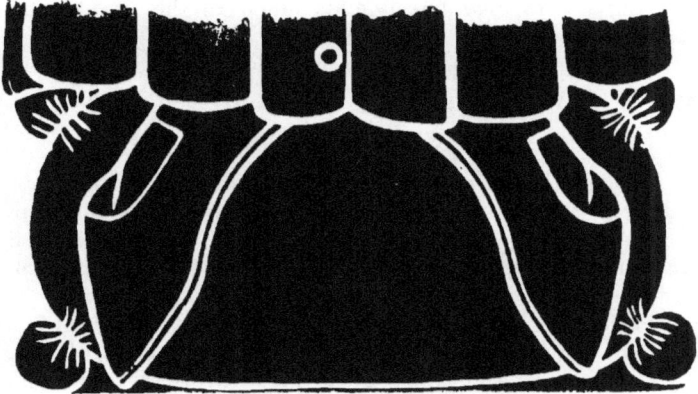

Fig. 17. Woolpack, C 1400, Northleach.

On her head the wife wears a close cap with its front edges plaited, carried strait across the forehead and down the sides of the face. Over this is a veil or kerchief falling down on the back and shoulders. The kirtle is seen at the neck and wrists, being in both places closely buttoned; at the neck the two top buttons are not fastened, and the upper edge of the kirtle is turned down so as to form a collar. On the fourth finger of her right hand she wears a ring with a jewel set in it. Over all is a mantle, fastened in front by the usual cord, the fermailes and slide are hidden, the ends hang down in front, and are terminated by tassels. At her feet lies a lap-dog (18) with a collar of bells.

The two effigies lie full-face with hands folded in the act of praying.

Fig. 18. Dog, C 1400, Northleach.

Illustrations.—— *Boutell's Series; Cutts (E.L.) Scenes and Characters of the Middle*

Ages, p. 522 (husband only), *Planché's Cyclopædia of Costume*, p. 8.

Portions lost.—All that remains of this memorial is in good condition, but from its being removed and the indent disappeared, it is impossible to say how much or what of this brass has been lost. The Rev. E. L. Cutts says that "over the effigy is an elegant canopy, which it is not necessary for our purpose to give, but it adds much to the beauty and sumptuousness of the monument."

Biographical Account.—It is not known to whose memory this brass is erected.

VII.—Chipping Campden.

William Grevel, citizen of London, "*flos mercatorum tauar tocius Anglie*," 1401, and wife Marion [daughter of Sir John Thornborough?] 1386, with canopy, merchant's marks, and marginal inscription (the end of which was loose Jan., 1860), very large, chancel.—*Haines*.

Position.—On the floor in front of the Communion rails.

Size.—8ft. 9in. x 4ft. 4in. Husband alone, 5ft. 4in. x 1ft. 4in.

Description.—The hair of William Grevel is short and removed from the temples like that of the reeve described by Chaucer in his *Canterbury Tales*. At this period the young men were clean shaven, their elders wore a moustache and beard. Chaucer tells us

A marchant was there with a forked beard,

and this fashion was duly followed by William Grevel. He wears a tightfitting tunic reaching to the ankles; from the waist it is fastened by buttons, of which three are visible above the girdle and eleven beneath it. The sleeves of this tunic are close-fitting, and from beneath them emerge the tighter sleeves of an under-dress with seven buttons showing on each wrist. The tunic is confined at the waist by a girdle made of leather profusely adorned, and passing through an oval buckle, the end is passed under the girdle hanging down in front, and terminated by a metal pendant, on which is engraved a rosette. On his left side is the anelace, or basilard, which is suspended from the girdle by a thong. The anelace is broad in the blade, sharpened on both sides and tapered from hilt to point. The scabbard is ornamented with little pateras at the top and middle. Over all is a mantle, fastened by three large buttons on the right shoulder, and, gathered over the left arm, hangs gracefully. Round his neck he wears a hood of which the buttons are not shewn. The shoes are pointed and fastened across the instep by a plain buckle. The background of the feet is plain.

Marion Grevel wears the nebule head dress, which consists of three rolls of frills worn only on the top of the head and shoulders. Round her neck is a frill. The kirtle and cotehardie are buttoned from the neck to the feet, and more than four score buttons are shown. In the *Romance of Sir Degrevant*, the writer describing the dress of an earl's daughter, says "To tell her botennes was toore" (*i.e.*, *dure*, hard)—to count her buttons would give much trouble. She wears neither mantle nor girdle, and closely buttoned mittens are seen on her wrists. The ends of the shoes are visible.

They have hands folded in the attitude of prayer, the wife being on her husband's left hand.

The figures lie under a double canopy crocketed and cusped: in each pediment is the merchant's mark. (19) This mark consists of a cross standing on a globe, and a streamer attached to the shaft. On either side and from the middle rise pinnacles. Between the finials and pinnacles are four shields. (20) It is very unusual to find the merchant's mark and his coat of arms on the same monument. The two outer pinnacles are continued down till their bases from the extremity of the diapered band at the bottom upon which the figures stand. The centre pinnacle has a foliated capital and is continued till its base rests on the diapered band.

Fig. 19. Merchant's Mark. 1401, Campden.

Inscription.—The inscriptions are placed exactly as on the French monuments, the husband's beginning under his feet, the wife's over her head. The legend round the verge comprises two distinct and complete commemorative inscriptions:—

✠ Hic iacet Wilelmus Greuel de Campdene | quondm' Ciuis London' & flos m'cator' lanar' tocius Anglie qui obijt p'mo die menſe Octobris An˜ | dn'i mill'm'o CCCC˜ p'mo. ✠ Hic iacet Mariona vxor | predicti Wilelmi que obijt Decimo die Menſis

---

For an account of Merchants' Marks see *Gloucestershire Notes and Queries* vol. v., p. 107 and vol. vi., pp. 9-12.

Septembris Anno d'n'i mill'm'o CCC⁰ LXXX⁰ V3⁰ Quor' a'i'ab' [p'picic]tur Deus. Amen.
which may be thus translated :

"Here lies William Grevel, of Campden, formerly a citizen of London, and the flower of the wool-merchants of all England, who died on the first day of October, A.D. 1401. Here lies Marion, wife of the aforesaid William, who died on the tenth of September, A.D., 1386. On whose souls may God have pity. Amen."

Heraldry.—The arms on the four shields, are :— Sable on a cross engrailed or, five pellets within a bordure engrailed of the second ; a mullet of the second in the dexter quarter for difference. The same still appears on the arms of the Earls of Warwick, but without the mullet.

Fig. 20. Arms of Grevel· 1401, Campden.

Illustrations.—Engravings of this brass may be found in *Gough*, vol. II. pl. IV., p. 10, *Bigland's Collections for Gloucesshire*, vol. I., p. 283, *Boutell's Series, Weekly Register*, No. 7, p. 105; *Boutell's Heraldry, Plate,* xxxvii. (coat of arms)

Portions Lost.—The lower portion of the central shaft, three crockets, the capital of the column at the wife's left hand *p'picie* of the inscription.

Biographical Account.—It is said that this family is of Norman extraction. John Grevill died before 33 Edward III., and was succeeded by his son William, who was seated at Campden. 21 Richard II. he had a son William, who was known as William Grevel of London, though afterwards he became of Campden, and is the subject of this memoir.

"William Grevel, woolmerchant, of Campden, who rebuilt Campden Church, co. Gloucester, lent to King Richard the Second, two hundred marks, on a promise of repayment at the ensuing Easter, 1398. He purchased in the same year, of Sir Walter Beauchamp, Knt., the manor of Millcote, and obtained a release of the same from William de Peto, Nov. 5, 1398. In 1400-1, 2 Henry IV., he entailed that estate by fine on the heirs of Joan, his then wife, sister and heir to Sir Philip Thornbury, Knt., and for want of such issue, to John and Lodowick, his sons by his first wife.

Male issue by his second wife Joan failing, he was succeeded in his estates by his eldest son John, and as an instance of the change in coat armour common at this period, it is deserving of note, that this John Grevel bore for his arms—Sable, on a cross engrailed within a bordure or, ten annulets of the first; in the dexter quarter, a mullet of the second. He was succeeded by his son John, who bore the arms without either annulets or pellets, but retained the mullet. The arms of the Grevilles as now borne by them are with the pellets, but without the mullet."—*Willis's Current Notes* (1857), vol. VII., p. 88.

"Speaking of the eminent clothiers† of Wiltshire, Aubrey states that 'the ancestor of Sir William Webb, of Odstock, near Salisbury, was a merchant of the staple in Salisbury. As Greville and Wenman bought all the Coteswold wool, so did Hall and Webb the wooll of Salisbury plaines.'"

For the subjoined interesting particulars, the reader is indebted to the Rev. T. P. Wadley. In a tax roll (numbered $\frac{19}{31}$ in the Public Record Office) which seems to belong to 2 or 4 Richard II; "*Will' Grenel mercator lan' Marie vx' ei*' xiijs. iijd. for both; his servants Thomas, William, John, and Robert, and Agnes, and Agnes were taxed iiijd. each.

"The *Inquis p. mortem* 3 Henry IV. No. 33 records that Wm. Grevil possessed property in Ullington and Pebworth.

"These occur on the ancient roll of the Guild of the Holy Trinity, &c., of Coventry, the name of William Grevel, of Campedene, and Mari*ota* his wife, and Richard Greuel his father.

"The will of William Grevel, who died in 1401, is registered at the Lambeth Library, in *Arundel*, vol. I., fol. 183. It was made 2 Apr., 1401, and proved at Lambeth, 8th Oct., 1401. He desired to be buried in the Church of the Blessed Mary of 'Campeden,' and bequeathed a 100 marks to the new work to be carried on there. Four chaplains were to celebrate daily in that Church for 10 years and be paid £200. Thomas Harewell, Richard, my priest, Thomas Geme, John Lawe, John Thurk, William Welde, Henry Foliot, Andrew Boteller, Wm. Cooke, were the legatees named. Residue of goods to the executors, namely, his wife Johan, John Grevell, and Richard Boschell (apparently Richard Bushell, then of Broad Marston,

† The general name for a clothier was a "a webbe," under which title Chaucer has introduced one into his Canterbury Tales.

in Pebworth), who were to dispose, *pro anima mea*, Sir Roger Hatton, abbot of Evesham, and Sir William Bradley, overseers."

The present Earl of Warwick is descended from Wm. Grevel and is entitled to quarter his arms. For particulars as to descent from William Grevel the reader is referred to "*Account of the Greville Family*," by J. Edmondson, 1766.

VIII.—Dyrham.

Sir Morys Russel [1401], and wife Isabel, with canopy (pediments only left), 6 Latin verses, large, South aisle. *Haines.*

Position.—Under a movable platform in south aisle.

Size.—7ft. 6in. x 3ft. 1in.

Description.—Sir Morys is represented in the armour which was commonly used during the end of the fourteenth and the first ten years of the fifteenth century. His armour is therefore very similar to that worn by Thomas Lord Berkeley, at Wotton-under-Edge, already described in No. II. of this series. Sir Morys wears the bascinet, camail, and habergeon of chain mail, breast and back plates, jupon with a a straight edge, and plate armour over the arms and legs. The hands are protected by gauntlets which are plain at the wrists, where the lining is visible, and they are armed with only one row of gadlings. He wears no collar. Gussets of mail are shown at the arm-pits, elbow-joints, and also at the knees and feet. The jupon is confined on the hips by a horizontal baldrick of square plates of metal richly chased and linked together, to which are attached the misericorde and sword. The misericorde, or dagger of mercy, which was used to give the *coup de grace*, is also called the basilard. It was a short dagger without a crossguard, worn on the right side, and attached to the baldrick by a short cord or chain. The upper part of the sheath for the sword is ornamented with rich tracery. The rowels of the spurs are clearly shown, and his feet are resting on a lion. (21)

Lady Russel wears the nebule head-dress. This consists of a caul of network arranged in three rows on the top of the head. Under this caul is a close-fitting embroidered cap, which keeps the hair off the forehead. The head-dress conceals the ears and falls in a wavy line upon the shoulders, where the network again appears. She is clothed in a mantle fastened

Fig. 21. Sollerets and Lion. 1401, Dyrham.

by a cord. Above the hands we see five buttons of the gown which is cut higher than that of Lady Berkeley. At her feet lies a little lap dog with a collar of bells. (22)

Fig. 22. Dog. 1401, Dyrham.

The figures are under a double canopy with oval cusped heads and crocketted ogee gables. Each tympanum is filled with a circular panel, containing a shield. The spandrils of the cusps are filled with leaves and terminate in trefoils.

They both are represented full-face, with hands folded

ready for devotion : the wife lying at her husband's right hand.

Inscription.—Under their feet are the following Leonine verses :

> Miles p'uatus vita iacet hic tumulatus
> Sub petra stratus Morys Russel vocitatus
> Isabel sponsa fuit huius militis ista
> Que iacet abscousa sub marmorea modo cista
> Celi solamen, trinitas, his conferat. amen.
> Qui fuit est et erit concito morte perit.

> Entombéd here bereft of life, behold a noble Knight
> Beneath this stone he lieth prone, once Morys Russel hight
> And Isabel his loving spouse in marble rare enclosed
> Hidden from sight of earthly wight hath here her limbs reposed
> The joy of Heaven bestow on these, blest Trinity of Grace
> Past, present, future, Death shall seize, who are of mortal race.

The two lines commencing with Isabel were also on a brass of about the same date at St. Mary's, Stafford : the names of the wives being the only difference. *Vide Ashmole's Collections for Staffordshire, Bodleian Library. No.* 583, *Vol. I. fol.* 12 *a.*

Fig. 23 a

Heraldry :—Over the husband, Argent, on a chief gules three bezants. The field is covered with diaper work, consisting of quatrefoils. (23 a)

Over the wife is, Russel as above, impaling quarterly 1st and 4th Argent, a bend wavy gules, between two bendlets of the last, Kingston, 2nd and 3rd, Ermine three annulets, one within the other gules, Fitton. (23 b)

Fig. 23 b

Illustration.—The effigies engraved in *Boutell's Series.*

Portions Lost.—The tops of the canopies and the flanking pinnacles, a portion of the guard of the sword

Biographical Account.—" It is traditionally asserted that Sir Maurice Russel, knight, built the church dedicated to St. Peter at Dyrham. He was Sheriff of Gloucestershire 1396."*Bigland.* He died seized of the manor 2 H. IV, and left two daughters Margaret and Isabel, the first married to Sir Gilbert Dennys, knight; who, with Sir John Drayton and Isabel his wife, the other daughter of Sir Maurice, (married before to Sir John St. Roe) were jointly seized of the manor of Dyrham 3 H. V.

But Sir Maurice, by a second wife, had a son Thomas, whose only child was named Margery, and died without issue.

IX. AND X.—Bristol, Trinity, or Barstaple Almshouse Chapel.

IX.—John Barstaple, burgess, founder of almshouses, 1411, canopy lost, small.

X.—Isabella [Gayner?] wife of No. IX., canopy lost, engraved *circa* 1411, small.—*Haines*.

Position.—In March 1882 these brasses consisted of loose and detached pieces in the custody of the Charity Trustees at Bristol. They were originally on two flat stones in the Chapel of the Trinity Almshouses. The erection of the new chapel was completed in 1882 when the brasses were recanopied and replaced on separate ledger stones in the chapel.

Size.—3ft. 7in. × 1ft. 9in. and 3ft. 5in. × 1ft. 9in.

Description.—Though these are separate memorials it will be convenient to describe them together. It was not usual to erect a memorial for a wife distinct from that of her husband in the same church.

John Barstaple has his hair cut short and a bifid beard. Round his neck he wears a hood fastened by buttons at the throat. His tunic reaches to his ankles, and is confined at the waist by an ornamental girdle, buckled in front, the end hanging down is terminated by a metal pendant, which formerly had a jewel in the cavity shown on the brass. From this belt is suspended a basilard or anelace on his left side. The sleeves are close and buttoned at the wrist. The shoes are large and fastened across the instep by a buckle. The ground beneath them is adorned with lilies (24)

Fig. 24. Feet.
1141, Bristol Trinity.

The figure of Isabella, the wife of John Barstaple, is a restored copy of an older one (*Haines, p. liii.*). The hair is represented on each side of the face; her head is covered by a veil or kerchief falling down on the back and shoulders; a gorget or wimple covers the neck, and is drawn over the chin. Round the shoulders is a cape fastened in front by a bow. She wears a long dress with tight sleeves slightly open in front showing the fur lining, and confined at the waist by a girdle which is tied in bow in front. Under her feet are three leaves of clover. (25)

They are both represented erect in the attitude of prayer.

Over each figure is a single canopy, crocketted and cusped with a panelled pinnacle on either side also crocketted and cusped; these pinnacles are continued to meet the inscription which is placed under the feet of each. The merchant's mark is below the inscription on the husband's brass and the coat of arms in a similar position on the wife's brass.

The merchant's mark consists of a cross with three streamers from the stem, which passes through a globe and terminates in another cross. (26)

Fig. 26. Merchants' Mark 1411. Bristol, Trinity.

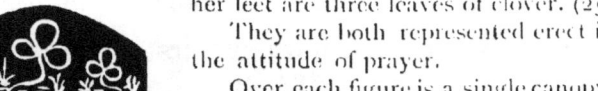

Fig. 25 Groundwork. c 1141. Bristol Trinity.

Inscription.—

Hic iacet Joh'es Barstaple Burges' Ville Bristo [ll' fudator isti loci qui] | obijt xv" kal'n Octob' l'ra d'o'cal' d A° d'ni M°mo CCCC°mo xj°mo cui' [a'ie p'piciet' d's Amen.]

The words in brackets have been restored to the inscription.

Here lies John Barstaple, burgess of the town of Bristol, founder of this place, who died 15th kalends of October, the Dominical letter D., 1411, on whose soul may God be merciful. Amen.

Hic iacet Isabella quonda vx' Joh'is Barstaple que obijt anno d'ni mill'o CCCC°mo .... l'ra d'o'calis .. .. cui' a'ie p'piciet' d's Ame.

Here lies Isabella wife of John Barstaple, who died in the year of our Lord, 14........the dominical letter being........ on whose soul may God have pity. Amen.

Fig. 27. Inscription. 1411, Bristol, Trinity.

The *da* of *quondam* and the *do* in *dominicalis* are conjoined and this contraction for *domini* is not usual. (27)

This use of the dominical letter is rare, and the Roman computation by Kalends seldom occurs.

Though John Barstaple and his wife were founders of the Trinity Almshouses, no one has taken the trouble of filling in the blanks on the brass of Isabella Barstaple with the date of her death. From her will it is clear she did not long survive her husband.

Fig. 28. Shield.
c 1411. Bristol, Trinity.

Heraldry.—The arms on the shield below the wife are "Azure, on a fesse between three roses or, as many bugle horns sa, Gayner." *(Simpson.)* (28)

Illustration.—*Bristol, Past and Present* vol. 2. p. 176.

Portions Lost.—The canopy on each brass and a portion of the inscription to John Barstaple were lost but are now restored, and the brasses are in perfect condition.

Biographical Account.—John Barstaple was bailiff in 1379, sheriff in 1389; and Mayor of the city in 1395, 1401, 1405. "When John Barstaple married his wife Isabella she was a spinster and the younger daughter of Walter Darby, the founder of St. Werburgh's Church."—*F. W. Newton.*

The will of Isabella Barstaple, widow of John Barstaple, a burgess of Bristol, was made 2nd March, 1411, and proved 30th March, 1412, (his will *see* 23 Marche) 1412. P. C. C. 24 Marche. To be buried in the Chapel of the Holy Trinity, "iux' portam Lafford." Names sons, Sir Nicholas, a chaplain, and Thomas and two daughters Alice and Joan wife of Robert Shepward. For further particulars see *Bristol Wills* p. 87.

XI.—Quinton.

Joan Clopton, widow of Sir (Wm. ?) Clopton, vowess, *circa* 1430, with canopy, and eight elegiac verses on marginal inscription. Altar Tomb.—*Haines.*

Situation.—On altar tomb at east end of south aisle.

Size.—6ft. 4in. × 2ft. 6in.

Description.—Her head is covered by the veil head-dress or hood. The veil is thrown over side cauls which causes the head-dress to assume somewhat the shape of the horned head-dress, and it hangs down covering the shoulders. A gorge or wimple covers her neck; this piece of attire is drawn over the chin in plaits and strained up each side of the face, the kirtle is long and has tight sleeves with narrow fur cuffs at the wrists. The mantle is fastened by a cord which passes through two metal loops with studs in front, termed fermailes, placed on each side of the mantle; this cord passes through a slide made of cord, and terminates below the waist in two tassels. Beneath is a tight-fitting gown not girt at the waist. On her right hand is a ring with a jewel. She is represented full face, with her hands raised in the attitude of devotion.

The effigy lies under a crocketted canopy, with a circular cusped head. The tympanum is filled with a circular panel containing a sexfoil, the spandrils being filled with quatrefoils, as also the upper two spandrils of the cusps. The canopy is terminated by a foliated finial. On each side rises a panelled pinnacle surmounted by a crocketted finial. The sides of the canopy are continued down level with the feet and beneath them are shields, as also between the pinnacles and the gable of the canopy.

As she was a "vowess" she is represented on a separate tomb. Her husband is commemorated by an alabaster effigy.

Inscription—the margin is the following inscription:—

☩ Criste nepos Anne Clopton' miserere Job'e
Que tibi sacrata clauditur hic vidua
Milite defuncto sponso pro te ih'u fuit ista
Larga libens miseris prodiga & hospitibus
Sic ven'abilibus templis sic fudit egenis
Mitteret vt celis quas sequeretur opes
Pro tantis meritis sibi dones regna beata
Nec premat vrna rogi sz bect aula dei

Vowed to a holy life when ceased her Knightly husband's breath
Joan Clopton here, Anne's grandchild dear; implores Thy grace in death
O Christ!—for Thee O Jesu blest, how largely hath she shed
Her bounteous gifts on poor and sick—how hath she garnishéd
Thy stately shrines with splendour meet—how hath she sent before
Her earthly wealth to Thee above, to increase her heavenly store!
For such blest fruits of faith, O grant, in Thine own joy her meed
Light-lies an earthly tomb on those whom Heavenly blessings speed!

Fig. 29. "Pear" c 1430, Quinton.

At the end of each line is a "pear" (29) the charge on the Besford arms, a punning allusion to "Pearsford."

At each of the four corners of the inscription round the verge are the symbols of the four evangelists:— St. Matthew, an angel clothed in amice and albe, at upper sinister angle; St. Mark, a winged lion, at lower dexter angle; St. Luke, a winged ox, at lower sinister angle; and St. John, an eagle, at upper dexter angle.

Over her head is a scroll with the following words, taken from Psalm xl.

Complaceat tibi Dne ut eripias me
Dne ad adiuuand' me respice.

Heraldry.—On the right hand at top is (1) Argent two bars gules, fretty, or, for Clopton, (30) on the left hand side at top (2) Gules, a fess argent, between six pears or, for Besford (31). At the right hand below the canopy is (1) impaling (2) (32), and on the left hand is (1) with the addition of a canton. These arms were originally filled in with composition, of which much of the red has remained. "According to Burke, one family of *Clopton* bore arms almost identical with those assigned to Besford, viz., Gu., a fess betw. six pears, or, the only difference being the tincture of the fess."—(Sir John Maclean, in the *Transactions of the Bristol and Gloucestershire Society*, vol. vi., p. 343.) The Clopton arms appear on the brass to Thomas de Cruwe, 1411, Wixford Church, Warwickshire.

Fig. 31. Shield.
c 1430. Quinton.

Fig. 30. Shield.
c 1430. Quinton.

Fig. 32. Shield.
c 1430. Quinton.

Illustration.—*Trans. Bristol and Gloucestershire Archæological Society*, vol. xiii p. 168.

Portions Lost.—The monument is in excellent condition, and at the east end of the tomb is—

T. Lingen, Ar. reparavit. Anno 1739.

Brasses composed of several distinct portions are rarely

found perfect; the inscription at the end of the tomb possibly explains why this memorial is so perfect.

Biographical Account.—Sir William Clopton was the son of Julian............by her first husband. Her second husband was Thos. de Crue, and the brass to both is at Wixford, 1411. The latter died without issue in 1418 and was succeeded by the family and representatives of his wife's former husband. Thomas de Crue, in his will, proved 23rd September, 1418, left his sister, Elizabeth (prioress of Chester), and William Clopton, and *Joan* his wife, executors. License was granted, 26 Henry VI., to Wm. Wolashull to found a chantry in connection with the Crewe Chapel at Wixford, co. Warwick; the chaplain to celebrate divine offices for the souls of Thomas Crewe and Julian, his wife, William Clopton Knight, and *Johan*, his wife, &c. She was second daughter and co-heir of Alexander Besford *alias* Pearsford of Besford co. Worcester.

Sir William Clopton died 7 Hen. V. (1419), and was buried at Quinton where is his effigy. He left a son and heir who must have died young and without issue for his two daughters became co-heiresses. The elder Agnes married 1st Roger Harewell of Wotton Wawen, co. Warwick, and 2nd Thos. Herbert. The younger Joane married Sir John Burgh, Knight who died 1471, the last heir of the Princes of South Wales. She had three daughters, the youngest of whom married Sir John Lingen, Knight, who was sheriff of Herefordshire in 1470 and again in 1476.

The above-mentioned "T. Lingen, Ar." a descendant of the Cloptons died in 1742.

XII.—Cirencester.

[Rich.] Dixton, Esq., 1438, under canopy, marginal inscription mutilated, large.—*Haines*.

Situation.—This brass is in Trinity Chapel, and lies with others, close to the reredos.

Size.—7ft. 6in. × 2ft. 6in.

Description.—The effigy is that of a warrior clothed in the characteristic armour of the XV century. He wears a complete panoply of plate armour. His head is protected by a globular bascinet, which over the forehead is ornamented by a narrow band of quatrefoils; the top of the cuirass is enriched by a similar ornamental edging. The clean shaven face of the knight is unprotected : this was by no means unusual during this period ; for the additional safety afforded by the vizor was dispensed with to obtain freedom of breathing as well as to be rid of the stifling heat and weight of the solid steel plate the vizor would entail. A gorget of plate which reaches the bascinet, protects the neck and both sides of the face ; its lower edge is escalloped. The body is protected by polished breast and back plates, which open with hinges at the sides ; the arms, from the shoulder to the elbow, by brassarts consisting of overlapping plates, which are seen on the right shoulder, and from the elbow to the wrist by vambraces. "The pauldron of the left shoulder is elaborately enlarged and strengthened to resist a blow, while the right shoulder is more simply and lightly armed so as to offer as little hindrance as possible to the action of the sword-arm."—*The Knights of the Middle Ages, Rev. E. L. Cutts.* The elbows are guarded by small plates, which are termed gardes-de-bras. The gauntlets are not divided into fingers but are hinged in two places to allow the fingers to be used more freely, and they have plain cuffs. To the cuirass is attached at the waist a skirt of taces which consist of a series of narrow overhanging plates, fastened to a leather lining. The taces had hinges on their left side, and were fastened by buckles on the right; here the separate plates of the skirt of taces are notched in the centre, and they are eight in number. As the arms are protected by a system of secondary defences or reinforcing, so are the legs ; the thighs are guarded by *tuiles* (so called because they resemble *tiles*), which are buckled on to the skirt of taces. A little rosette covers the fastening of the two straps to each tuile and the two outer straps are fixed to the seventh tace, the two inner ones to the eighth tace. The legs are protected by plate armour : under the tuiles may be seen the cuissarts which protect the thighs and beneath the knees, the jambarts—the knees are guarded by genouillières, while extra pointed plates defend the shins. The feet are protected by sollerets of overlapping plates ; and he wears rowelled spurs. His feet are resting on a dog with head uplifted (33). Across the skirt of taces from right to left stretches diagonally a narrow sword-belt to which is attached on the left side, the scabbard

Fig. 33. Dog. 1438, Cirencester.

ornamented at the top. The sword is long and narrow, with a long, curved crossguard (34).

On the pommel appears his coat of arms. This does not often occur. His spurs are guarded so that they might not get entangled. By some this is thought to be a sign that the wearer was a courtier. At any rate Dixton was one, as we shall see later on.

Inscription.—The inscription, the lost part being supplied from Bigland runs thus:

[Hic jacet Richardus] Dixton Armiger qui obijt die Sancti Laurencij [Martyris anno Domini] Millesimo CCCC° xxxviij° Cuius anime propicietur [Deus Amen.]

Here lies Richard Dixton, Esq., who died on the day of Saint Lawrence the Martyr, [*i.e.* Aug. 10] in the year of our Lord 1438. On whose soul may God have pity. Amen.

The figure is erect, with the hands folded in the attitude of prayer, while over it is a very fine canopy with an oval cusped head, and a crocketted ogee gable, which is quite perfect, terminating in a foliated finial; there is a soffit moulding of quatrefoils running above the cusps; the two lower cusps are filled with trefoils. The tympanum is filled by a circular traceried panel divided into seven compartments, each of which is sub-divided and cusped; in the eye of the panel is a quatrefoil. The spandrils are filled with quatrefoils and trefoils. On either side are panelled pinnacles, which are continued downwards and end level with the feet, but unfortunately all the upper portions of them are gone.

Heraldry.—His arms are engraved on the pommel of the sword (34) and are Or, a pile azure, over all a chevron gules; the same coat appears on the North wall of the [Trinity] chapel.

Fig. 34. Pommel of Sword. 1438, Cirencester.

Illustrations.—Bigland vol. I., p. 341; Waller pt. xii; Boutell's Mon. Br. p. 69 (placcates).

Portions Lost.—The end of the sword, portion of the cross-guard, the misericorde, portions of the inscription, and two flanking pinnacles, and two shields, one on each side of the gable of the canopy.

Biographical Account.—Beyond the fact that Richard Dixton was squire to the ill-starred Richard of York, (father of Edward IV.) I have found no other record, except his will (P. C. C. Luffenam 119,) in it he desires to be buried "withyn the new chapell of the Trinite at Siscetre." He bequeaths vestments to this chapel and its priests, also to other religious bodies, " iij of my best hors to my Lord of York," "to my wyf all my stuff beying at the Fasterne." One of the executors was William Prelett of Siscetre *see* No. 24. His will is printed *in extenso* in *Trans. Bris. and Glos. Archæol. Soc.* vol. xi, p. 155.

XIII.—Bristol, St. Mary Redcliff.

Sir John Juyn, recorder of Bristol, Baron of the Exchequer, Chief Justice of the King's Bench, 1439, marginal inscription and eight Latin verses, Lady chapel.—*Haines*.

Position.—On a flat stone in the Lady chapel.

Size.— 6ft. x 2ft. 7in.

Description.—Sir John has a close cap covering his head, and he is clean shaven. Round his neck is a hood and over his shoulders a tippet edged with fur, which is to be seen under the mantle on the right shoulder. The tunic is long, reaching to the ankles, and the sleeves are full and slightly open at the wrists, showing the fur lining; beneath them fastened close to the wrists are seen the sleeves of an underdress. His mantle is not so long as his tunic: it is fastened by one button on the right shoulder, and being gathered up it falls in folds over the left arm; it is lined with fur. His shoes have pointed toes. He is represented full face with hands folded in prayer.

Inscription.— Round the verge is—

Hic iacet Johes Juyn Miles Capitalis Judiciari' D'ni Regis ad pli'ta Coram ip'o rege tenenda qui obijt xxiii° Die Marcii Anno Dni Millmo CCCCXXXIX° cui' a'i'e p'picietur De' Amen.

Here lies John Juyn, Knight, Chief Justice of our Lord the King for Pleas held before the King himself, who died on the 23rd day of March in the year of our Lord, 1439, on whose soul may God have mercy. Amen.

Beneath his feet are eight Leonine verses:—

    Juste deus paciens Judex miserere Johannis
    Juyn qui ius faciens miles fuit ci' in annis
    Urbe recordator fuit hac Baro Sccioq3
    Sumus et in Banco Judex capitalis vtroq3
    Justiciam voluit conixam cu pietate
    Miliciam coluit subnixam nobilitate
    Juste ihu fortis miles iam ppiciatus
    Esto fores mortis sibi claude remitte reatus.

"O Just God, patient Judge, have mercy upon John Juyn, who was in his time a soldier, but practising the law he became Recorder of this City, Chief Baron of the Exchequer, and Chief Justice in both benches, he tempered justice with clemency; maintained himself, being a soldier, in honour. Just Jesus! brave soldier! now be thou propitiated; shut the doors of death upon him, pardon his sins." Between each word of the legend round the verge the same ornament is repeated (35).

Fig. 35. "Break."
1439, Bristol, St. Mary Redcliff.

Heraldry. Beneath are two shields, the sinister being, Or, a fess azure between three unicorn's heads coupled argent, within a bordure of the same, quartered with . . . a lion rampant (36a) . . . The dexter being . . . a lion rampant . . . impaling . . . (36b) *Pryce.*

Fig. 36a. Shield.
1439, Bristol, St. Mary Redcliff.

Fig. 36b. Shield.
1439, Bristol, St. Mary Redcliff.

Illustrations.—*Anastatic Society*, 1860.
Portions Lost.—None.
Biographical Account.—*Pryce*, p. 183, says "beyond what is stated in the inscription little is known of him." but more is known of him now than was in Pryce's time.

Rev. T. P Wadley, M.A., suggests that his name may have been Inyn, and adds, "There were anciently Bristol people of the name of *Innyn* or *Inhyme.* A Philip *Guyn* was among the burgesses of Bristol in 1430. Again, the episcopal registers at Worcester record that William *Inyne*, Canon of Cirencester, was ordained a religious acolyte and sub-deacon in the year 1407, December 17th, possibly his name was *Juyne.*" From *Judges of England* by Foss the following is taken :—

John Juyn is so called in the Rolls of Parliament, and the Acts of the Privy Council, but sometimes spelt Joyn, and on his monument Juyn and so in Bishop Bubwith's will of which he was one of the executors, which seems most probably correct, as his mansion is now called " Inne Court." He was one of a Somersetshire family, his country seat being at Bishopsworthy (now called Bishport) in that county. He first appears in the Year Book of II Hen. IV; after which his name is of frequent occurence. He held the office of Recorder of Bristol, and about eight months after the accession of Henry VI, he was appointed, on 5th May, 1423, to the double office of Chief Baron of the Exchequer, and Judge of the Common Pleas. (*Acts Privy Council iii.* 71.) He was knighted in 4 Hen. VI ; and on 9th Feb., 1436, he was made Chief Justice of the latter court. About three years later he became chief justice of the King's Bench and presided there to his death, on 24th March, 1439-40. He was buried in St. Mary's Chapel, Redcliffe Church, Bristol By his wife Alice he left a son.

XIV.—Cirencester.

Robert Page, wool merchant, 1440 (?) and wife Margaret, with six sons and eight daughters; canopy; marginal inscription in six Latin verses (stating he repaired churches and roads) lost. The date is given from *Wood's* M.S. (D. 11. No. 8,517, fol. 29) at the Ashmolean Library.—*Haines*.

Position.—On a flat stone in the Trinity Chapel.

Size.—7ft. x 2ft. 10in.

Description.—"There is a very fine brass, with double canopies, representing a merchant and his wife, with fourteen children at their feet. There is no name, as the whole of the inscription is lost ; but the style of the execution of the brass would place the date about the latter half of the XV century (temp. Edw. IV. or Rich. III). The male figure is depicted wearing a loose gown, with large sleeves, gathered in tighter at the wrist; the collar is standing up round the neck, and there is a girdle round the waist; the female figure is draped much in the same style. At the foot of the male figure, and above the canopy are escutcheons charged with a merchant's mark, and a letter " R " in old English. This is probably one Robert Pagge and his wife, who are stated in the *History of Cirencester* as being commemorated by a fine brass in the church. A scroll issues from the mouth with these words

'*That to the Trinite for us*,' the rest is lost, but the words most probably were '*pray, singe or read*,' as examples are to be found in other parts of the kingdom."

Rev. W. E. Hadow, M.A.

The figures are under a double canopy with circular cusped heads, and crocketted ogee gables terminated by a foliated finial characteristic of the period. The tympana are filled in with circular panels, within which are sexfoils; the spandrils being filled in with trefoils as also the spandrils of the cusps. On either side and between the canopies are panelled pinnacles terminated with crocketted finials; the outer pinnacles are continued down on either side forming a border, but the centre one is terminated by a moulded and foliated pendant. The feet of Robert Page rest upon a woolsack. Beneath the husband are six sons, and beneath the wife eight daughters. The sons are dressed like their father, and the daughters have long dresses with sleeves like their mother's, but lower at the neck. Their hair is confined by caps with side cauls covering the ears. Unfortunately the heads of the first three daughters have vanished, but Mr. Blake of Stroud has very kindly lent a rubbing taken before they disappeared, and on that is shown that all eight daughters wore similar caps. Scroll work separates each child. All are represented standing with hands folded in the attitude of prayer. His merchant's mark consists of a cross with streamers standing on a lozenge charged with the letter "R" in old english.

Inscription.—" Bigland has preserved the inscription of this and other memorials, stating in a note that he 'has given them as before the mutilation from a manuscript of Thomas Carles, M.A., vicar, dated Dec. 8, 1673, obligingly communicated by the Rev. Mr. Kilner.'

Hic jacet Robertus Pagge cum Margareta sibi sponsa prole fecunda.

Vicinis gratus fuerat mercator amatus
Pacificus, plenis manibus subventor egenis
Ecclesiisque viis ornator, et bis reparator,
Mill' C quater X quater anno, sed Aprilis
Octava luce mortem p' transit ipse,
Cell solamen Deus, illi conferat. Amen.

" He states that on a Pilaster between him and his wife is engraven the usual diagram of the Trinity, and on a label '*That to the Trinite for us pray, singe or read.*' Pagge's label it would seem was already lost."

Fig. 37. Pendant.

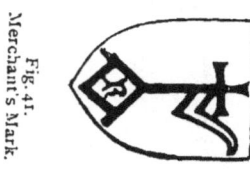

Fig. 41. Merchant's Mark.

Fig. 38. Woolsack. 1440. Cirencester, Robert Pagge. Details.

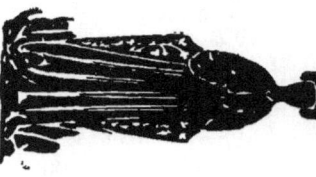

Fig. 39. Son.

Fig. 40. Daughter.

The inscription may thus be rendered into English :—
Of good report, beloved of all, this peaceful man of trade,
With liberal soul his plenteous dole to needy brethren made,
The beauty of God's house he sought, our ways he well sustained,
In fourteen-hundred-fortieth year, when showery April rained,
On the eighth morn death's gate he passed :— O ruler of the skies,
On him Thy heavenly grace bestow, and grant the eternal prize.

Illustrations.—None known.

Portions Lost.—The inscription, the label over the husband's head, the finials of the pinnacles, a portion of the side, the heads of the first three daughters.

Biographical Account.—The inscription states that he repaired churches and roads. His will is in the Prerogative Court of Canterbury 27 Luffenham.

XV.—Cirencester.

Reginald Spycer, merchant, 1442, and his wives, Margaret, Juliana, Margaret, Joan.—*Haines*.

Position.—On the floor in the Trinity Chapel.

Size.—2ft. 5in. × 1ft. 10in., not including the merchant's mark.

Description.—" The date of the brass to Reginald Spycer and his four wives is 1442 (20 Henry IV.) The male figure in the centre is clothed in a close-fitting gown, reaching nearly to the ankles, girded at the waist; the sleeves are somewhat full, but fit tolerably close at the wrist; the collar is an upright one; the gown is buttoned from the neck to the breast; beneath appears the collar of the under-tunic. Of the wives, the two on the husband's left hand wear that peculiar shape of the horned head-dress, which may be distinguished as the 'heart-shaped,' the folds of the head-dress descend in front of the figures on to the breast; the kirtles are long and flowing over the feet, the sleeves shaped like their husband's; the collar is opened so as to fall back, and no buttons are visible; the kirtle is confined round the waist by a girdle. The two wives on the husband's right hand wear the coverchef, falling in folds in front on the breast; and the wife on the extreme right has the hair in a sort of caul, or close cap; both of these dresses are of

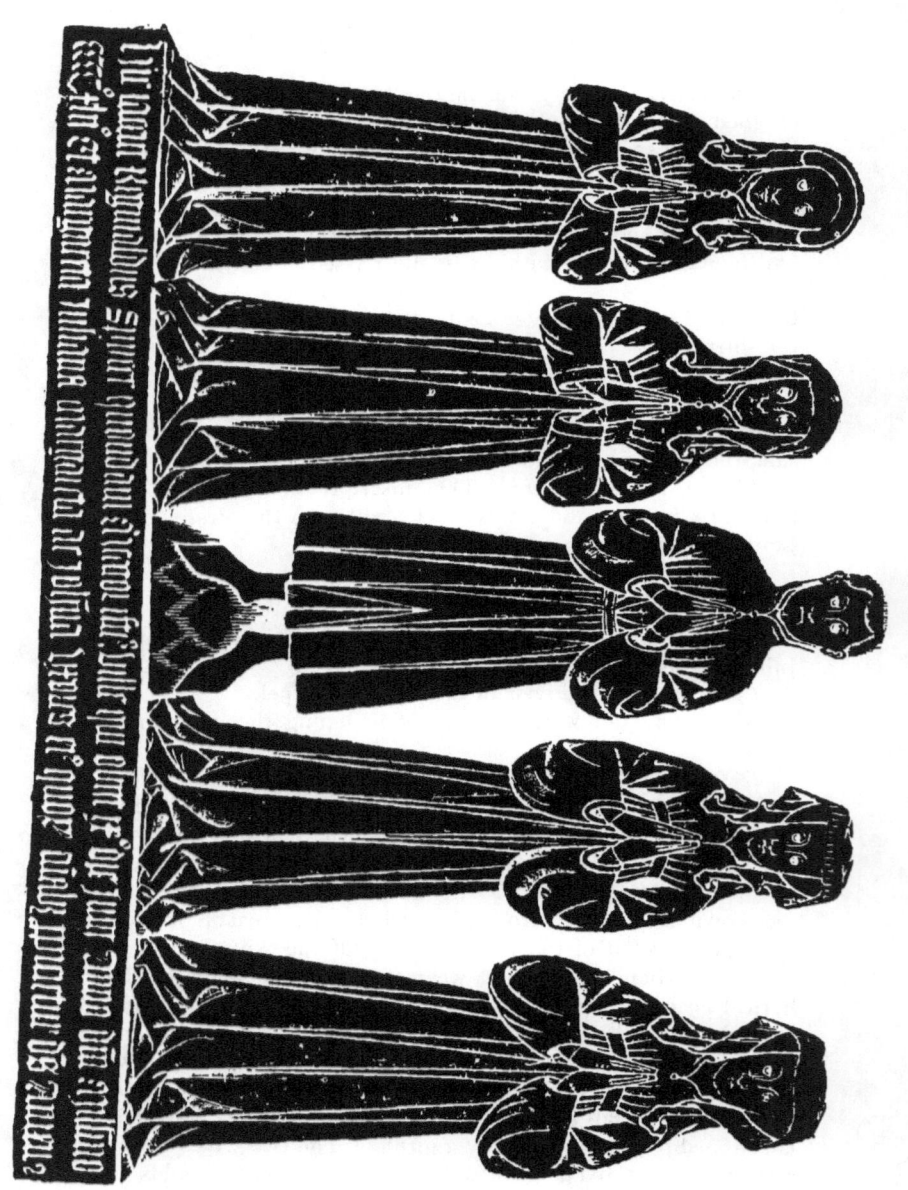

Fig. 42. Reginald Spycer and four wives, 1442, Cirencester.

older date than the heart-shaped, and thus on the same brass we have examples of the styles in which ladies dressed their hair from the latter part of the 14th to the middle of the 15th century. The kirtles of both the earlier wives are flowing like the others, but the sleeves are quite of a different pattern, being cut straight and are not so full. There are buttons from the neck to the breast; both also wear girdles." (42)—*Rev. W. E. Hadow, M.A.*. They are all erect with hands in the attitude of prayer, the husband having two wives on each side of him.

Beneath the figures is an escutcheon charged with a merchant's mark (43) between the letters ℞ and S. The merchant's mark may be described as a cross with two streamers and a semicircle on the stem opposite to the streamers. The cross passes through a globe and the foot of the stem has a long horizontal line cutting it.

Fig. 43.
Merchant's Mark.
1442 Cirencester.

Inscription.—The inscription at the foot is as follows.—

𝕳ic iacent Reginaldus Spycer quondam m'cator isti' ville qui obijt ix° die Julij Anno d'ni mill'mo CCCC° xlij° et Margareta Juliana Margareta ac Job'na vxores ci' quor' a'i'abus p'picetur d's. Amen.

The inscription in English reads thus:—" Here lie Reginald Spycer, formerly a merchant of this town, who died on the 9th of July, A.D. 1442, and Margaret, Juliana, Margaret, and Joan, his wives on whose souls may God have mercy. Amen."

Illustrations.—*Transactions of the Bristol and Gloucestershire Archæological Society* for 1877-8, p. 154.

Portions Lost.—None.

Biographical Account—Nothing is known of Reginald Spicer, but the will of a Joan Spicer, of Cirencester, probably his widow, was proved 1444. P.CC. Luffenham.

XVI.--Newland.

A man in armour, legs gone, and wife *circa* 1445, with curious crest, marginal inscription nearly all lost. South Chancel.—*Haines.*

Position.—On the floor in the Chapel of SS. Nicholas and John.

Size.—This brass originally was 7ft. 10in. × 3ft., but all that remains is 3ft. 9in. × 2ft 2in.

Description—The husband is represented wholly in plate armour. His hair is cropped close but the beard is full. His head rests on a helmet of which the visor is raised. (44) The

Fig. 44. Head and Helmet. c 1445. Newland.

body is protected by a cuirass, the shoulders are defended by épaulières. " The left or bridle arm is more fully protected than the right, by large plates placed outside the elbow, and in front of the armpit ; they were secured by small spikes or spring-pins fitted into staples affixed to the armour underneath, the loops of which passed through holes in the centre of the plates. The right, or sword arm, which was required for action, has slighter defences ; thus a small and peculiar-shaped plate called a moton, protects the armpit, and the elbow-piece is much smaller."—*Haines. p. cxci.* The gauntlets have long pointed cuffs and have no gadlings. To the cuirass is attached a skirt of seven taces; to this skirt are buckled two pointed tuiles which hang over and protect the thighs. Across the skirt is stretched a sword-belt obliquely from right to left, to this belt is fastened a sword, and on the right side the pommel of the misericorde is seen. The thighs are covered by cuisses ; the rest of the figure has disappeared.

The wife wears the fashionable horned head-dress of the period. The embroidered band of the crespine closely fits the face and entirely conceals the hair and ears. The side cauls of the crespine are much raised above the forehead, thus forming that variety of the horned head-dress known as the acutely-pointed. Over all this is thrown a veil which is gathered in folds and falls gracefully on the shoulders. The caul is enriched by bands of embroidered cinquefoils which alternate with slightly narrower bands upon which are worked a neat pattern. Her dress is long, and being girt high by an ornamental girdle makes the figure short-waisted. The sleeves are wide and hanging, but narrow at the wrists. At the neck the dress is low, leaving the upper portions of the shoulders as well as the neck bare.

They are both represented erect with hands in the attitude of prayer, the wife being on the husband's right hand.

Inscription. The late Mr. J. D. T. Niblett, F.S.A., kindly gave me a rubbing on which are **Anno d'ni Mill'o CCCC**⁰, these words have now disappeared but they are here reproduced (45). In the illustration in the *Antiquarian Repertory*, 1780, two more words are given, **die Maie**, but now all traces of the inscription have disappeared. The late Sir John Maclean suggested that *moie* may have been a misreading of *m-nsis*. On the slab between the figures are incised these words: SIR CHRISTOPHER BAYNHAM, KT., and these have been filled in with mortar.

Heraldry.—The four shields originally on this memorial are lost, but in the centre above is a square plate (46) which in 1780 was reported as lost but now is in place. Mr. Nicholls in his *Forest of Dean* (p. 217) thus describes it:—

"The heraldic crest gives a curious representation of the iron miner of that period equipped for his work. (46) It represents him as wearing a cap, holding a candlestick between his teeth handling a small mattock with which to loosen as occasion required, the fine mineral earth lodged in the cavity within

Fig. 45. Inscription. c 1445. Newland.

which he worked, or else to detach the metallic incrustations lining its sides, bearing a light wooden mine-hod on his back, suspended by a shoulder strap, and clothed in a thick flannel jacket, and short leathern breeches, tied with thongs below the knee. Although in this representation the lower extremities are concealed, the numerous shoe-footed marks yet visible on the moist beds of some of the old excavations prove that the feet were well protected from injury by the rough rocks of the workings. Several mattock-heads exactly resembling the one which this miner is holding have also been discovered; and to enable us, as it were, to supply every particular, small oak shovels for collecting the ore, and putting it into the hod, have in some places been found."

Fig. 46. Crest, c 1445. Newland.

Illustrations.—*Antiq. Repert.*, 1780, p. 259, and 1808, Vol. II. p. 387, *Nicholls' Forest of Dean* (crest), cover, title-page and p. 217, *Bristol and Gloucestershire Archæological Society Trans.*, vol. vii, and *Cardiff Naturalists' Society Trans.*, vol. xviii (1886) p. 48 (Crest only, litho. by T. H. Thomas).

Portions Lost.—The brass has suffered very rough treatment, it is much worn, and the portions lost are:—the whole of the marginal inscription, four shields, and the legs of the husband.

Biographical Account.—In the *Transactions of the Bristol and Gloucestershire Archæological Society*, vol. vii, is a paper by the late Sir John Maclean, F.S.A., entitled "Notes on the Greyndour Chapel and Chantry, in the Church of Newland, co. Gloucester, and on certain monumental brasses there," the writer assigns these brasses to Robert Greyndour and his wife dame Joan Barre. He died 19 November, 1443. His widow Joan, was daughter and heiress of Thomas Rugge, or Rigge, of Charlecomb, co. Somerset. She obtained letters patent, dated 6 November, 1445, to found a perpetual Chantry in the Church of Newland. She married Sir John Barre, of Rotherwas, co. Hereford, knight, who died 14 January, 1482-3, and dying 17 June, 1485, was buried in Newland Church with her first husband, Robert Greyndour. Her will is in the Prerogative Court of Canterbury, 16 Logge.

XVII.—Northleach.

Thos. Fortey, woolman, repaired churches and roads, 1447, (head lost); William Scors, tailor, 1420, and their wife Agnes (head lost), with two groups of children, two daughters (3 [?] other children gone) and two sons and four daughters, canopy and marginal inscription mutilated, North Aisle.—*Haines.*

Position.—On the floor in the North Aisle behind the organ.

Size.—8ft. 3in. x 3ft. 3in.

Description.—This brass represents Agnes Fortey and her two husbands—Thomas Fortey and William Scors.

She wears a robe with full sleeves, open and turned back at the wrists and lined with fur. Her dress is short-waisted and girt with a narrow plain girdle. The lady is now unfortunately headless. But this brass is illustrated in *Lysons' Gloucestershire Antiquities*, plate 42; and in it she is represented as wearing the veil head-dress.

Both her husbands wear tunics or gowns which reach half way down the leg, and are fringed with fur; the lower part of each is slit up in front to allow greater freedom in walking; the collar of each is buttoned up close to the chin; the sleeves are moderately full, but close at the wrists, where they are turned back and reveal the fur lining; the sleeves of an underdress are shown beneath. The tunic is girt round the waist by a narrow belt, which is plain on William Scors, but two studs or ornaments appear on Thomas Fortey's girdle. The hair of William Scors is cropped close, and he is clean shaven. The shoes are distinct from the hose; they have pointed toes and are fastened by buckles.

Under Thomas Fortey is what Lysons calls a woolpack, but it is now so worn as to render it difficult to say what it represented; under William Scors is a pair of shears (47). The woolpack" was the sign of the wool merchant, and the "pair of shears" that of a clothier, but in the inscription Scors is recorded as being a tailor. In Seend Church, Wilts, a "pair of scissors" is exhibited on the one side of the west window of the north aisle, and a "pair of shears" on the other side; and Mr. Kite, in his *Monumental Brasses of Wiltshire*, says that they are "in allusion to the occupation of the founder who was doubtless a clothier." Perhaps it may be well to note

Fig. 47. Feet of William Scors. 1447. Northleach.

that on the west wall of the tower of Cranham Church, a parish which touches Painswick on the north-east, there is carved the representation of a "pair of scissors" or "shears." It would be interesting to know whether the whole, or any part, was built by a "clothier."

The figures are erect with hands folded in the attitude of prayer; they are under an elaborate and enriched canopy, which has been much mutilated. Agnes is standing between her two husbands, having Thomas Fortey on her right hand, and William Scors on her left hand.

Inscription.—Beneath the figures there is a two-line inscription, which with the help of Lysons, from whom is taken the portions enclosed in brackets, reads thus:—

Hic jacet Thom's ffortey Wolma, Will's Scors Taylour & Agnes vx' corude q' quide Tb (om's obiit) | p'mo die deceb aº d'n'i Mº CCCC 47* Will's obiit die aº d'ni Mº CCCCxxº Agnes obiit die / Aº (d'ni MCCC).

This may be thus rendered into English:—

"Here lie Thomas Fortey, Woolman, William Scors, Tailor, and Agnes their wife, which Thomas indeed died on

---

* These figures (47) are very quaintly formed; this date has, therefore puzzled antiquaries. *Lysons* reads it as 84; *Bigland* gives it as being XX;

the first day of December, A.D. 1447, William died day of   A.D. 1420, Agnes died day of   A.D. 14 . ."

The date 1447 is shown in facsimile in the annexed engraving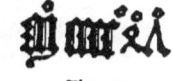

Fig. 49.

Beneath were two groups of children, with scrolls above them. The group of Thomas Fortey's children has disappeared, but the scroll remains with these words—"**Pray for ye children of Thomas Fortey.**" The other group consists of two sons and four daughters, and over them is a scroll inscribed with "**Theyse be ye childen of Willia Scors, vi.**

Round the verge is this inscription, the spaces between each word being filled with various ornaments:—

✠ **Sub** (rose) **pede** (rose) **morte** (rose) **jacens** (rose) **Thomas** (rose) **ffortey** (rose . . . . scroll) | (quadruped) **Et** (cock) **sua** (leaf) **sponsa** (boar) **placens** (hedgehog) **Agnes** (cinquefoil) **sibi** (fleur-de-lis) **consociatur** (rose and scroll work) [**Mercator dignus iustus uerarq; benignus**] (two dogs fighting) **Noscitur** (cinquefoil) **in** (crab) **signis** (blank) **non** (two fleurs-de-lis) . . . . . [**gaudens Jpe malignis**] | **Ecc'liarum** (castle) **suar;** (dragon) **viarum** (fabulous monster) **fit** (?) **Reparator** (. . .) |

while *Rudder* has XA, thus avoiding the difficulty by giving a very poor illustration of the first numeral. The inscription round the verge records 47. In *Journal of the Archæological Association*, 1846-7, Vol. II, pp. 146--163, and 283 are devoted to the antiquity of dates expressed in Arabic Numerals. From this we learn that the so-called Arabic numerals have not been found in inscriptions, in this country, before the fifteenth century. The earliest authentic date yet discovered in England appears on a stone in the interior of the tower of Heathfield Church, Sussex, and carries us no further back than the year 1445, so that probably this date on the brass in Northleach Church is the earliest to be found in Gloucestershire, and is only two years later than that of Heathfield.

𝕮𝖗𝖎𝖘𝖙𝖊 (goose) 𝖘𝖚𝖆𝖗𝖚𝖒 (leaf) 𝖘𝖎𝖘 (branches) 𝖒𝖎𝖘𝖊𝖗𝖆𝖙𝖔𝖗 (rose and scroll work) . . . . [𝖒𝖎𝖑𝖑𝖊] (an acorn between two oak-leaves) 𝖖𝖚𝖆𝖙𝖊𝖗 (slug) x (fighting cock) 𝖘𝖊𝖕𝖙𝖊𝖒 (snail) 𝖒𝖔𝖓𝖚𝖒𝖊𝖓𝖙𝖚 (eagle displayed and scroll-work) [𝖕𝖗𝖎𝖒𝖔 𝖉𝖆𝖙' 𝖋𝖑𝖆𝖒𝖊𝖓 𝖉𝖊𝖈𝖊𝖓𝖎 𝖅𝖇𝖊 𝖇𝖚𝖈 𝖇𝖊𝖆𝖙 . . .] (48)

The words in square brackets are supplied from Rudder. At the corners were the symbols of the four evangelists, of which St. Matthew only remains at the upper sinister angle.

Illustrations.—In *Lysons' Gloucestershire Antiquities*, plate 42 is devoted to this brass. It is represented much more perfect than it is at present, but even then it was mutilated.

Portions Lost.—Part of the right sleeve of Agnes, part of the right hand skirt of Fortey, part of the right and left hand skirt of Scors. The end of both lines of the inscription beneath Scors. The heads of both Fortey and his wife. All the children of Thomas Fortey. The whole of the right side and two portions of the left hand side of the canopy, a portion of the middle pinnacles, several portions of the legend round the verge, and three of the emblems at the corners. On rubbing the brasses in 1894, at least one portion was found to have disappeared since making a rubbing in 1883.

Biographical Account.—"Mr. Fortey, a wealthy clothier of this town, and his wife are both interred in this church, in the Abbey before the pulpit, upon whose gravestones are inchased their effigies in large plates of brass. The inscriptions on the brass are not perfect."—*Abel Wantner's Collections.*

In the marginal inscription unfortunately so imperfect he is described as having restored churches and roads.

XVIII.—𝕮𝖍𝖎𝖕𝖕𝖎𝖓𝖌 𝕮𝖆𝖒𝖕𝖉𝖊𝖓.

William Welley, merchant, 1450, and wife Alice, chancel, now within altar rails.—*Haines.*

Position.—On the floor in the chancel.

Size.—2ft. x 1ft. 10in., the slab measures 7ft. 10in. x 4ft 4in

Description.—The dress of William Scors, in the last description (vide No. xvii. of this series) resembles that worn by William Welley.

At the wrist are seen the sleeves of the under-dress, these sleeves are deeper than those of William Scors. The tunic is kept in place by a narrow belt round the waist. His hose and shoes are all in one piece, and it may be noticed that they are made right and left. His feet rest on ground from which grass is springing—emblem that "all flesh is grass."

Alice Welley wears the veil head-dress which consisted of a kerchief thrown over the head, concealing the ears and falling in folds on the shoulders and back. She has a long flowing gown, with deep full sleeves, in that respect resembling her husband's, and like his they are narrow at the wrist, where the end of the sleeve is turned back, and shows the fur lining. It does not fit the neck closely, but the top is turned down so as to form a little collar. The gown is girt high by a narrow girdle.

They are both erect with hands folded in the attitude of prayer, the wife being on the husband's right hand, and distant from him 11 inches.

Inscription—They stand on a brass plate, which bears the following inscription :—

𝔥𝔦𝔠 𝔦𝔞𝔠𝔢𝔱 𝔚𝔦𝔩𝔩'𝔪𝔰 𝔚𝔢𝔩𝔩𝔢𝔶 𝔮𝔬'𝔡𝔞 𝔪'𝔠𝔞𝔱𝔬𝔯 𝔦𝔰𝔱𝔦' 𝔙𝔦𝔩𝔩𝔢 𝔮𝔲𝔦 𝔬𝔟𝔦𝔦𝔱 𝔛𝔙° 𝔡𝔦𝔠 𝔄𝔭𝔯𝔦𝔩𝔦𝔰 𝔄° 𝔡'𝔫'𝔦 𝔆𝔆𝔆𝔆„𝔏°, 𝔢𝔱 𝔄𝔩𝔦𝔠𝔦𝔞 𝔳𝔵𝔬𝔯 𝔢𝔦𝔲𝔰 𝔮𝔲𝔬𝔯' 𝔞𝔦𝔞𝔟𝔷 𝔭'𝔭𝔦𝔠𝔦𝔢𝔱' 𝔡𝔠.' 𝔄𝔪𝔠.

Which may thus be translated into English :—"Here lies William Welley, formerly a merchant of this town, who died on the 15th day of April, A.D. 1450, and Alice his wife, on whose souls may God have mercy. Amen."

Illustrations.—None known.

Portions Lost.—Beneath the figures are the matrices of two shields.

Memoir—The inscription records that he was a merchant, of Campden.

The pedigree of the family of Weoley or Welley is in the *Visitation of Gloucestershire.*

XIX.—Lechlade.

A wool merchant and wife *circa* 1450, about six children, and inscription lost. Perhaps the brass of John Townsend, wolman, 1458. See Harl. MSS., No. 6,072, fol. 114. *Haines.*

Position.—On the floor in the Nave (March, 1882).

Size.—3ft. 2in. x 2ft. 5in.

Description.—The hair is close cropped and brushed back from the temples in a similar fashion to the reeve described by Chaucer in his *Canterbury Tales* :—

"His heer was by his eres rounde i-shorn."

His dress is like to that worn by the Campden merchant last described, viz., a long tunic reaching half way down the legs, open a little up the front, with the lappets turned back so as to show the fur lining. The sleeves are full, with narrow cuffs. Round the neck the top is turned over to form a collar. On this brass the opening of the upper portion of the tunic is clearly shown, it reaches a little below the belt, which is plain. The lower edge of the tunic is not fringed with fur. The shoes and hose are formed of one piece, and his feet rest upon a woolsack. (50)

Fig. 50. Feet. c. 1450. Lechdale.

"Mr. Gough says, the figures of shoes. as worn 37 Hen. VI., may be seen in Leachlade church; and that the figures as naturally show that the persons were woolmen as if there there had been inscriptions." †—*Fosbrooke's Gloucestershire*, vol. ii., p. 458.

The wife wears a modified form of the "horned" head-dress, called the "heart-shaped" headdress. The side cauls are unadorned and of moderate size, with their outer edges

---

† *Introd. Sepulch. Monum.*, v. i., pp. cxxvi.-vii.

elevated a little above the forehead and covering the ears, and over this is thrown a kerchief or veil, which covers the forehead and hangs down on the back and shoulders. She wears a long gown which completely covers the kirtle except at the wrists; it is girt under the breasts by a plain narrow girdle, and has very deep sleeves, close and edged with fur at the wrists; at the neck it is turned down so as to form a collar. The gown hides her feet.

Inscription.—The following extract from the Harleian Manuscripts in the British Museum is referred to by Mr. Haines:—

"In Lachlaide Church in com' Glocester.
Orate pro bono statu Jobis Towensend mercatoris et wollman' istius ville qui obijt, 19 August, 1458." No. 6,072, fol. 114.

Heraldry.—By the side of the above extract is tricked the following coat of arms:—*Sable, three woolpacks. Argent.*

Illustration.—*Bigland,* vol. ii., p. 141.

Portions Lost.—The marginal inscription, some six children, and four shields, one over head and one under foot of husband and wife respectively.

Biographical Account.—"There is," says *Atkyns,* "a monument in the church (Lechlade) in memory of John Townsend, merchant and woolman, of this place, who died 1458, and had been a good benefactor to the church and poor."—*History of Gloucestershire,* p. 280.

The will of John Townsend is in the Prerogative Court of Canterbury, 24 and 25 Stokton.

XX.—Northleach.

(John Fortey) 'wolman,' 1458, marginal inscription mutilated with six merchants' marks (one in private possession) large, Nave.—*Haines.*

Position.—On a flat stone in the Nave.

Size.—8ft. 10in. × 4ft. 1in.

Description.—His hair is closely cut, and brushed back from the temples, and he is clean shaven. He wears the long tunic then commonly worn, extending halfway down the legs but without any fringe of fur. The lower portion of the tunic is open for a short distance up the front, and the lappets are turned back revealing the fur lining. The tunic is fastened at the top, and two of the buttons are seen above the hands, the part round the neck is turned down to form a collar, and shows the fur lining. The sleeves are large and full, they reach nearly to the hips, but are narrow at the wrists, where they terminate in small fur cuffs. Portions of the underdress appear at the wrists and neck. The waist is girt by a strap, which passes through a large round buckle from which the unused portion of the girdle depends in front, and is terminated by a pendant on which was probably engraven his initial, in this portion of the belt are three holes so that the strap might be loosened at the wearer's pleasure. His shoes and hose are not distinct, and they have long pointed toes. His right foot rests on the back of a sheep, and the other on a wool-pack. (51) The figure is erect, with hands clasped in prayer.

Fig 51, Feet 1458. NORTHLEACH

John Fortey is represented under a trefoil arched canopy, the outer foils being smaller than the central one; all of them are moulded and cusped. Above is an ogee crocketted gable terminated by a moulded and foliated finial. The tympanum is filled by a circular panel (52) containing a rose

Fig. 52. Detail and Canopy. 1458. Northleach.

with four petals and four barbs, the spandrils being filled with trefoils, as also the spandrils of the cusps. The quatrefoil soffit moulding of the arches is continued down the sides. There are four pinnacles, two rise above the intersections of the trefoil arch, and have plain shafts, and the remaining two spring from the side shafts, forming the sides of the canopy, and are panelled. The side shafts are buttressed and have moulded offsets and bases.

Fig. 53. Merchant's Mark. 1458. Northleach.

At each corner of the slab, and in the middle of the inscription on the two longer sides were his marks. (53) This consisted of a cross standing on a woolpack; from the upper part of the stem a streamer is flying, whilst the lower part is ornamented: the initials of John Fortey, 𝔍. 𝔉. are placed on either side. These are surrounded by a small wreath formed of two ivy stems artistically intertwined, in the interstices of which alternately are placed an ivy leaf and a bunch of ivy berries seven times repeated.

Inscription.—Under the feet are the following Leonine verses :—

> Respice quid prodest presentis temporis evum
> Omne quod est nichil est preter amare deum.

Think what the things of present life have brought to thee in store.
Yet all is nought till thou hast sought thy Maker to adore.

" According to Weever, *Funeral Monuments*, p. 748, a similar inscription was to be found at Long Melford, Suffolk."—*Haines, i. p. xciv.* " The inscription at Northleach was at the Mercer's Chapel at London, on the tomb of John Riche, 1469, see Weever, *Fun. Mon.* p. 401." *Do. ii., p.* 259.

Round the verge was an inscription which cannot now be given in its entirety, the portion in brackets, taken from *Lysons*, supplies some thirteen words :—

[. . . . prayeth God his soule to socoure, and after his disese the rofe made . . . .] wherfor God rewarde him as he is all witty: As he bequathe him his soule in the yere of grace riiij boundred wynter and viij and fifty: In the celestiall . . . . . .

Illustrations.—*Lysons' Gloucestershire Antiquities* pl. 41. Cutts (E.L.) *Scenes and Characters of the Middle Ages*, p. 523 (effigy only) p. 526, (merchants' mark.)

Portions Lost.—The greater part of the marginal inscription, the finial of the gable, and portions of the flanking pinnacles. Some years ago a hole was clumsily knocked through the figure, near the right wrist, in order to fix a stove. !

Biographical Account.—" The roof of the nave was considerably raised at the expense of John Fortey, a wealthy clothier of this town [Northleach], who died in 1458, and was buried in the middle aile."—*Rudder*, p. 580.

" John Fortey, a clothier, built the body of the church."— *Atkyns*, p. 305.

His will was proved in the Prerogative Court of Canterbury, 1458, 24 and 25 Stokton.

XXI.—Temple Church, Bristol.

A priest in cope, on reverse a lady in mantle both engraved *circa* 1460, relaid.—*Haines.*

Position.—On the chancel floor. The Rev. Chas. R. Manning, in his "*List of Monumental Brasses,*" London, 1848, says of this brass, "A priest in cope, on the reverse a female (loose in the Vicarage kitchen)!"

Size.—27in. x 8in.

Description.—This brass is remarkable for being palimpsest, *i.e.*, there is an engraving on the reverse side of the plate. Mr. Haines chronicles that in this case the brass is cut out of a larger one which had been engraved with the representation of a lady in a mantle. (54) Very probably as the dates of the two engravings are nearly identical the reverse side may have been inaccurately engraved or for some other reason never laid down. The priest is represented with hair long enough to cover his ears, but the tonsure is clearly shown. He is dressed in processional vestments, which are a surplice, under which the cassock is visible, the almuce and cope. The cassock covers the feet, and has close sleeves; it formed the ordinary dress of the clergy. The surplice comes just below the knees, with very deep sleeves. (55)

The figure is erect, and the hands are placed in a devotional attitude. When this brass was rubbed in April, 1882, it was fixed to a slab in the chancel floor, and consequently it was impossible to see the reverse side or to take a rubbing thereof. By the kindness of the late Mr. J. D. T. Niblett, F.S A., who gave me a rubbing of this brass before it was fixed, an illustration of the reverse side is given. (54)

Illustration.—In Pryce's "*Notes*" is a sketch on p. 118 fig. 8.

Portions Lost.—The inscription. This brass is now so carefully scoured and brightened that in a few years the finer lines must inevitably disappear.

Biographical Account.—It is not known what persons the brass on either side commemorates.

XXII.—St. Peter's' Bristol.

Robert Lond, chaplain 1461, with chalice and host, Chancel.—*Haines.*

Fig. 54 Lady c. 1460. Temple Church, Bristol. Fig 55, Priest c. 1460, Temple Church, Bristol

Position.—On the floor at the east end of the south aisle, formerly the chantry of the Blessed Mary of Belhouse.

Size.—2ft. 5in. x 1ft. 6in.

Description—He is represented as wearing the eucharistic vestments, which are the amice, albe, maniple, stole, and chasuble; they were put on in the above order when the priest robes, and a short prayer was said as each vestment was assumed.

He is holding a chalice in his hands. The chalice in use in Robert Lond's days was a lighter and more elegant one than is generally seen at the present day, though copies of the old chalices are becoming more common. Placed erect over the chalice stands the host, or consecrated wafer: so that here is represented both the elements of the sacrament of the Lord's Supper. At the wrist are seen the tight-fitting cuffs of an under dress. His feet are shod with shoes having pointed toes. He is represented full-face, holding the chalice and host on his breast.

Inscription.—Beneath his feet is this inscription:

Hic iacet Magist' Rob'tus Lond Capellanus qui | obiit xxiij^o die ffebruarij Anno d'ni Mill'mo | CCCC^o lxj^ocuius anime propicietur deus. Amen.

which may thus be translated—"Here lies Master Robert Lond, chaplain, who died on the 23rd day of February, A.D., 1461, on whose soul may God have mercy. Amen."

Illustration.—*Pryce's Bristol*, p. 203, fig. 24. Bristol and Gloucestershire Society Transactions vol. xv., pl. xii. p. 163.

Portions Lost.—None.

Biographical Account.—His name occurs in the Churchwarden's Accounts for St. Ewen's, Bristol (1455-6) among the donors to the "Weel of the aforseid cros of Syluer and ouer Gylt." "Item of Mr. Robert Lond............iiijd."

XXIII.—Rodmarton.

John Edward, lord and patron of the manor, lawyer, 1461. Chancel.—*Haines*.

Position.—On the south wall of the chancel.

Size.—2ft. 8in. x 1ft. 10½in.

Description.—This is probably the only instance in Gloucestershire where a civilian is represented on a brass wearing a cap. Mr. Haines notices this peculiarity by saying

"John Edward, 1461, Rodmarton, Gloucestershire, *famosus apprenticius in lege peritus* wears simply a round cap in addition to his ordinary habit."—*Manual of Monumental Brasses I. xc.* Mr. Gough reports that 'the cap resembles that of the sizars at Cambridge, or the blue-coat boys of Christ's Hospital, London." *Sepulchral Monuments II. p.* 196, and Fosbrooke *(Gloucestershire* I. 384) says that this "sepulchral effigy is noted by Mr. Gough to have a cap like that of the *President au Mortier (Introd. Sep lchral Mon. i. p. clxiv)."* In the church of Norton St. Philip, Somersetshire, is a stone effigy surmounted by a similar cap. This cap seems to be made of some soft material such as velvet, with a band round the lower edge. Probably it was the cap or coif worn by serjeants-at-law. (56)

Fig 56. Head, 1461. Rodmarton.

No hair is visible and he is clean shaven. The gown is very similar to the gowns described in Nos. xvii to xx, of this series. It reaches nearly to the ankles, and is slit up in front for a short distance, thus showing the fur lining. The fur edging is seen round the skirt, at the neck and wrists. The sleeves are moderately full and of uniform breadth Mr. Gough terms it "a serjeant-at-laws' gown." (II p. 196.) The girdle is plain and shows no fastening, and is lower than on the other brasses before described (Nos. xvii to xx). Beneath is seen "the little standing cape of the coat" *(Gough)*, and the sleeves of the same at the wrist. No distinction is shown between the shoes and hose, and the toes are pointed: the feet are represented on a grassy sod. The figure is full face, and erect with hands raised in prayer.

Inscription.—Beneath the feet is the following inscription :-

Hic iacet Job'es Edward qu'd'm'd'n's Manerij de Rodmarton | & verus patronus eiusdem ffamosus apprentici' in lege p'itus qui | obijt viij° die Januarij A° d'n'i M°CCCC° lxj° cui' a'ie p'picietur de' ame.

which may be thus translated :—

"Here lies John Edward, formerly lord of the manor of Rodmarton, and a true patron of the same, a famous apprentice skilled in law, who died on Jan. 8. A.D., 1441 : on whose soul may God have pity. Amen!"

Illustrations.—*Grose's Antiquities of England and Wales,* vol. i., pl. viii, fig. 2. *Gough*, vol. II., pl. lxxv., p. 305; *Lysons' Gloucestershire Antiquities*, pl. 11.

Portions Lost.—This brass is in very good condition, a small portion of the cap (the right-hand corner) only being lost.

Biographical Account.—"William Fitzwarren, a family seated at Woodmancote, in Dursley, of whom very little is known in the county notices, passed the manor and advowson (of Rodmarton) by fine 19 Henry VI. to Sir Ralph Boteler and *John Edwards*, and his heirs, which John dying seized in 1461 of this manor and Torleton, left Margaret only daughter and heir, wife of Thomas Whittington, by whom she had only another daughter and heir, wife of William Wye, who left a memorial of his possessions by placing his arms in the North Isle."—*Fosbrooke's Gloucestershire*, i., 384.

In *Bigland's Continuation, s. v.* RODMARTON, may be read : " 1446 John Edward presented to the Rectory ; and 1468, he died Lord of the Manor."

This brass was originally on a ledger stone of grey marble in the chancel, and *Rudder* records that on the same stone was another brass plate with the following inscription :—

"Hic jacet Stephanus Collier, A.M., nuper hujus Ecclesiæ Rector. Obiit decimo die mensis Augusti Anno Domini 1772, annoque ætatis suæ 79."

In English thus, " Here lies Stephen Collier, M.A. late Rector of this Church. He died on the 10th of August, A.D. 1722, and in the 79th year of his age."

XXIV.—Cirencester.

Wm. Prelatte, Esq., a very special benefactor to the chapel of Holy Trinity, and two wives Agnes, and Joan.—*Haines*.

Position.—On the floor in the Trinity Chapel.

Size.—3ft. 5in. x 3ft. 2in.

Description.—" Close to Robert Pagge's monument is the valuable brass of William Prelatte, and his two wives: dated 1462 (2 Ed. IV.), and the costume may well be compared with that of Richard Dixton, [vide No. xii] which is only a quarter of a century earlier. The variations in the dress will fully repay careful study."

Prelatte wears a helmet of the kind termed *salades* (Germ. *Schale*, a 'shell' or 'bowl'); the salade was originally a close-fitting helmet which protected the sides of the face and the back of the head; in this instance it is cupola-shaped. The visor is raised, and the face is destitute of beard or moustache. His neck is protected by a haussecol of mail, and his armpits also by gussets of mail,—the one at the right armpit is very clearly shown; from this we learn that the use of mail armour which had been discontinued for a time again came into fashion. On his breast immediately above his finger he wears a "sun" which the Rev. W. E. Hadow says is "the emblem of the House of York." The system of reinforcing or strengthening the armour by secondary plates is well shown on this brass. The shoulders are protected by pauldrons, the left one being crested and larger than the right one. The elbow-pieces or coudières are fanshaped and beginning to take the extravagant size which afterwards was so much in vogue. The mode of fastening the coudière of the right arm is distinctly visible: (57) a staple from the under armour comes through the coudière and by means of a spring-pin, which is thrust through the staple, this extra defence was fixed. The skirt of five taces is plain and to the last tace are fastened two tuiles, which are large, scalloped and five-pointed, and between which a baguette of mail is seen. Gauntlets, very much resembling a tortoise-shell cover the back of the hands, the fingers are bare. The genouillières are large with plates behind them the legs are protected by the usual plate armour, The sollerets are laminated throughout and the rowelled spurs have no strap beneath the feet: the spurs are "guarded by a thin plate of steel over the rowels to prevent their entangling or penetrating deep."—*Haines, i. clxxxviii.* The sword has a circular pommel with a fringe and an adorned hilt; the sword hangs diagonally in front of him suspended from a belt of which

Fig. 58. Defence of Arm, 1462. Cirencester.

the ornamental buckle is shown. On his right side is fastened a miséricorde. He stands on a ground on which, between his feet is a plant bearing three conventional flowers. The husband is placed between his two wives and all three have their hands placed in the attitude of prayer. The two wives wear the horned head-dress—a peculiar costume long in high favour with the ladies, in spite of the severe censures launched against it both by the clergy and the laymen—the hair being visible beneath. They are clad in long kirtles, with high waists, the sleeves and collars, which open and lie back leaving the neck bare, are guarded with fur. One wife wears a ribbon with a sun like her husband; the second one wears a cross in lieu of the sun. At the feet of each wife lies a little dog with a collar of bells.

Inscription.—The inscription is thus worded :—

Hic sepeliuntur Willius Prelatte Armiger specialissim' benefactor hui' Capelle Agnes nup' uxor Johannis Martyn et Johana | filia et heres Ricardi de Cobyndon [Relict] a Johann is Twynybo de Cayforde in comitatu Som's Armigeri uxores ipius | Willi qui quide Willius Prelatte obi [t in] vigilia Ascencionis d'nice xxvj° die maij Anno d'ni M° CCCC° LXij° quor' p'picict' de' A.

The inscription in English reads thus :—" Here are buried William Prelatte, Esquire, a most special benefactor of this chapel, Agnes late the wife of John Martyn, and Joan, daughter and heiress of Richard de Cobyndon and the widow of John Twynho of Cayforde in the county of Somerset, Esq, wives of the above William; which William died on the eve of the Ascension of our Lord, the 26 May, A.D. 1462, on whom may God have mercy.—Amen."

Heraldry.—In the extract from *Lysons'* are given his arms: but in the west window of the nave occurs a shield :—Argent, an escallop gules, impaled with azure, a chevron gules, differenced with a crescent, for Prelatte and his second wife Joan the heiress of William Cobyndon.

Illustration :—" The Brass of William Prelatte and his two wives engraved is in *Lysons' Gloucestershire Antiquities*, pl. 16. where the inscription is not correctly given, either in the letter-press or on the engraving; in both *aibus* is inserted, which word is omitted in the inscription—simply because there was not room for it and in the former, after *heres* is ommitted *Ricardi de Cobyndon relicta*. The arms of their two husbands Prelatte and Twynyhow, are in the spandrels of the east window of Bagendon Church."—*Rev. W. E. Hadow.*

Portions Lost.—Five shields, one over each figure and two below the inscription.

Biographical Account.—The inscription relates that he was a very special benefactor to the Chapel of Holy Trinity. "A part of Wm. Prelatte's benefaction to this chapel appears to have been a painting representing the martyrdom of St. Erasmus, discovered a few years ago on the north wall, since his arms—argent, a chevron gules, charged with a crescent, are represented under it. * This William Prelatte appears to have been in the service of Richard Duke of York, the father of King Edward IV., by a letter from him preserved among the MSS.

Fig. 59. Feet. 1462, Cirencester.

at Holm Lacy, directed 'to oure trusty and well-beloved squier and Servant William Prelat, oure Recever and Feodier in Gloucestershire,' which accounts for the figure of the Duke having been placed in the east window, and his cognizance

---

* In the *Archæologia* vol. xv. p. 405 are a sketch and description of this painting, by Mr. Samuel Lysons.

(the falcon and fetterlock) being carved in several parts of this chapel, as it does not appear that the duke himself had any connection with Cirencester."—*Lysons's Gloucestershire Antiquities.*

He was an executor of Richard Dixton's will (vide No. xi), and receiver-general of the Gloucestershire estates of Richard Duke of York. His house was in Laurens St., i.e, Gloucester St. (Register of Lady Chapel, f 19. a.)

XXV.—Chipping Campden.

John Lethenard, merchant, 1467, and wife Joan. Nave.—*Haines.*

Position.—On a flat stone in the nave, a portion being under a movable platform. (Feb., 1882.)

Size.—3ft. 3in. × 2ft. 5in.

Description.—John Lethenard has his hair cropped across the temples and above the ears; he is also clean shaven. He wears the ordinary civilian's gown characteristic of the period, edged with fur, and slightly open at the lower part of the skirt. The sleeves are full, but close at the wrists where the fur lining is exposed. The upper portion of the gown is turned down, showing the fur lining and reaching down the front, till hidden by the hands. At the wrists and neck portions of the underdress are visible. The waist is confined by a narrow plain belt. The shoes are distinct from the hose, and the fastening at the side is shown. Between the feet are three sprays of trefoils. (60)

Joan Lethenard wears a modified form of the horned headdress, of which a description is given in No. XIX. Her gown is long and flowing, covering her feet; it has a v-shaped opening, which extends below the girdle, and is edged with fur. The sleeves are close, and of uniform breadth, with large cuffs lined with fur. It is very short-waisted, the girdle used being plain and narrow. (60)

They are both represented erect, and in a devotional attitude, the wife being on her husband's left hand.

Inscription.—The figures stand on a plate of brass, on which is engraved the following inscription :—

Hic iacent Johes Lethenard quondam M'cator isti' ville q. . . . | Anno d'ni Mill'mo CCCC° lxvij° et Joh'na vxor eius quor' . . .

Fig. 60   John Lethenard and wife Joan.   1467, Chipping Campden.

In English thus—"Here lie John Lethenard, formerly merchant of this town (who died) in the year of our Lord 1467, and Joan his wife, on whose (souls may God have mercy. Amen.")

Illustrations.—None known.
Portions Lost.—Part of the inscription,
Biographical Account.—Unknown.

XXVI.—Cirencester.

William Notyngham, 1427 (head gone), and wife Cristina, 1434, engraved *circa* 1470. South aisle.—*Haines.*

Position.—On the floor in the Lady Chapel.
Size.—2ft. 5in. x 2ft. 4in., not including the shield of arms.
Description.—"The earliest dated brass in Cirencester Church is in the Lady Chapel. It is that to the memory of William Nottingham and his wife. . . . Next to the brass of the wine merchant and his wife* comes the brass of W. NOTTINGHAM, which, as I before stated, is the earliest brass in the church; it bears the following inscription:— Orate pro a'i'abus Will'i Notyngham et Cristine vxoris eius qui quidem Will'mus obiit xxj° die mensis Nouembris Anno d'ni Mill'mo CCCC° xxvij° Et predict' Christina obiit iiij° die Julij A° d'ni M°CCCC° xxxiij° q'r a'i'abs, p'piciet' deus.—Amen. "This fixes the dates at the 5th and 12th years of Henry VI. The effigy of the man who is headless, is clothed in the usual civilian's gown of the period with a rosary on the right hand side of the belt, the end of which is visible. The female figure wears the 'horned' or 'mitred' headdress, but no hair is visible beneath; the kirtle is long and flowing to the feet; the sleeves are tight, and no cincture is visible at the waist. The collar is remarkable as coming down in a loop to the waist."—*Rev. W. E. Hadow, M.A.*

They are represented full-face with hands in the attitude of prayer, the husband having his wife on his left hand.

The style of engraving is very much later than the date on the brass and as appears above. Haines assigns it to the period 1470. It is of course possible that Sir William Nottingham a baron of the Exchequer may have placed this memorial to his father.

---

* Vide No. V. of this series.

Inscription.—The above inscription may be translated thus:—"Pray for the souls of William Notyngham and of his wife Christiana, which William died on the 21st of November, A.D., 1427, and the aforesaid Christiana died on the 4th July, A.D., 1433. On whose souls may God have mercy. Amen."

Illustrations.—None known.

Portions Lost.—The head of the husband, and a shield of arms between the husband and wife.

Biographical Account.—In Atkyns's *Gloucestershire* it is recorded that "there is an inscription, upon a marble stone, in the south aisle for Sir William Nottingham, and his wife. He died 1427," and in his account of the chantries, &c., he says, "the office of St. Thomas the Martyr, founded by Sir William Nottingham, baron of the Exchequer, whereof Thomas Neal was the last chaplain." It would seem that Atkyns' has confused the two William Nottingham's.

Rev. E. A. Fuller records that this William Nottingham was a clothier and father of Sir William Nottingham. He quotes this extract from Sir William's will:—" to the support and maintenance of one priest which shall be fit and which shall say Divine prayer in the said church of Saint John, at the altar of St. Thomas the Martyr, where the bodies of William Nottingham and Christine his wife, my parents, were buried."

XXVII.—Bristol, St. Mary Redcliffe.

Philip Mede, Esq., 1475 (?) in tabard and two wives, one in heraldic mantle, with demi-figure of our Saviour (?), inscription lost, quadrangular plate, mural North Aisle.—*Haines.*

Position.—Affixed to the north wall under a canopy.

Size.—22½ in. x 18½ in.

Description.—His helmet lies on the ground in front of him. His head is uncovered, and his hair is long and flowing. Over his armour he wears a tabard or surcoat. The tabard is slit at the sides and portions of the armour are to be seen beneath. Round his neck is a standard of mail. The arms are protected by pieces of plate armour whilst the hands are bare. To the skirt of taces are fastened large tuiles. The legs are encased in armour, the tying of the genouilliéres

Fig. 61. Philip Mede and his two wives. 1475, Bristol, St. Mary Redcliff.

being most plainly shown; on the feet are large sollerets or sabbatons.

Both the ladies wear the kennel head-dress and the long flowing robe cut low at the neck; the lady to the left of the husband wears a heraldic mantle. Her gown is confined by a girdle fastened in front, with an ornamental pendant at the end. The other lady wears no adornment nor mantle, and so her dress is seen to fit tightly to the body, the sleeves being close fitting with deep cuffs.

From the husband's hands proceed a label '**S'ca trinitas vn' de' miserere nobis**', 'Holy Trinity, one God pity us,' and from the hands of the lady in the heraldic cloak is '**Pater de celis deus miserere nobis**,' 'O God the Father of Heaven pity us.' All the figures are kneeling; the tips of the fingers of the husband and the wife behind him are merely touching; the lady in the heraldic mantle is holding up her hands in supplication. The husband is turned a little to the left to face the lady in the mantle, who is turned a little to her right; the lady behind the husband is turned a little to her left. The background is plain.

At the top of the brass is a demi-figure representing our Saviour in a blaze of light and his head surrounded by a nimbus. He is holding his hands in the attitude of blessing.

Inscription.—Lost.

Heraldry.—His surcoat is charged with the following armorial bearings:—*Sable, a chevron ermine, between three trefoils slipt argent;* these bearings are shown twice,—on the breast and skirt, and on the right arm,—the left side is not visible.

The mantle of his first wife bears the following arms : . . . *two lions rampant.* . . . She has a necklace with an ornament hanging in front.

In the British Museum is an example of his seal as Mayor of Bristol. It is thus described:

4696 [A.D. 1459] Red. (Add Charters 26,474)

Ob.—On the left a view of Bristol castle, with three storeys of embattled masonry, on one of the corner towers a watchman, half-length to the left, blowing a horn, on the battlements a flag charged with a cross, on another turret another watchman blowing a horn. The secret quay is open and a ship is sailing out from behind the castle, with high forecastle and flag of the Royal Arms of England, as used by Edward III., viz. quarterly 1 and 4, and semy-de-lis, for FRANCE; 2, 3, ENGLAND. In the field over the forecastle the initial letter B.

SIGILL' MAIORITATIS VILLE. BRISTOLLIE.

R.—A small round signet, ⅜in. from a chased ring. An eagle rising with expanded wings, cf. crest of MEADE, an eagle displayed with two heads between two indistinct initial letters in black letter.

Illustration.—*Bristol: Past and Present*, vol 2 p. 208.

Portions Lost.—The inscription.

Biographical Account.—" Philip Mede was at the battle of Nibley Green. He was present at "the unduly summoned" parliament held at Coventry which attainted the Duke of York and his friends.

" The first name of the wife of Philip Mede is all that Barrett mentions, and we, therefore, only know that it was Isabel, and that their son John lies with them. Isabel* their daughter, married the fifth Maurice, Lord Berkeley,† who was disinherited by his brother, William, Marquis of Berkeley, because he had married the daughter of a Bristol merchant whose parentage was not considered sufficiently honourable for an alliance with a Berkeley! The will of Philip Mede was proved January 11th, 1471, in which he directs his body to be interred at the altar of St. Stephen, in the church of St. Mary Redcliffe, to which he was a benefactor. He served the office of Bailiff in 1444; Sheriff in 1454; Mayor in 1458, 1461, and 1468; and was returned Member of Parliament for Bristol in 1460, and which met both at Coventry and Westminster."—*Pryce*, pp. 187, 188, 189.

Philip Mede was the son of Thomas, son of Thomas, decended from the Meads of Mead-place in Feyland, in Wraxall, co. Somerset'.—*Smyth's Lives of the Berkeleys, p.* 165.

His will is in the Great Book of the Wills, and proved Mar. 1476. It is also in the Prerogative Court of Canterbury 21 Wattys. His inquisition post mortem shows that he had lands in Faryeland *alias* Feylond, Wraxhall, Rolleston, Bedmyster, Somerset.

---

*A full account of the ceremonial of this lady's funeral will be found in *Smyth's Lives of the Berkeleys*, pp. 166, 167.

†Born at Berkeley 1435, married at 30 years of age, died 22 Hen. VII., anno 1506. They had four children.

XXVIII.—Bristol, St. John.

Thomas Rowley, merchant and sheriff, deceased 1478, and wife Margaret, under moveable floor, Nave.—*Haines*.

Position.—On the floor in the centre of the Nave.

Size.—3ft. 1in. × 2ft. 4in.

Description.—The hair is combed over the forehead, but shewing the ears, and he is clean shaven. His mantle is fastened at the right shoulder and falls over the left arm; the lining is edged with fur. The mantle was worn at that period as a distinctive garment of civic functionaries. The collar of the tunic is seen above the mantle; the tunic reaches to the ankles, the lower edge has a fur border. The sleeves are moderately full with narrow fur cuffs, beneath them are the tight fitting sleeves of an under-dress. The tunic is kept in place by a plain narrow belt, which is buckled on the left side. From this girdle hangs a *gypcière* or pouch and a rosary, (62) both on the right side. When Chaucer described a "Franklein" he said that a

Fig. 62. Purse and Beads, 1478, Bristol St. John.

"..... Gypser al of silk
Heng at his gerdul, whit as morne mylk."

The gypciére was worn by women as well as by men, for when Chaucer described the carpenter's wife he says:—

And by hire girdel hung a purse of lether
Tasseled with silk and perled with latoun.

The gypciére served as an external purse, and was worn much earlier, but rarely seen on effigies before the time of Edward IV. The anelace which figured so conspicuously on earlier brasses is now superseded by the rosary. "This was a chaplet composed of various numbers of beads strung loosely on a cord or thread."—*Haines, i. cciii. n.*

The shoes are long with pointed toes and fastened across the instep, and on the ground between the feet is a trefo l.

Margaret Rowley wears a variety of the horned head-dress called the heart-shaped. Her gown covers her feet and is girt high by a broad girdle. The gown has a v-shaped opening from the shoulders below the girdle with a border of fur at the edges; the sleeves are close, of uniform breadth throughout and have deep cuffs lined with fur and turned back. The kirtle is seen at the neck and wrists. From Thomas is a label with the inscription 𝔖𝔠'𝔞 𝔐𝔞𝔯𝔦𝔞 𝔬𝔯𝔞 𝔭𝔯𝔬 𝔫𝔬𝔟𝔦𝔰 ("Holy Mary pray for us"). And from Margaret proceeds a label with the words 𝔖𝔠'𝔞 𝔗𝔯𝔦𝔫𝔦𝔱𝔞𝔰 𝔳𝔫' 𝔡𝔢' 𝔪𝔦𝔰𝔢𝔯' 𝔫𝔬𝔟 ("Holy Trinity one God, pity us"). Both are erect, with hands folded, the wife being on her husband's left. Above each figure is a shield containing his merchant's mark :—a Maltese cross with a streamer from its summit, the cross bar seems to be the Arabic numeral 2 and on the lower part of the stem are "T.R.," his initials. (63)

Fig. 63. Merchant's Mark, 1478, Bristol, St. John.

Inscription.—The inscription beneath the figure is:— 𝔥𝔦𝔠 𝔦𝔞𝔠𝔢𝔱 𝔗𝔥𝔬𝔪𝔞𝔰 𝔑𝔬𝔴𝔩𝔢𝔶 𝔮𝔲𝔬𝔡'𝔪 𝔪'𝔠𝔞𝔱𝔬𝔯 𝔞𝔠 𝔙𝔦𝔠𝔢𝔠𝔬𝔪𝔢, 𝔥𝔲𝔦𝔲𝔰 𝔳𝔦𝔩𝔩𝔢 𝔅𝔯𝔦𝔰𝔱𝔬𝔩𝔩, 𝔢𝔱 𝔮𝔲𝔦 𝔮𝔲𝔦𝔡'𝔪 | 𝔗𝔥𝔬𝔪𝔞𝔰 𝔬𝔟𝔦𝔦𝔱 𝔵𝔵𝔦𝔦𝔦° 𝔡𝔦𝔢 𝔪𝔢𝔰𝔢 𝔍𝔞𝔫𝔲𝔞𝔯𝔦𝔦 𝔄𝔫𝔫𝔬 𝔡'𝔫𝔦 𝔐𝔦𝔩𝔩𝔦𝔬 𝔠𝔠𝔠𝔠° 𝔩𝔵𝔵𝔳𝔦𝔦𝔧° 𝔈𝔱 𝔐𝔞𝔯𝔤𝔞𝔯𝔢𝔱𝔞 | 𝔳𝔵𝔬𝔯 𝔢𝔦 𝔮𝔲𝔢 𝔬𝔟𝔦𝔧𝔱 𝔡𝔦𝔢 𝔪𝔢𝔰𝔢. 𝔄° 𝔡'𝔫𝔦 𝔐°𝔠𝔠𝔠𝔠° 𝔩𝔵𝔵 𝔮𝔲𝔬3 𝔄𝔫𝔦𝔪𝔞𝔟3 𝔭'𝔭𝔦𝔠𝔦𝔢𝔱' 𝔡𝔢 𝔄𝔪𝔢.

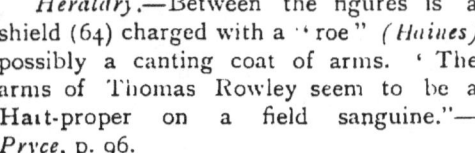
Fig. 64. Shield, 1478, Bristol, St. John.

In English thus —" Here lies Thomas Rowley, sometime a merchant and sheriff of this town of Bristol, who died on the 23rd January, 1478, together with Margaret his wife, who died 1470. To whose souls may God be merciful. Amen."

Heraldry.—Between the figures is a shield (64) charged with a "roe" *(Haines)* possibly a canting coat of arms. ' The arms of Thomas Rowley seem to be a Hart-proper on a field sanguine."—*Pryce*, p. 96.

Illustration.—*Pryce, p.* 96.

Portions Lost.—None.

Biographical Account.—" Much difference of opinion has obtained as to this Thomas Rowley. It is known that he founded a chauntry in this church, and it is recorded that he was one of the bailiffs of the city in the year 1466, and sheriff in 1475."—*Pryce, p.* 98.

" Thomas Rowley was appointed executor to the will of his son, William Rowley, burgess of Bristol, 25th November,

1478, but died before the will was proved ; 18th March, 1478, old style, was the date of probate."—*Rev. T. P. Wadley, M.A.*

His will was proved in the Prerogative Court of Canterbury, 36 Wattys. There is extant a view of Bristol Castle as it appeared in 1440, with this name in the corner "T. Rowleie Canonicus delin, 1440."

XXIX.—Cirencester.

Ralph Parsons, 1478, with chalice and host, much worn.—*Haines.*

Position.—On the floor at the east end of the Trinity Chapel.

Size.—3ft. 3in. by 1ft. 5½in.

Description.—" In Trinity Chapel also is the brass of an ecclesiastic, vested in alb, stole, amice, chasuble, and maniple; and valuable as having the chalice and host in the hands."

Inscription.—The inscription is :—

" Orate pro anima dni Radulphi Parsons quondam capellani p'petue cantarie S'te Trinitatis in hac cc'lia fundate qui obiit xxix die Augusti A° d'ni MCCCC° lxxviij cuj a'i'e p'picict' deus. Amen."

The inscription reads thus in English :—" Pray for the soul of Sir Ralph Parsons, formerly chaplain of the perpetual chantry of the Holy Trinity founded in this church, who died on the 29th day of August A.D. 1478, on whose soul may God have mercy. Amen."

From the mouth proceeds a circular label, but the lettering is indistinct.

Illustration.—None known.

Portions Lost.—A shield above the head, a portion of the scroll issuing from the mouth, and a part of the surname has been chipped out. The whole brass is much worn.

Biographical Account.—From the inscription we learn that Ralph Parsons was a chaplain of the Chantry of Holy Trinity in Cirencester Church. It appears that he bequeathed to the church his cope, which was afterwards altered into a pulpit cloth. It has been thus described :—" The cope was cut into long strips and sewed up into its present shape. It is made of blue velvet with a wide border, which is now quite faded, but was perhaps purple. Both the middle and border are covered with spangles and embroidered with cherubim standing on stars of Bethlehem with pine apples in gold and colours. The border at the upper part seems meant to be worn round the neck, as the pine apples are inverted. One of the cherubim holds a shield of armorial bearings :—Argent on a chevron sable, three roses or, under which is a scroll with the words *Orate pro anima domini Radulphi Parsons.* Under the other cherubim are the words *Gloria tibi Trinitas;* over the pine apples on the border are the words *Da gloriam Deo.*" Rev. E. A. Fuller says that "Part of the embroidery is the six-winged seraphim of Ezekiel's vision, which appear also on the outside of the Great South Door, and in the remains of ancient glass in the Trinity Chapel and the Garstany Chapel."

XXX.—Bristol, St. Mary Redcliff.

John Jay, and wife Joan, *circa* 1480, with 6 sons and 8 daughters, canopy and shields.—*Haines.*

Position.—On a ledger-stone on the south side of the Chancel.

Size.—7ft. 9in. x 2ft. 9in.

Description.—His hair is worn over his ears, and covers the forehead, reaching nearly to the eyebrows: he is clean shaven. His tunic reaches to his feet, and is edged with fur. It is slightly open up the front and reveals the fur lining. It is cut square at the neck, and here appears a small portion of the collar of his under-dress, as also the manner in which it was fastened by means of a lace passing through holes, of which two are visible. The sleeves are ample and of uniform breadth, they are turned back at the wrists and form moderately deep cuffs. Beneath them are seen the tightly fitting sleeves of an under-dress. The tunic is confined at the waist by a very narrow girdle, from which hang a purse and a rosary. (65) John Jay's shoes have pointed toes.

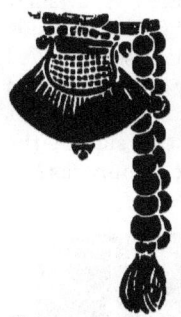

Fig. 65. Purse and Beads c. 1480 Bristol St. Mary, Redcliff.

Joan Jay is dressed in the usual long close-fitting gown covering the feet, and confined at the waist by a narrow and ornamental girdle. Above the girdle the gown is thrown back nearly to the shoulders, and has a border of fur at the edges of the v-shaped opening, and beneath the kirtle is visible fitting up to the neck. The sleeves are narrower than those of her husband's tunic, of uniform breadth with much deeper fur cuffs, and at the wrists are seen the sleeves of her kirtle. On her head is a variety of the horned headdress.

Beneath the husband are six sons dressed in long plain tunics, with stand-up collars, but their hair is long, especially in the first two, where it reaches their shoulders. These two are taller than the rest. Under the wife are eight daughters, dressed in gowns which do not cover the feet: the gowns are made after the fashion of their mother's with the wide v-shaped opening in front. Nos. 3, 6 and 8 have long hair and caps somewhat similar to the fashionable 'mob' caps (66) they are also shorter than the others. The remaining 5 wear the butterfly headdress.

Fig. 66. Dau. c. 1480. Bristol St. Mary Redcliff.

The figures lie under a double canopy, with oval cusped heads and crocketted ogee gables, with a foliated finial. The pediments are filled in variously, (67) and the groining is shewn; there is a soffit moulding of quatrefoils. On either side and between the canopies rise panelled pinnacles set on diagonally and terminated in crocketted finials; the outer pinnacles are continued down by the side of the figures, and the centre one terminates in a pendant.

Fig. 67. Rose. c. 1480. Bristol St. Mary Redcliff.

There are four shields, one above the husband between the gable and the outer pinnacle; the same is repeated below the daughters. Mr. Haines suggests that it is charged with a fuller's bat. (68) Another shield is above the wife, between the

Fig. 68 Shield c. 1480. Bristol St. Mary Redcliff.

Fig. 69. Merchant's Mark c. 1480. Bristol St. Mary Redcliff.

gable and the outer pinnacle; the same is repeated below the sons. This shield contains a merchant's mark, (69) which consists of a cross with two short legs and a streamer flying from the shaft. At the bottom of the shaft extends a cross each way horizontally: the legs and crosses pass through a small circle, of which the end of the shaft forms the centre

John and Joan Jay are represented erect and full-face, the wife being on her husband's left hand: the sons are erect and turned half a turn to the left and the daughters are also turned half a turn to the right.

Inscription.—The effigies are standing on a band of brass which bears this inscription:—

Hic iacent Johes Jay Quondam Vicecomes istius ville et Johanna vx' ei' q' quidem Johe | obijt——die mense——A°d'ni M°CCCC lxxx°——Quor' a l'ab3 p'piciet' de' ame.'

Which reads thus in English, "Here lie John Jay, formerly sheriff of this town, and Joan his wife, which John died on the——day of the month of——A.D. 148—. On whose souls may God have mercy. Amen."

Illustrations.—Bristol, past and present, vol. 2, p. 208. Journal of Archæological Association, vol. ii, p. 115 (Mark).

Portions Lost.—None.

Biographical Account.—The will of a John Jaye is in the Prerogative Court of Canterbury under date 1468, 23 Godyn; and it occurs in the Great Orphan Book, and Book of Wills. He had a wife Joan and desired to be buried in the choir of St. Mary of Redcliff, Bristol. His brother John Jaye to be executor, and this most probably is the person here commemorated. This Joan was sister to William Wyrcestre, the fifteenth century topographer and antiquary. The will of a Joan Jaye is to be seen in the Prerogative Court of Canterbury, 29 Dogett.—1492 John Jay was sheriff in 1472.

The following is extracted from Harper's Magazine vol. 25, 1893, pp. 436-7. "Other rich merchants might be instanced were it necessary to enlarge on the prosperity of Bristol such as May, Young, and Spelly, the builder of the chapel on the bridge, but we have only space to speak of John Jay, who in 1480, sent out two ships under the command of the most scientific mariner in England, one Thlyde, or Lloyd, in search of the much-talked-of Isle of Brazil supposed to lie to the west of Ireland. This is the first recorded expedition from England

Fig. 70. Priest c. 1480, Cirencester.

to discover America, and it was followed by numerous others but until the year 1497 none of these voyages was continued sufficiently far to be crowned with success. The connection with America thus begun has continued to the present day."

XXXI.—Cirencester.

A priest, circâ 1480, in cassock, small, inscription lost, south aisle.—*Haines*.

Position.—On the floor in the Lady Chapel.

Size.—2ft. 4in. by 1ft. 3½in.

Description.—"In the Lady Chapel there is another ecclesiastical figure clad only in a cassock, valuable on account of its rarity. The fragments of inscription at the foot have no relation to the figure."—*Rev. W. E. Hadow, M.A.*

The cassock was generally worn as an undergarment but here the priest is represented in it as his ordinary dress. There is another example of a priest habited only in a cassock on the brass commemorating Thos. Awmarle, *c.* 1400, Cardynham Cornwall.

The cassock formed a portion of the processional or canonical attire, and as such is seen on the brass in Temple Church, Bristol. In the west window of Cirencester Abbey is represented an ecclesiastic with a red cassock.

The hair is worn long enough to cover half of the ears and the tonsure is clearly shown. The shoes have pointed toes. Beneath the feet is the word **suorum**, which could not have formed a portion of the inscription. The figure is erect with hands in a devotional attitude. (70)

Illustration.—*Haines* i. p. lxxvii.

Portions Lost.—A circular label issuing from the mouth, and the inscription beneath the feet.

XXXII.—Cirencester.

A civilian and wife in mantle, circâ 1480, worn, another wife, inscription and children lost. South aisle.—*Haines*.

Position.—On the floor in the Lady Chapel.

Size.—The portion that is left measures 3ft. × 2ft. 1in.

Description.—"In this same chapel (Lady Chapel) are the brasses of a merchant and his wife, which have been much injured. They lie close to the north wall. The male figure is dressed in a long gown, descending to the feet, bound round the waist by a girdle, which falls down the front of the figure, and supporting on the right side a rosary, the sleeves are loose at the wrist, showing the sleeves of the under tunic. The female figure wears a kirtle, falling in folds over the feet, surmounted by a robe with a standing collar, fastened at the throat; the head is covered with a coverchief falling behind the figure. There is no name or inscription of any kind, nor trace of any, but the brass is most probably late in the 14th century or early in the 15th century."—*Rev. W. E. Hadow, M.A.*

Illustration.—None known.

Portions Lost.—One wife, some children, and the inscription; the husband has lost the upper half of his head.

XXXIII.—Chipping Campden.

William Gybbys, 1484, and wives Alice, Margaret, Marion, with seven sons and six daughters. Nave.—*Haines.* Atkyns incorrectly gives the name as Dobbins.

Position.—On a ledger-stone in the centre of the nave. The effigies of the husband and one wife are under a movable platform.

Size.—4ft. 5in. x 3ft.

Description.—William Gybbys wears his hair long but brushed back behind the ears, it presents an arched appearance across the forehead, and he is clean shaven. His tunic is long and reaches to his ankles, it has a tight-fitting collar at the neck, above which is seen the collar of an under-dress fastened in the same manner as that of No. XXX. The sleeves are full and of uniform breadth, at the wrists they are turned back and form slight fur cuffs, beneath which the sleeves of an underdress are visible. The gown is confined by a girdle, of which the hanging portion is seen on his left side; from it on the right side hangs a rosary, to the two ends of which are fastened two tassels, on the string are twelve beads equally divided. The shoes are long, with pointed toes, and fastened across the instep. Between the feet is represented a conventional plant of seven leaves.

The three wives all wear the modified form of the horned headdress, termed heart-shaped. Each lady wears a long gown, which falls in graceful folds, hiding the feet; it has a turn-over collar, v-shaped, of fur or velvet, terminating below the girdle in a point, and thrown back nearly to the shoulders, revealing an under-vest or stomacher of a different colour. The sleeves are full and of uniform breadth, but not so ample as those of the husband, while the cuffs are very much deeper. The gown is girt high by a plain cincture.

All four are represented erect, full-face with hands in the attitude of prayer.

Beneath the figures are two groups of children, on the right hand corner seven sons with long hair and tunics like their father, on the left hand corner six daughters in butterfly headdresses. The figures are too much worn to distinguish their dresses, which, however, hide the feet. The sons are turned to their left to face the daughters, who are turned to their right.

Inscription.—The figures stand on a fillet of brass, which bears the following inscription :—

Orate pro a'i'abus Will'i Gybbys Alicie, Margarete et Marione Consortes sue qui quid'm Willi us obiit viij" | die mensis Januarii Anno Domini mill'mo CCCC lxxxiiii. Quorum animabus p'piciet' de'. Amen."

In English thus :—"Pray for the souls of William Gybbys, Alice, Margaret, and Marion his consorts, which William died on the 8th of January, A.D. 1484: To whose souls may God be merciful. Amen."

Illustration.—*Bigland's Gloucestershire*, vol. i., p. 284.

Portions Lost.—Over the head of the outside wives are the matrices of two scrolls, one of which is shown on the engraving in *Bigland* to have the words, *Jhu merci, ladye help.*

XXXIV.—Micheldean.

Thomas Baynham, Esq., 1444, and two wives Margery and Alice, all lost but the effigies of the wives which are loose, engraved *circa* 1485.—*Haines.*

Position.—Hanging on two nails in the vestry. In *Bigland's* time they were inlaid on a large blue stone "in the farther North Aisle."

Size.—Each effigy measures 2ft. 6in. x 1ft. 6in.

Description.—In this interesting brass the most striking feature is the totally different shape of the headgear each wife affects. The vagaries of fashion are here brought into close and sharp contrast, and it is difficult without the aid of illustrations clearly to picture in words the great divergence in form and mode of wearing the head-dresses of these two ladies. To those interested in such matters it may be stated that illustrations of both these forms of the head-dress are given in any work on costume.

Fig. 71.   Margaret Baynham.   c. 1485, Micheldean.

Margaret Baynham wears the wired or butterfly head-dress, which was much in vogue especially among ladies of rank. This remarkable head-dress was composed of a framework of wire fastened to a cap or caul into which the hair was strained back so as to be completely hidden. This caul was made of coloured silks oftentimes embroidered in gold or silver thread and sometimes enriched with jewels. Over this wirework foundation a veil of gauze, lawn or other light material was thrown. Planché in his history of British Costume shews that these butterfly head-dresses are prototypes of those worn even at the present day in Normandy. (71)

The head-dress of Alice Baynham is very different from that of Margaret Baynham. Alice is represented as wearing the pedimental, kennel, or diamond-shaped head-dress; as this head-dress is to be found on many of the brasses in Gloucestershire it is worthy of description. Mr. F. W. Fairholt, F.S.A., in his account of Ladies' Head Gear thus speaks of this head-dress. "A perfectly geometrical form, which might have been invented by some clerical architect, succeeded to the butterfly head-dress in the reign of our Henry VII. An angle, like the penthouse of an old timber mansion, was formed over a lady's forehead, and a straight ugly line was brought down the sides of the face; the whole thing was formalism run mad." *St. James's Magazine*, No. XII (March 1862), p. 459. Like the butterfly head-dress it was "supported by wires and confined the hair in a round cap at the back of the head, but it was destitute of the veil projecting behind, its leading characteristics were long frontlets or lappets which formed an angle over the forehead, and hung down on each side, and similar lappets depended behind." *Haines*, i. p. ccxii. As the head is turned to the right, the lappet hanging behind is clearly seen; all the lappets are plain.

The dresses of the ladies, though similar, differ somewhat in detail. Both are close-fitting, small waisted and long, and gathered in graceful folds round the feet. They are fastened in front, but the method of fastening is not shown. Fur is to be seen at the neck, and round the hem of the skirt. The sleeves are narrow and fit tightly.

The gown of Margaret is cut low at the neck, and the cuffs are large, slashed, and turned back, disclosing the fur lining. The waist is encircled by a long narrow girdle, which, passing through a large buckle on her right side, hangs down in front with a pendant terminating in a tassel; the mode of fastening is curious, for the tongue of the buckle does not pass through the strap, but beneath it; the strap is adorned with embossed or embroidered scroll-work. The neck is bare and she seems to be wearing a small chain; the kirtle or underdress is seen.

Alice is wearing a gown cut square at the neck, and at the

top of the fastening of the gown is a brooch (?). The cuffs, instead of being turned back, cover the hands reaching to the knuckles. The buckle of her belt is on her left side, and the tongue of the buckle passes through a hole in the belt, which is enriched with scroll-work.

Both the ladies are represented erect with hands clasped in a devotional attitude, Margaret being slightly turned to her left to display her butterfly headdress, (71) and similarly Alice is turned to her right to match, and probably the husband was placed full face between them.

Illustration.—*Transactions of the Bristol and Gloucestershire Archæological Society*, Volume VI, Plates VII and VIII.

Portions Lost.—This brass was mutilated in Bigland's time. He records that over the man's head the escutcheon with a mantle and crest was then gone; there were " four corner Escutcheons, three remaining; 1. Gules, a Chevron between three Bulls Heads caboshed Argent for BAYNHAM; 2. A Fess surmounted of another indented, for HODYE; 3. Quarterly 1st and 4th, BAYNHAM; 2nd and 3rd, on a Chief three Mullets;—impaling, Per Pale Or and Vert, twelve Guttés counterchanged, for GREYNDOUR, and Crusilly a Fess, for . . . ." *History of Gloucestershire* i. p. 446, *s.v. Dean Michel.*

Memoir.—Thomas Baynham was son and nearest heir of Robert Baynham, and at his father's death, 12th September, 1436, he was aged 14 years five months and three days.— (*Inq. p. m.* 15, Henry VI, No. 15.)

" Thomas inherited from his father, with other lands, the first moiety of the Manor of Dene Magna, or the purparty of Johanna, the senior co-heir of William de Dene. He married, as his first wife, Margaret, daughter of Richard Hody, one of the King's Justices—it is so stated in an old pedigree recorded in the Heralds' College in 1582, nevertheless it would seem to be doubtful; there was never a *Richard* Hody, a justice in either of the King's Courts—and by her had a son and heir named Alexander. He married secondly, Alice, daughter and heir of William Walwyn, with whom he acquired also, in her right, the other moiety, or purparty, of Isabella, the second co-heir. By her he had a son Christopher, heir of his mother and other children."

Much further information respecting the Baynham family will be found in a paper on the " Manors of Dene Magna and

Abenhall," by Sir John Maclean, F.S.A. in the "Transactions of the Bristol and Gloucestershire Archæological Society," Vol. VI.

XXXV.—Northleach.

A woolman and wife, *circâ* 1485, with two sons and two daughters, merchant's mark and marginal inscription. North aisle.—*Haines*.

Position.—On the floor in the north aisle.

Size.—6ft. 8in × 2ft. 8in.

Description.—The husband has his hair long, parted down the middle and brushed back behind the ears. He wears a tunic, which does not quite reach the ankles; it is edged with fur round the skirt, wrists, and neck. The sleeves are full and flowing with wide openings at the wrists, where the sleeves are turned back to form narrow fur cuffs. The gown is kept in place by a girdle, which has an ornamental stud visible in front. The gown is closed the whole way down; the mode of fastening is concealed. Round his neck is a narrow collar, possibly of his underdress, above the band of fur. At the

Fig. 72. Feet of Husband. c. 1485. Northleach.

wrists the tight-fitting sleeves of the underdress are seen. He has neither anelace. gypcière, nor rosary. He wears low shoes with rounded toes. The right foot rests on a sheep, and the left on a woolpack, on which is shown his merchant's mark. (72).

Beneath are two sons dressed like their father.

The wife has unfortunately lost the upper part of her head, but seemingly she wears a heart-shaped head-dress, which ends in three tiers; her ears are not visible. The gown is long, full, and straight, with a v-shaped opening at the neck, and terminates below the girdle; the edges are trimmed with fur, so also is the bottom of the skirt. The chest is protected by an underdress, also v-shaped and leaving the neck bare. The sleeves are long and narrow, reaching to the wrists, where they terminate in wide cuffs of fur. The gown is confined by a girdle ornamented with rosettes. The supporters of her feet, which are concealed by the gown, are the same as her husband's except that the merchant's mark is not visible

Beneath is a plate representing two daughters, who are attired in the same fashion as their mother, with the following exceptions, their girdles are loose and fastened at the side, and their headdresses belong to the butterfly kind. (73)

Fig. 73. Daughter, c. 1485 Northleach.

The merchant's mark (74) consists of a cross, from the stem of which a streamer is

Fig. 74. Merchant's Mark. c. 1485, Northleach.

flying, standing on an inverted old-fashioned W. The figures are erect, full face with hands clasped in a devotional attitude; the wife is on her husband's left hand, and she is also represented shorter in stature than her husband. The sons are turned to their left to face their sisters, who are turned to their right. All the children are represented erect with their hands folded in prayer. Above the husband is a scroll inscribed **Jh'u Mercy**, below the sons is a similar pious ejaculation. Above the wife the matrix only is left, whilst below the daughters **J'hu Mer**...is all that is left.

Inscription.—Round the verge are the following verses ;—
✠ a ffarewell' my frendes the tyde abideth no man (1)
I am departed from hense and so shall' ye
But in this (2) passage the best songe that I can
Is requiem eternam now (3) Jhu graunte it me
When I haue ended' all (4) myn aduersite
Graunte me in paradise to haue a (5) mansion
That shed' thy blode ffor my redempcion. (6)

The inscription commences over the husband's head, and at each corner as well as at the middle of the sides were ornamental plates ; a part of one remains at the upper dexter corner (6), on it is engraved the symbol of the Apostle St. John—an eagle ; at the middle of the side near the wife (2) is a part of a winged ox, the symbol of St. Mark ; whilst at the lower sinister corner (3) is a shield containing the merchant's mark described above ; the plates have been torn away from (1), (4), and (5).

"This inscription occurs with slight variations at Royston, Herts, and according to Weever, it was at Baldock in the same county ; at Maldon and Romford, Essex ; and at St. Martin's, Ludgate, London (Fun. Mon., pp. 545, 610, 649, 387)."—*Haines, i. p. clxxxi. note.*

Illustration.—Cutts (E. L.) *Scenes and Characters of the Middle Ages*, p. 524 (effigy only), p. 526 (merchant's mark.)

Portions Lost.—The upper half of the wife's head, the scroll above her, a part of the scroll beneath the daughters, the ornamental plates at (1), (4), and (5) and parts of (2) and (6), (see inscription).

Memoir.—As each effigy is represented standing on a sheep and a woolpack, it is very probable that Haines' supposition that the brass represented a "woolman and his wife" is correct.

XXXVI.—Nortbleach.

[John Taylour], wolman, and wife Joan, *circâ* 1490, with eight sons and seven daughters, Evangelical symbols, marginal inscription mutilated, Holy Trinity lost, south chancel.—*Haines.*

Position.—On floor.

Size.—6ft. 9in. x 2ft. 4in.

Description.—John Taylor has hair long enough nearly to reach his collar and cover his ears. The face is clean shaven, and he is represented well advanced in years by the wrinkles on his forehead. He wears the ordinary long gown of the period, but it is destitute of fur edging either at the skirt or sleeves. To his girdle are fastened a gypcière on his right side, and on his left a rosary of twelve beads, *i.e.*, five small beads and one large one on each string, one end terminates in a tassel, and to the other end is attached a signet ring. The gown covers the ankles so that the mode of fastening the shoes is not seen—only the wide rounded toes are visible. Between his feet is represented a conventional flower.

Joan Taylor wears the butterfly headdress, but it is not so large as that of Margaret Baynham. Her gown is long and very low-necked, it has not the V-shaped opening. Below the gown is her kirtle or stomacher protecting her chest. The sleeves are narrow with long fur cuffs, and fit tightly at the wrists. The hip girdle is narrow and hangs loosely.

Beneath John Taylor are eight sons dressed like their father, and beneath his wife are seven daughters dressed like their mother. Above the husband and wife and beneath their children are plates on which are engraved the evangelical symbols, but they are much mutilated.

In the centre of the bottom of the brass is represented a sheep, head to left, standing* on a woolpack, between its fore and hind feet is John Taylor's mark viz., two shepherd's crooks placed one vertically turned to the left the other crossing it horizontally turned to the right, a crook lies in front of the woolpack. (75)

Fig. 75. Sheep on Woolpack. c. 1490. Northleach.

Inscription.—Round the verge is the following inscription, the portion in brackets being supplied from Rudder:—

Fig. 76. End of Inscription. c. 1490. Northleach.

[John Taylour] A᷃ Thousand CCCC and Joone bys wyfe. . . . The yere of O[wre Lord God A° Thowsand]CCCC. . . . . on whois soulis J'bbaue m'cy. Amen. (76)u

---

* "Couchant" *Rudder's Gloucestershire.*

From John's mouth proceeds a label *S'ca trinit* [as ora pro nobis]. His wife's label probably bore a similar inscription but "*is*" is all that is left.

Illustration.—*Cutts (E.L.) Scenes and Characters of the Middle Ages*, p 524 (effigy only) p. 526 (Merchant's Mark.)

Portions Lost.—Representation of the Holy Trinity, most of the marginal inscription, the symbol over John's head, and parts of the other three, the left hand lower corner of John's gown.

Memoir.—The will of a Johane Taylour of Northleach is in the Prerogative Court of Canterbury, 1510, 32 Bennett.

XXXVII —Tormarton.

John Ceysyll, "famulus" of *Lord John Sendlow, 1493, marginal inscription Nave.—*Haines.*

Position.—On a ledger stone in the centre of the nave.

Size.—6ft. 2in. x2ft. 3in.

Description.—His hair is worn long, it conceals his ears and the greater part of his forehead. The face is clean-shaven, and furrows are represented shewing that he was an old man. He wears the long tunic customary of the period, this has no border of fur at the edge of the skirt nor at the neck and wrists. The sleeves are full and of uniform width. At the

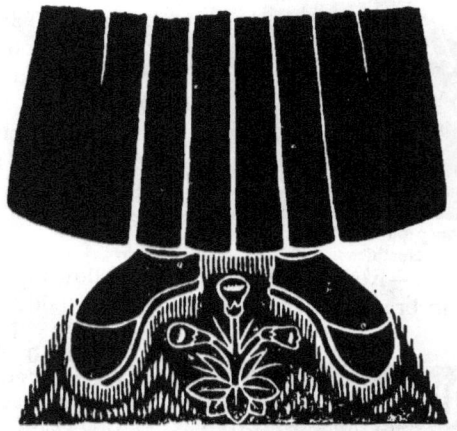

Fig. 77. Feet. 1493. Tormarton.

---

*It is evident that Mr. Haines strangely enough overlooked the fact that "Dominus" in this case is merely the equivalent of "Sir" and does not mean Lord." *Ed.*

neck is the small standing collar of the underdress of which a portion of the lacing is shewn. At the wrist the tight-fitting sleeves of the underdress are to be seen. The line shewing where the tunic is fastened down the front is very evident. The waist is confined by a narrow girdle, but the buckle is not shown. From this girdle hang a gypcière on the right side, and a rosary on the left side. The rosary has, instead of a tassel at one end, a ring, probably a signet-ring. The feet are shod with mis-shapen round-toed shoes with thick soles. Between the feet and springing from the centre of seven leaves is a conventional flower of three blossoms displayed somewhat in the form of a cross. (77)

The figure seems to be spare and the hands are clasped in the attitude of prayer.

Inscription.—The inscription (78) is round the verge and is as follows:—*Orate* (oak leaf), *pro* (three leaves springing from a crown), *Anima* (cinq-foil), *Johannis* (two acorns), *Ceysyll* (double triangle), | *Quondam* (a clover [trefoil] leaf) *famulus* (leaf), *Reuerendi* (Tudor rose, boss), *d'ni* (leaf), *Joh'is* (a flowered square), *Sendlow* (heart), *militis* (rabbit), *qui* (quadruped), *quide* (oak leaf and acorn), *Johannis* (leaves), *Ceysyll* (bunch of three cherries), *suum* (lily blossom), *clausit* (cherry and leaf), *extremu* (coventional), *in* (do), *Vigilia* (cap) *Sancti* (rose) *Bartholomei* (hare), *Apostoli* (a pod bursting and revealing the seeds), *Anno* (leaves), *d'ni* (goose?) *Mill'mo* | (a spread eagle), *CCCC°* (bird flying), lxxxxiii° (goose preening her wings), *et* (goose with neck arched), *Anno* (crown), *Regni* (a rose barbed), *Regis* (leaf and double square), *Henrici* (a berry between two leaves), *septimi* (trefoil), *nono* (bell), *Cuius* (stringed instrument resembling a violin, *Anime* (pair of bellows), *propicietur* (apple?) *de'* (?), *Altissimus* (leaf), *Amen*.

In English it may be rendered thus:—Pray for the soul of John Ceysyll, formerly servant of the reverend Sir John Sendlow, Knight, which John Ceysyll ended his last day on the eve of St. Bartholomew the Apostle, [August 23], A.D., 1493, and in the ninth year of the reign of King Henry VII. To whose soul may the Most High be merciful. Amen."

Illustrations.—None known.

Portions Lost.—None, and the brass is in excellent condition.

Memoir.—Nothing known of John Ceysyll.

Fig. 7 Inscription. 1493. Tonvarton

XXXVIII.—Cirencester.

John Benet, 1497 (head gone), and two wives, Agnes and Agnes. One wife and children gone. Marginal inscription nearly all lost.—*Haines.*

Position.—On the floor in the Lady Chapel.

Size.—All that is left measures 6ft, x 1ft. 8in.

Description.—" There is also the brass of a man and his wife, evidently another wife has been there, and children† also. The man wears a gown falling to the feet, the sleeves are large at the wrist and lined and faced with fur; from the girdle hang a rosary on the right, and the gypcière on the left side; on the right shoulder rests a cap of a peculiar construction, in high favour with all classes of persons during the reign of Henry VI., and very often worn throughout the remainder of the 15th century; in form the cap was circular like a turban, and was made of a roll of cloth, or some rich material from which on one side a long and broad band or scarf hung down to the ground unless tucked in the girdle or wound round the neck; while to the other side of the cap was attached a kind of loose hood, which fell negligently, about the head or shoulders. In this brass the scarf is represented as hanging down in front of the figure. The wife's figure is clad in a flowing kirtle down to the feet, with a tightly-fitting bodice, cut low and square on the breast showing the under tunic round the throat; the sleeves have large cuffs of fur, and there is a cincture round the waist; she wears the horned head-dress hanging in folds behind the figure.

Inscription.—Part of the inscription only remains, and reads thus:—*Qui quidem Johannes obijt decimo nono die;* and in another part of the chapel are the following words, which evidently, from the style of lettering, belong to this brass: *Mensis Julij anno domini millimo cccc^o nonages' septimo quor' a'i'abus.* From the mouths of the two figures are scrolls issuing and bearing the following words:—Man's scroll—*S'cta Trinitas vnus De' miserere nobis.* Woman's—*Spiritus s'ti* (sic) *de' miserere nobis.*

This inscription is also preserved by Bigland I. 357. *Orate pro a'i'abus Johannis Bennett ac Agnetis uxoru' suar', qui quidem Joh'es obiit decimo nono die mensis Julij, anno*

---

† According to Bigland there were *eight* children.

d'ni Millimo cccc nouages' septimo quorum o'i'bus. From the other wife a label with *Fili redemptor mundi miserere nobis.*

The inscription may be thus translated:—
Pray for the souls of John Bennett [Agnes] and Agnes his wives, which John died on the 19th day of July, A.D. 1497, on whose souls [may God have mercy. Amen.] The portions in brackets seemed to be lacking when Rev. Thos. Carles, M.A., vicar of Cirencester made a copy of the inscriptions in the church in 1673.

His merchant's mark (79) resembles a cross with knops at each end; and on the long staff, a St. Andrew's cross with similar knops.—*Rev. W. E. Hadow, M.A.*

Fig. 79. Merchant's Mark. Cirencester. 1497.

Both the effigies are erect, full face, with hands clasped in the attitude of prayer, the wife being on her husband's right hand.

The lower portion of the stone has been utilised by placing upon it a brass plate with the following inscription in ordinary Roman letters:—" Here lieth the body of | Tho son of Tho and | Jane Nicholls, | obiit June 19th, 1752, | aged 32 years.

Illustrations.—None known.

Portions Lost.—Head of husband, lefthand corner of the wife's gown; and according to Haines, the wife and a group of children, the name, effigy, and scroll of the second wife, the marginal inscription is much mutilated.

Biographical Account.—His will and that of one of his wives are in the Prerogative Court of Canterbury 11 Horne, and 7 Moone.

XXXIX.—Sevenhampton.

A Civilian, c. 1490, lately lost (?) feet, and inscription, perhaps covered by a step. Chancel.—*Haines.*

John Camber. 1497.

Position.—On the floor in the Chancel, the feet and inscription, being covered by a moveable step.

Size—2ft. 6in. x 1ft. 1in.

Description.—The figure is two feet three and a half inches in length, and the costume that of a well-to-do yeoman of the time of Henry VII. His hair is full and long covering the ears, and is cut so as to form a fringe which almost touches the eyebrows; not a vestige of beard, whisker, or moustache is visible. He wears a long tunic which reaches below the ankles, this opens down the front, but here it is closed, and the mode of fastening is not shown; at the waist it is confined by a wide girdle devoid of ornament. The sleeves are ample, wider at the wrists than at the elbows; they have broad fur cuffs, which are returned inside, where the fur forms a narrow edge. The collar of the tunic is merely a narrow band. At the neck a quaker-like collar of the underdress is represented; this is fastened by means of a lace; at the wrist the closely-fitting sleeves of the underdress are seen. From the girdle depends on his left side a purse, or bag sewn to a metal frame of a semi-circular shape while from his right side hangs a rosary of twenty small beads and two larger ones the ends of the cord are terminated by tassels. Over the right shoulder is thrown a hood, which usually was of a dark colour. In this instance it consists of a cap which is shaped somewhat like a Scotch 'bonnet' and to it is attached a long streamer or scarf, which reaches below the knees; it was sometimes called a liripipe, and was used for wrapping round the head when required. The tunic covers the fastening if any of the shoes, which are pointed, a fashion which was soon superseded by broad round toes. He is full-faced with hands raised in the attitude of prayer.

Inscription.—Beneath the figure is a plate of brass on which is engraved the following inscription:—

Ibic iacet Job'es Camber qui obijt vicesimo | Sexto die mensis ffebruarij A^o d'ni m^o | CCCCXC vij^o cuius a'i'c p'picier' de' amen

Which may be thus translated, " Here lies John Camber, who died the 26th Feb A.D., 1497, to whose soul may God be merciful. Amen.

It is observable that the inscription affords an early instance of the modern fashion of writing the number '*Ninety*' with the '*X*' to the left of the '*C*' it being far more common in the fifteenth century to express it thus, LXXXX.

Illustrations.—Sevenhampton *Parish Magazine,* June 1869, continuation of *Bigland* s.v. Sevenhampton. *Bristol and Gloucestershire Archæological Society,* vol. *xiv, p.* 343.

The excellence of the material is evident from the fact that though close upon four hundred years old, the lines and indentations, the hair, features. fur on cuffs, &c., are as clearly cut as at the time of its execution; although, on account of its position before the altar rails, many generations must have walked over it.

Portions Lost.— No portion is lost.

Biographical Account.—The Rev. J. Melland Hall, M.A., rector of Harescombe and Pitchcombe, and formerly vicar of Sevenhampton, very kindly sent me the following account, and to him I beg to express my indebtedness:—"The Rev. Herbert Haines, after a visit subsequently to the publication of his well-known work on *Monumental Brasses* (an extract from which will be found at the head of this notice), kindly furnished some additional particulars concerning the interesting memorial remaining in the church. As the inscription was supposed to be lost, the style of the execution was his sole guide as to its date, and he consequently assigned it to about the year 1490. He believed that it might probably be the monument of John Camber, who is said, by Sir Robert Atkyns, to have built the church (dying in 1497), this, however, can only refer to the fifteenth century portions: but whether he asserts this on any authority, or merely as a tradition doth not appear.

As Mr. Haines remarks, while the lower part of the effigy, and a possible inscription were concealed by the altar step, it appeared very tantalizing to the wandering and enthusiastic antiquary to find that, until the obstruction was removed, uncertainty must hang over the person commemorated. It was, therefore, most satisfactory when the matter was investigated and the step removed to find that it was indeed the memorial of JOHN CAMBER, and also that the assigned date was not very far removed from the real one, viz., A.D. 1497.

The inscription, it will be seen, simply records the name and date of the decease of John Camber; and hardly anything more is known concerning him, except that his '*anniversary service*' was to be performed on the 26th of February, for which 'the Parishioners were enfeoffed of a House, with Close, and Dovehouse, at Prestbury, yearly value, vjs. viijd.—*(Valor. Eccles.)* His will is in P.C C. 21, Horne and printed in *Gloucestershire Notes and Queries* II., 444.

It may, however, be mentioned that the name Camber occurs at Tilbury, Essex, and also in Norfolk early in the sixteenth century, where, in the parish Church of Hedenham, a small brass inscription to a John Camber [John Camber, 16th cent., loose, inscription only. *Haines Manual* ii. 139] still remains. Whether the subject of this interesting and well-preserved brass was connected with these families we know not; but it is evident that he was a man of considerable note in his day, and as the probable restorer or rebuilder of the Tower and other portions of the parish Church of Sevenhampton, "*zealous of good works.*"

XL.—Fairford.

John Tame, Esq., 1500, and wife Alice (Twynihow) 1471. Marginal Inscription, Altar Tomb, Chancel.—*Haines.*

Position.—On an altar-tomb, lying partly in the Lady Chapel—*Northe Chappell*—and partly in the Chancel.

Size.—7ft. 8in. x 3ft.

Description.—"This stately memorial of Purbeck marble, which forms a conspicuous ornament of the chancel, was raised by his son and successor, Sir Edmond Tame, Knight, who finished the church after his father's death. This tomb has a somewhat uncommon character from the circular panels which ornament its sides. Upon the top are full-length figures in brass of John Tame and Alice his wife, with their respective shields of arms separate, and also with the same arms impaled together. In this effigy it is to be noted that John Tame is represented, not as a citizen or merchant, but as an *armiger* or Esquire, clothed in mail and wearing spurs. It is also observable that the *affirmation* attached to his will, a short time previous to his decease, attested by the names of the vicar of Fairford, and the vicar of Southrop, styles him 'John Tame, *Squier*,' quite in accordance with this fact"—*The Fairford Windows.*

This brass is in an unusually fine state of preservation, and gives a very good illustration of the armour worn at the end of the fifteenth and the commencement of the sixteenth centuries.

John Tame's hair is so long as to reach to his shoulders; it covers his ears and is parted down the middle. The face is clean shaven. The head is uncovered and the helmet is not shown. He wears a cuirass having a tapul, *i.e.*, a projecting edge, in front. To the right side of the cuirass is affixed a kind of bracket of iron in order to support the lance, whence its name—lance-rest. (80) His shoulders are protected by paldrons, which were still the fashion—but they resemble each other very closely both in size and shape; they are rounded and have high projecting edges round the neck, the left one being a little higher than the right one; there is also a demiplaccate. The coudiéres are of moderate size and plain. The skirt consists of five taces, slightly invecked in the centre; to this skirt are attached two tuiles in front, and on the right side is seen a third, so that probably there was a fourth on his left side. Mail is shown at the neck, a skirt of the same material is also seen below the taces, and gussets of mail are at the armpits, the one under the right shoulder only being visible,

Fig. 80. Lance Rest. 1500. Fairford.

Fig. 81. Sabbatons. 1500. Fairford.

and at the insteps. The legs are protected by plate armour, and the genouillières have small extra plates both above and below them, the mode of fastening is shown on the left knee. The feet are encased in large wide-toed sabbatons, (81) to which the spurs were most probably screwed. On his right side is a dagger, and on his left a sword which passes diagonally behind him.

Alice wears the then fashionable kennel head-dress with plain lappets. Her gown is long and close-fitting to the body and arms; the sleeves fit tightly at the wrists where there are deep fur cuffs slashed and reflected. The gown is cut low and square at the neck, thus displaying her kirtle over which a ribbon apparently crosses; the kirtle fits close to the neck. The girdle is long and adorned with scroll work, it passes through a buckle on her left side and the tongue of the buckle pierces the belt but as there are no holes made for it, most probably the belt was made of woollen material and not of leather.

The figures are erect with the hands joined in an attitude of prayer, John being turned slightly to his left and Alice much more to her right, she is on the left of her husband, whose effigy is larger than hers.

Inscription.—On a fillet of brass at their feet is this quatrain in English :—

ffor Jhus loue pray for me | J may not pray nowe pray ye
With A pater noster and aue | That my paynys Relessyd may be.

which is repeated at the end of the marginal inscription.

Round the moulded edge of the slab is a narrow ribbon of brass bearing the following words cut in relief, commencing at the lower left hand corner :—

Orate pro animabus Jobis Tame Armigeri et Alicie uxoris eius qui quidem Jobes obiit octauo die Mensis Maij Anno d'ni Millesimo quingentesimo et Anno Regni | Regis Henrici Sept'i sextodecimo et predicta Alicia obiit vicesimo die | Mensis Decembris Anno Domini mill'imo CCCC septuagesimo primo quorum a'i'abus propicietur dc'. ffor jhus lou pray for me J may not pray now pray ye | with A pater noster ande ave that my paynes relessid may be.

Which may be thus translated :—" Pray for the souls of John Tame, Esq., and Alice his wife, which John died on the 8th of May, A.D. 1500, and in the 16th year of King Henry VII. And the aforesaid Alice died on the 20th December, A.D. 1471, on whose souls may God have mercy.

Heraldry.—The following account of the heraldry on the brass and in the church is taken from that most valuable and interesting monograph "*On the Fairford Windows,*" published in 1872, by the late Rev. J. G. Joyce, M.A., F.S.A.

"The armorial shield which occupies the centre of the west parapet of the tower of Fairford Church, exhibits a marked difference from the heraldry of the other three faces, as the lateness of its origin is manifest in the character of the charge. This is such as to suggest that the science of heraldry was already on the wane when these arms were first assumed. But this shield on the west parapet fills nevertheless the most important function of all in the indisputable record it perpetuates. This is a memorial of the man to whose munificence Fairford is indebted for its noble church. John Tame the merchant.

"The charge which is somewhat rudely sculptured in relief is a wyvern on the dexter side, combating a lion crowned on the sinister. The same charge is repeated on a shield of quite a different shape inside the porch, on the corbel of the inner doorway on the right as one enters the church. It is particularly to be noticed that the one is not a mere reproduction of the other; the two are perfectly distinct in style.

Fig. 82. Shield. Fairford. 1500.

"There is, however, in Fairford Church a different and a still later version of the arms of John Tame. It is that incised on the brasses which adorned his tomb. The arms of Tame upon the tomb (82) vary from those on the tower and in the porch. The heraldic charge upon the two latter as described above, is reversed upon the brasses of the tomb, the beasts having changed places, so that the crowned lion occupies the dexter side in the brass. There is a second variation in the circumstances that the wyvern of the stone shields receives the addition of hind legs, and so becomes a dragon on the tomb.

"All these, whether in stone or brass, are equally commemorative of John Tame's connexion with the church, because the same arms when used by Sir Edmund his son, who completed the building, are invariably differenced by a crescent." In the paper on the '*The Tames of Fairford*' by Henry F. Holt, Esq., published in the *Archæological Journal*, 1871, is the following :—" In the year following Henry VIII.'s visit to Fairford [July 1520], John Tame's tomb was completed by the addition of the armorial bearings granted to Sir Edmund Tame, on that occasion, and added thereto were those of the Twynihoe family, *argent*, a chevron *gules* between three popinjays proper, (83) varying the escutcheons by arranging the several arms of the Tame and Twyn'hoe families per pale." (84)

Fig. 83. Shield. 1500. Fairford.   Fig. 84. Shield. 1500. Fairford.

Illustrations.—Bigland vol. p. 567, Gentleman's Magazine vol. lvii. pt. ii. p. 345, Cambridge Camden Society Illustrations. No. IV. p. 115.

Portions Lost.—None.

Biographical Account.—The life of Edmond Tame may be found in the following works :—Joyce (J. G.) *On the Fairford Windows;* Holt (H. F.) *The Tames of Fairford;* Cambridge Camden Society, *Monumental Brasses.*

John Tame married Alice, a daughter of John Twynihoe, a merchant of Cirencester. The Twynihoe coat may be seen in the Abbey Church at Cirencester. They had four children, William, Thomas, Elnore and Edmund.*

Thomas Tame was parson of " Castel Eton." He and his sister " Dame Elnore " received bequests, to Edmond was

---

*Of whom an account will appear Vide No. LXII.

bequeathed all the property John Tame held. William's name is not mentioned in the will so he very probably predeceased his Father. John Tame's will is in P.C.C., 3 Moone.

Mr. Holt thus sums up in one paragraph his opinion upon the tradition respecting John Tame and the Fairford Windows.

"It may here be convenient I should state, as the result of my researches, that I have satisfied myself—1st, that John Tame did *not* acquire the glass in 1492, or at any other time, by conquest or piracy; 2nd, that he did *not* found Fairford Church, or dedicate it to the Virgin Mary; 3rd, that he did *not rebuild* the Church; 4th, that he had nothing to do with the painted glass, and never contemplated its purchase or erection; 5th, that the painted glass windows were expressly *made for* the Church, and not the Church for the windows; 6th, that John Tame *never was* Lord of the Manor of Fairford."

XLI.—Cirencester.

A civilian, *circa* 1500, mutilated, head restored, inscription gone.—*Haines*.

Position.—On the floor in the Trinity Chapel.

Description.—The Rev. W. E. Hadow in his account of the Monumental Brasses at Cirencester rightly terms this a "nondescript figure," for the head evidently has no relation to the remaining portion of the figure. The body is clothed in a furred robe open above and below but closed at the waist by a girdle. The sleeves are ample and of uniform breadth; at the wrists the hemmed sleeves of the underdress are visible. The hands are in the posture of prayer. All that is left of this brass is the body from the neck to the edge of the skirt.

With this memorial may be classed another nondescript one, in which the head of a man has been fastened to a female waist!

XLII.—Minchinhampton.

A civilian and wife, *circa* 1500, inscription and other wife (?) lost. Relaid, perhaps incorrectly, now in the belfrey.—*Haines*.

Position.—On the north wall at the west end of the church. Mr. Bigland records that "in the south cross aisle are two figures with legends but no inscriptions."

Size.—1ft. 6in. x 1ft. 7in.

Description.—The husband has long hair covering his ears and cut in a pointed fashion over the forehead, somewhat resembling the kennel headdress of the wife. Not a vestige of hair adorns the face. The tunic reaches below the ankles, and is open at the neck where the wide fur edge is plainly shown; the sleeves are very full at the wrists with deep fur cuffs. The waist is encircled by a plain girdle from which hangs a rosary, of which only four beads are visible, and a large gypcière.

At the neck is seen the tight-fitting undergarment, having a little stand-up collar; the tightly-fitting sleeves with narrow cuffs of the under-dress appear at the wrists. Below the gown are seen the toes of his wide and misshapen boots or shoes. Attention has been drawn to the long pointed shoes in vogue in the XV. century; and now in the XVI. century, the fashion had gone to the other extreme, and boots and shoes were "so excessively square-toed that the law, which had formerly limited the length, was now called on to abridge the the breadth of these pedal terminations." *Planché's Cyclopædia of Costume*, p. 47, *s.v.* BOOT.

The wife wears a pedimental headdress as described in No. 34 and her dress is very similar to that worn by Margaret Baynham, and described in the same number. It is a long flowing robe, narrow-waisted, and has tight-fitting sleeves with deep fur reflexed cuffs. The skirt has a plain edge. A long, plain girdle loosely encircles the waist, fastened by a simple buckle, through this passes the other end of the belt which almost reaches the feet and terminates in an ornamental pendant.

Both the figures are erect with hands clasped in prayer; the husband is full face and the wife is on her husband's left hand, but turned a little to her left, so that most probably there were originally two wives, one on either side of the husband. When the brasses were re-laid in a fresh stone perchance the effigy of the wife formerly on the left hand being lost, the remaining wife was by mistake put on the wrong side, and made to turn her back to her husband.

Illustrations.—None known.

Portions Lost.— As the brass is not in its original slab, it would be difficult to say positively what has been lost, but very likely another wife and the inscription. Mr. F. Stanley, of Margate has a rubbing shewing a scroll between husband and wife thus worded :—𝔇e' miserat' n'ri & . . . dicat nobis.

XLIII.—Northleach.

Robert Serche, 1501, and wife Anne, with three sons and one daughter.—*Haines*.

Position.—On the floor.

Size.—5ft. 2in. × 2ft.

Description.—Robert Serche has long hair covering the ears; over the forehead the hair is cut like the fringe of these days; the face is beardless. His gown is similar to that worn by a civilian *circa* 1500, at Minchinhampton, from the plain narrow girdle hangs a gypcière but no rosary. The tightly-fitting under-dress has closely-buttoned sleeves. The shoes are wide and fastened across the instep.

Anne Serche is dressed very similarly to the wife of the civilian *circa* 1500, at Minchinhampton, viz., a kennel head-dress, tight-fitting gown, and loose hip girdle.

Beneath the father are three sons, with tunics fitting close to the neck, and covering the ankles, the sleeves are wide mouthed. They have no girdle.

Beneath the mother is one daughter, she wears a kennel headdress, but instead of the lappets behind is a long veil reaching far below her waist. Her dress is of the same fashion as that of her mother, but it is not so long, and consequently the wide-toed shoes are visible.

The figures are all erect with hands in a devotional attitude: the husband being turned a little to his left to face his wife, who is on his left hand; while the wife is turned a little to her right to face her husband. Similarly the sons are turned a little to their left, and the daughter a little to her right.

Inscription.— Robert and Anne Serche stand on a fillet of brass which bears the following inscription: –

Fig. 75. Scroll. 1501, Northleach.

"Pray for the soules of Robt Serche and Anne hys wyfe, whych Robt deceesed the xx day of Janever the yere of our Lord MVc and oon. On whose sowlys Jhu haue mercy Amen."

At each corner of the slab is a scroll (75) on which is engraved J'hu mercy, Lady helpe.

In the middle of the slab above the husband and wife are these letters on a circular plate (76):—R. & A., i.e., R(obert) and A(nne.)

Illustration.—None known.

Portions Lost.—None, and the whole brass is in splendid preservation. This memorial is mentioned by Rev. H. Haines in his Manual I, p. *ccli, n.* as an instance of a brass consisting of several pieces and yet remaining perfect, which rarely is the case.

Fig. 76. Monogram, 1501, Northleach.

Memoir.—His will is to be found P.C.C. Blamyr 6.

XLIV. Olveston.

Morys Denys, Esq., son and heir of Sir Gylbert Denys, lord of the manors of Alveston and Irdecote, and his son Sir Walter Denys, 1505, in tabards, holding a scroll mural.—*Haines.*

Position.—On the wall under the east window of the north aisle.

Size.—2ft. 6in. x 2ft. 7in.

Description.—Morys Denys (77) and Sir Walter, his son, are both in armour, similar to that worn by John Tame, but neither of the two wear spurs. Their armour consists of a cuirass, paldrons, condières, skirt of taces, tuiles, below these a skirt of mail appears, cuisses, genouillières, and wide-toed sabbatons. Most of the armour is concealed by a tabard.

Both the figures are kneeling on an embroidered cushion, and facing each other. Their hands are uplifted, showing the inside of the brassarts: the left hand of Morys (77) and the right hand of Sir Walter are holding a scroll on which is engraved this inscription:—**Miseremini n'ri miseremini nostri | saltem vos fiij et amici nostri quia | manus domini tetigit nos.**

From the mouth of Morys proceeds a scroll with these words:—**Unicus et trinus bone Jhu sis nobis Jhus.**

Similarly from Sir Walter's mouth is a scroll on which is engraved the following :— **Jn trinitate p'fecta sit nobis requies et et'na vita.**

Fig. 77. Morys Denys. 1505, Olveston.

Inscription.—Below the figures is a plate of brass thus inscribed :—

Ther lyeth buryed in ye midd' of the quere Morys Denys, Esquyer, sonne and ! heire of Sr Gylbert Denys, Knyght, lorde of the Manor of Alveston and of the | Maner of Frocecote, and also Sir Walter Denys, Knyght, sonne and heire to the | seid Morys Denys, Esquyer, ye whiche Sr Walter Denys, decessed the first | day of the Moneth of Septembre, in the xxj. yere of the

reigne of kyng henry the vij., whose soules Jhu p'don ame. All ye that this rede and see | of yor charite seye.for their soules a pater noster and an ave.

Heraldry.—On the tabard of Morys Denys (77) are the following armorial bearings:—" Quarterly—1 . . . a bend engrailed . . . between three leopard's faces, jessant de fleur de lis. DENYS.—2 . . . on a chief . . three balls. —3 Lozengy . . . a chevron . . . —4 . . a cross moline . . ."—*Bigland,* s. v., Olveston.

Fig. 78. Shield. 1505, Olveston.

No. 2 above (81) is Argent on a chief gules, three bezants, Russell, for Margaret, daughter of Sir Maurice Russell. married to Sir Gilbert Denys, father of Morys Denys here commemorated.

The same quarterings appear on a shield under Morys. (78)

Sir Walter's tabard is charged with similar bearings, except that —4 is ". . . a chevron . . . . between three roses . . ."—*Bigland*; and the same shield is repeated beneath him. (79)

Over Morys' head is a shield containing the DENYS coat of arms, and (80) over Sir Walter's head is a shield charged with the RUSSEL coat of arms. (81)

Illustration.—In the volume of the *Anastatic Society's Publications* for 1876 is a sketch of this interesting monument.

Portions Lost.—None.

Memoir.—" A pedigree in my possession says tha Sirt Walter Dennys, of Alveston, Siston, and Dyrham, which estates respectively came into his family through the heiress of Fitzwarine, Corbet, and Russel, ought on the Lancastrian

Fig. 79. Shield. 1505, Olveston.

side, was taken prisoner at Redemore, near Bosworth, and had to pay a great ransom, 'his life being saved through his youngest son, John, then in the service of King Henry VII.' This Sir Walter Dennys married four times, but had no children by any of his wives excepting the second one, who was Agnes, the daughter and co-heiress of Sir Robert Danvers, or Davers, a Justice of the Common Pleas, who died 1467. Sir

Fig. 80. Shield. 1505, Olveston.   Fig. 81. Shield. 1505, Olveston.

Walter died September 1, 1505. His third and youngest son, John Dennys or Dennis, was settled in the parish of Pucklechurch, and died, I believe, in 1521. This John Dennis had a grandson, John Dennis of Pucklechurch, who died August 7, 1609."—*H. B. Tomkins* in *Notes and Queries* 4th, S. IV. Aug. 28, '69. p. 197.

The will of Sir Walter is to be seen P.C.C. Adeane 9.

XLV.—Lechlade.

John Twinyhoe, merchant, founder of a chantry *circa* 1476, deceased *circa* 1510, about four children, inscription, etc. lost.—*Haines.*

Position.—On the floor in the centre of the nave.

Size.—The effigy of the husband measures 3ft. 2in. by 9in.

Description.—John Twinyhoe wears long hair but his face is clean shaven. His tunic reaches to his ankles and is faced with fur, a customary garment among the civilians at the end of the 15th century and commencement of the 16th century. The large open sleeves hide the girdle which most probably he wore. The under-garment is seen at the neck, and again at the wrists, where its sleeves appear to be tightly buttoned. The feet are encased in the large square-toed shoes of the period.

The figure is erect and slightly turned to his left with his hands uplifted in a prayerful attitude.

Illustration.—Bigland's *Gloucestershire* ii. p. 144.

Fig. 82. Merchant's Mark. C 1510, Lechlade.

Portions Lost.—The effigies of his wife and children, together with the marginal inscription, two scrolls, and four plates, on which were most probably the evangelistical symbols, have disappeared. The matrix of his merchant's mark shews that his 'mark' was' in the shape of a tau cross combined with a Latin cross. (82)

Biographical Account. — In the Prerogative Court of Canterbury 14 Logge (1485) occurs the will of John Twinyhoe of Cirencester.

XLVI.—Minchinhampton.

John Hampton, gent., 1556, and wife Elyn in shrouds, with 6 sons and 3 daughters (the eldest dame Alice), engraved *circa* 1510.—*Haines.*

Position.—Rudder, in his *History of Gloucestershire*, 1799, records that this monument was on a flat stone in the north aisle ; but it is now to be found affixed to the north wall at the west end of the church.

Size.—4ft. x 2ft. 3in.

Description.—Though the date on this brass is 1556, Mr. Haines in his *Manual* says that it was engraved about 1510, and the date 1556 subsequently added.

This memorial presents a marked contrast to all those which have been previously described in these columns. On all the brasses hitherto noticed, the effigies of the persons

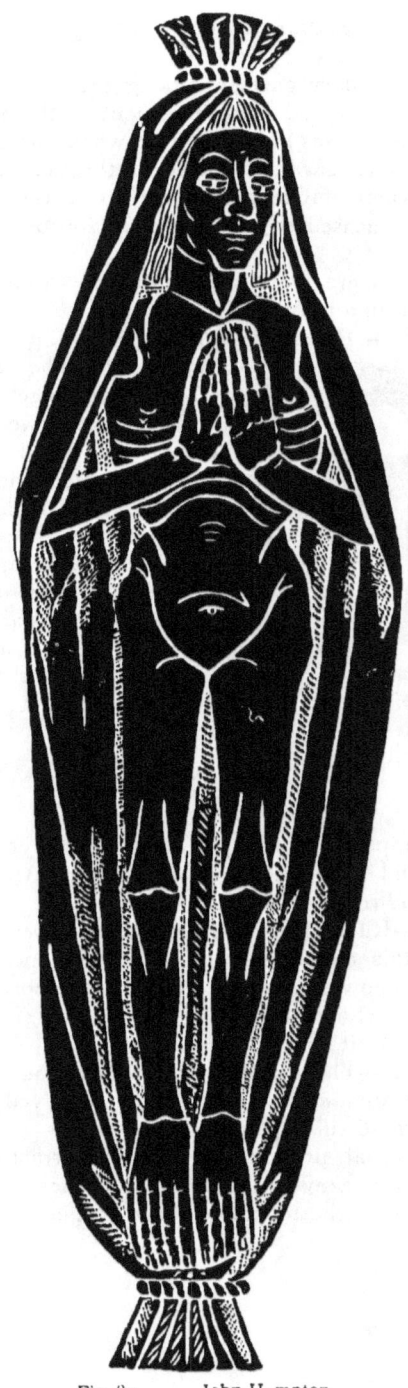

Fig. 83. John Hampton.
C 1510, Minchinhampton.

represented were engraven as they appeared in life, but John and Elyn Hampton are represented in their shrouds.

The shrouds are tied above and below the figures, which are recumbent
"In an attitude of prayer,"
but the head of the husband is turned a little to his left (83), and the head of the wife is turned a little to her right ; the wife being on her husband's left hand.

On the Continent it was customary to represent the deceased enshrouded, even as early as the commencement of the 14th century. An example may be seen at Bruges of the date 1339, and very probably this fashion was introduced from the Continent into England, where the fashion found much favour.

Fig. 84.
Eldest Son.
C 1510,
Minchinhampton.

Below the inscription are two groups of children, six sons under the father, and three daughters under the mother. The eldest son is clothed in the garb of a monk (84). This is very interesting, as the brasses of monks are seldom met with. This is not to be wondered at considering the vows made by them on entering the Order, and especially the one of poverty by which they were bound. This son, whose name is not given, wears the tonsure, and closely cropped hair, a large hood or cowl, and a long vestment with long open sleeves similar to the surplice-sleeves of that date. The remaining four sons wear a loose-fitting gown, without fur facings. The sleeves are ample and very wide at the wrist Their hair is long.

The eldest daughter Alice is dressed as a nun (85). She wears the veil headdress, a cape over her shoulders, a mantle open in front revealing her gown with tight sleeves, and girt by a loose hip girdle, from which hangs in front a rosary of 14 beads. The other two daughters were probably young at

Fig. 85.
Alice Hampton.
C 1510,
Minchinhampton.

the time of the execution of the brass, or had died young, for they are represented bareheaded with flowing hair, reaching below the waist. Their gowns fit the body well, with close sleeves. All the children are erect with hands upraised in prayer, the sons being turned a little to their left to face the daughters who are turned to their right; the eldest son and daughter being of a larger size than the others.

Inscription.—On a plate of brass beneath the effigies is this inscription :—

𝔒𝔣 𝔶𝔬 𝔠𝔥𝔞𝔯𝔦𝔱𝔢 𝔭𝔯𝔞𝔶 𝔣𝔬𝔯 𝔱𝔥𝔢 𝔰𝔬𝔲𝔩𝔢𝔰 𝔬𝔣 𝔍𝔬𝔥𝔫 𝔥𝔞𝔪𝔭𝔱𝔬𝔫 𝔤𝔢𝔫𝔱𝔦𝔩𝔪𝔞𝔫, 𝔈𝔩𝔶𝔫 𝔥𝔦𝔰 𝔴𝔶𝔣 | 𝔞𝔩𝔩 𝔱𝔥𝔢𝔦𝔯 𝔠𝔥𝔦𝔩𝔡𝔯𝔢𝔫, 𝔰𝔭𝔢𝔠𝔦𝔞𝔩𝔩𝔶 𝔣𝔬𝔯 𝔱𝔥𝔢 𝔰𝔬𝔲𝔩𝔢 𝔬𝔣 𝔡𝔞𝔪𝔢 𝔄𝔩𝔦𝔠𝔢 𝔥𝔞𝔪𝔭𝔱𝔬𝔫 𝔥𝔦𝔰 𝔡𝔞𝔲𝔤𝔥 | 𝔱𝔢𝔯, 𝔴𝔥𝔦𝔠𝔥𝔢 𝔴𝔞𝔰 𝔯𝔦𝔤𝔥𝔱 𝔟𝔢𝔫𝔢𝔣𝔦𝔠𝔦𝔞𝔩𝔩 𝔱𝔬 𝔱𝔥𝔦𝔰 𝔠𝔥𝔲𝔯𝔠𝔥, 𝔭'𝔦𝔰𝔥, 𝔴𝔥𝔦𝔠𝔥𝔢 𝔍𝔬𝔥𝔫 𝔡𝔢𝔠𝔢𝔰𝔰𝔢𝔡 | 𝔦𝔫 𝔱𝔥𝔢 𝔶𝔢𝔯𝔢 𝔬𝔣 𝔬ʳ 𝔩𝔬𝔯𝔡 𝔪ᵃ 𝔠𝔠𝔠𝔠𝔠𝔩𝔳𝔧, 𝔬𝔫 𝔴𝔥𝔬𝔰𝔢 𝔰𝔬𝔲𝔩𝔢𝔰 𝔦𝔥𝔲 𝔥𝔞𝔲𝔢 𝔪𝔢𝔯𝔠𝔶. 𝔄𝔪𝔢𝔫.

The letters *clvj* were evidently added at a later period, so that the brass may have been engraved at an earlier date even than that assigned by Mr. Haines, perhaps at the end of the 15th century.

Illustration.—Dame Alice will be found in Haines' *Manual* i., lxxxvii.

Portions Lost.—None.

Memoir.—Sir R. Atkyns (p. 237) says that John Hampton was High Sheriff of Gloucestershire in the reign of King Edward II. Sir R. Bigland (ii., p. 6), quoting *Fuller*, reports that "in 1314, King Edward II., John de Hampton was Sheriff of this county, and was continued for four years." A Sir William Hampton was sheriff of London in 1462, and Mayor in 1472. Fosbroke *Gloucestershire* i., 375, records that "Amberley is a large tract of common given to poor housekeepers by the supposed benefaction of Alice Hampton, daughter of John Hampton," and, according to Bigland, "her Will or Deed of Gift is said to be preserved among the Tower Records."

"The monastery of Syon was founded by Henry V. in 1414. It was established according to the modified order of St. Saviour and St. Bridget. As the monastery had the manor of Minchinhampton granted it by its founder, it is most probable that Dame Alice Hampton was a member of that society."—*Haines* i., lxxxviii.

XLVII.—Cheltenham.

[Sir William Greville, of Arle Court, justice of Common

Pleas], 1513, and wife [daughter of —— ?] with 3 sons and 8 daughters. Chancel.—*Haines.*

Position.—On the floor near the font, it was originally in the chancel, and in its present position it is liable to much injury for it is at the bottom of a step.

Size.—4 ft. 2 in. x 2 ft. 8 in.

Description.—In this county are four " brasses " commemorating judges, viz., Sir John Cassy, Deerhurst, 1400; Sir John Juyn, Bristol, St. Mary Redcliffe, 1439; Sir William Greville, and John Brook, St. Mary Redcliffe, 1522. This brass is so much worn, that it is with great difficulty that the various lines incised on its surface can be determined. On his head Sir William wears the coif which became a distinguishing feature in the costume of a serjeant-at-law. But the Judicature Act has extinguished that order, and all judges created since 1873 have their white wigs unspotted with that circular black patch, which was one of the relics of the middle ages.

Following the custom of the times Sir William's hair is long, reaching to his shoulders. Round his neck is a tippet, and he wears a long robe with narrow sleeves, and over it a mantle fastened on the left shoulder. The shoes are large and round-toed. There seems to be a gypcière, but the brass is too much worn to distinguish it plainly.

His lady wears the then fashionable pedimental headdress, a long close-fitting gown, tight sleeves with deeply reflexed fur cuffs, and a loose hip girdle.

Under Sir William are three sons, in long tunics, with large bell sleeves. The hair is reaching the shoulders but cut to form a fringe across the forehead ; the shoes are wide.

Beneath the wife are eight daughters dressed somewhat similar to their mother ; but the robe is not so long, and thus it may be noticed that the girls as well as the boys wore wide-toed shoes.

All the figures are erect, with hands clasped in prayer. Sir William is turned to his left to look towards his wife who is turned to her right. In like manner the sons are turned to their left and the daughters to their right.

Illustrations. —None known.

Portions Lost. —More than half of the marginal inscription. The whole brass is very much worn.

Inscription.—Round the verge are these words:—

"and Slavghter whiche William decessid the ix day | of Marche the iiijth yere of the reigne of King Henry the viij."

This stone has been utilised at a later date by the addition of a brass plate (16 in. x 11½ in.) bearing this inscription:—

" Neare lieth ye Body of Elizabeth
Wife of William French Gent &
daughter of ye Rev. James Ingram
D.D. & formerly Rector of Whittington
in this County she died ye last of his
Fourteen Children on ye 10th of Septr
in ye 65th year of her age, and in ye
year of our Lord 1727.
Also ye body of Margarett the
daughter of ye abovesaid Eliz. French
she died the 15 March 1729 aged 44."

Biographical Account.—"William Greville, son of Richard Greville, Esq., of Leamington in Gloucestershire, attained the sergeant's coif in November, 1504. He was made a judge of the Common Pleas on May 21st, 1509, 1 Hen. VIII., and so remained till 1513, when he died, and was buried in Cheltenham Church, where there is a monument to his memory."—Foss, *Judges of England*, p. 311.

17 Mar., 1513, Letter to Abp. of Canterbury, Chancellor —Walter Rowdon to be keeper of the Rolls in the Co. of Gloucester, vice Wm. Grevile, late justice of the Common Pleas.

Fosbrooke (II. 374) says that "Arle near Cheltenham belonged to a family which took their name from that place. Robert Greville married—daughter and co-heiress of John Arle (*Hart MS.* 6174) and sold this estate to his brother William, a judge of the Common Pleas, 2 Hen. VIII., whose sole daughter and heiress took it to Sir Richard Lygon. (Lygon Pedigree in Nash's *Worcestershire*, &c.)"

His will is in the Prerogative Court of Canterbury, 12 Fetiplace.

XLVIII.—Bisley.

Katherine, wife of Thomas Sewell, 1515, with five sons and seven daughters. Nave.—*Haines.*

Position.—On a ledger stone close to the north side of the Chancel Arch.

Size.—3 ft. × 1 ft. 6 in.

Description.—This lady is attired in the usual dress of the times. She is represented full face, and consequently only the long front lappets of her kennel headdress are shewn: they are plain and reach half way down the arms, concealing the shoulders. As in the preceding examples the gown is tight-fitting, and cut low at the neck, where is a border of fur. The sleeves are of uniform breadth, fitting closely to the wrist; the cuffs are of fur, slashed underneath, and long enough to reach nearly to the elbow. At the neck is seen the kirtle beneath the gown. Beneath the lower fur border of the skirt of the gown peep the tips of her large round-toed shoes. The waist is encircled by a loose hip girdle, long and fastened in front. The pendant and buckle are made of ornamental metal work; and the tongue of the latter passes behind the embroidered front of the girdle, probably through loops made in the back to receive it.

Beneath the inscription are two groups of children, five sons on the left and seven daughters on the right. The sons have long hair, loose tunics reaching to the ankle and open in front with wide sleeves. The daughters are represented bare headed, and the hair of the last reaches far below her waist: they wear long gowns but high necked. Both the sons and daughters are wearing the then fashionable round-toed shoes. The figures are all erect, with hands in a prayerful attitude, the sons being turned a little to their right, and the daughters a little to their left.

Inscription.—Beneath the figure is a plate of brass on which is engraved this inscription :—

    Pray for the soule of Kateryn Sewell late the
    Wyf of Thomas Sewell. whiche Kateryn de=
    cessed the viij day of January the yere of o' lord
    MD·xv, on whose soule Jhu have mercy, ame.

Illustration.—None known.

Portions Lost.—None.

Biographical Account.—According to Rudder, she lived at Ferrie's Court, near Upper Lypiatt.

In the P.C.C. 23 Spert is the will of Thomas Sewell of Strode, dated 1543.

XLIX. Eastington.

Elizabeth [daughter of Sir William] Knevet [1518] in heraldic mantle, marginal inscription mutilated; chancel.—*Haines.*

Position.—On a ledger stone in front of the altar rails.

Size.—4 ft. 8 in. x 1 ft. 8 in.

Description.—Elizabeth Knevet wears the pedimental head dress with the front lappets embroidered with quatrefoils.

It may have been noticed that knights and squires occasionally displayed their armorial bearings on the tabard which they wore over their armour, *e.g.,* Morys Denys and his son Sir Walter, wear tabards. Ladies, too, wore arms on their dresses, and more especially on the mantle.

This mantle is fastened by a cord which passes through the loops at the back of the fermailes, and hangs down in front, the two ends terminating in tassels. Not much is to be seen of the underdress, the cuffs and collar are made of fur. The shoes are large and round-toed (87).

Heraldry.—The brass of Elizabeth Knevet (now being described) is quoted by Mr. Haines (*Manual,* i., p. cxiii.) as "a good example of a lady in an heraldic mantle." It bears the following arms—"Quarterly 1. Argent, a Bend Sable, within a Bordure engrailed Azure, Knevet. 2, Argent, a Bend Azure, and chief Gules, Cromwell. 3, Chequy Or and Gules, a chief Ermine, Tatshall. 4, Chequy Or and Gules, a Bend Ermine, De Cailly or Clifton. 5, Paly or six within a Bordure bezanté . . . . 6, Bendy of six, a Canton. . . . . "—Bigland's *Gloucestershire,* p. 539.

Fig. 86. Shield 1518. Eastlington.

At each corner is a coat of arms; Nos. 1 and 4 (86) are on ordinary shields, 2 and 3 on lozenges. Nos. 1 and 3 (86) are charged with the same bearings as are on her mantle. No. 2 on a lozenge quarterly. 1, *Knevet.* 2, *Cromwell.* 3, *Tatshall.* 4, *Cailli.* 5, *De Woodstock.* 6, Paly of six within a bordure. 7, Bendy of six, a canton. 8, or a chevron gules, *Stafford.* 9, Azure, a Bend cotised between six Lioncels rampant,

Fig. 8.— Elizabeth Knevet, 1518, Eastington.

or *De Bohun*. No. 4 similar to No. 1, with the omission of 2 and 3.

Inscription.—Round the verge was the following inscription, the portion now missing, in brackets, being supplied from Bigland :—

🙵ere lyeth | Elizabeth Knevet, daugh[ter of Sir Will Knevet] knight whiche Elizabeth decessed the first day of Novembre in ! [the yere of our Lord God M.D. and xviii. On whose soule Jesu have Mercy. Amen.]

Illustration.—*Haines' Manual*, i., p. cxiii.

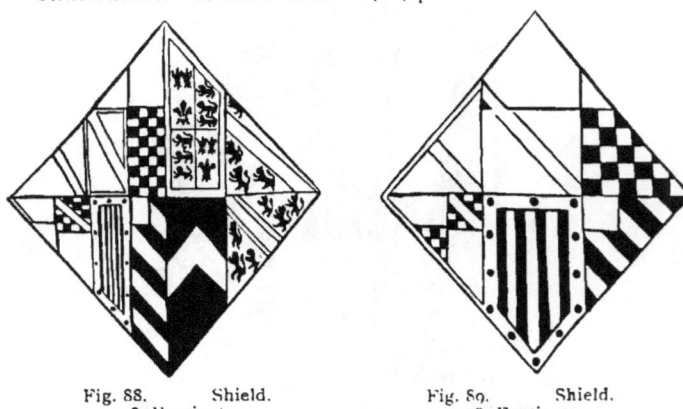

Fig. 88.   Shield.
1518. Eastington.

Fig. 89.   Shield.
1518. Eastington.

Portions Lost.—Part of the inscription.

Memoir.—"She was the daughter of Sir William Knevet, Knight, of Buchenham Castle, in the county of Norfolk, by Joan, his second wife, sister of Edward, Duke of Buckingham, commonly styled Lady Beaumont."—*Blomefield's Norfolk*. vol. i., p. 257.

The will of Sir William Knevet is in the P.C.C. F 18 Holder.

L.—Gloucester. St. Michael.

William Henshawe, bell-founder [5 times] mayor [1503-1520] and wives Alys 1519, and Agnes, male effigy and about three sons and three daughters lost. Nave.—*Haines*.

Position.—Originally on a ledger stone in the Nave, but now affixed to the west Wall of the south aisle.

Size.—2 ft. 11 in. x 2 ft. 6 in. There is now only 6 in. space between the wives; but before the memorial was moved from the floor there was a space of 14 in. between them.

Description.—Rev. W. C. Lukis, M.A., F.S.A., in his very interesting paper on *The Bell-Foundry at Gloucester*, which appeared in "*The Journal of the British Archæological Association*," 1871, gives the following particulars:—

"It is remarkable how little information of a positive kind has come down to us respecting bell-founders prior to the reign of Henry VIII. We have to feel our way in the dark in the pursuit of faint glimmerings of facts, and frequently meet with disappointment where we hoped to be satisfied. We should like to gaze upon a mediæval bell founder of the West of England, to study his physiognomy and to notice any peculiarity in his dress; and in Gloucester we meet with disappointment. In St. Michael's Church William Henshaw was buried, and a sepulchral brass records the decease of his first wife Alice. The brass was laid down in the husband's lifetime and a space was left for the date of his own decease. The figures of the two wives remain, but that of the founder exists no longer.

"Fortunately we have examples at Norwich of brass effigies of two bell-founders named Brasyer, of the exact date of William Henshawe, and from these we may obtain a notion of his figure. There is nothing to distinguish the bell-founder from civilians of the period. He is habited in long furred robe, and wears very broad-toed shoes. He is represented with his hands raised in prayer; and from his girdle hangs a rosary on the left side, and a gypciere or pouch on the right. His hair is flowing to his shoulders, parted in the middle, and cut square over the eyebrows. In the North of England is another example of a bell-founder's portrait, viz., in the curious and most interesting 'bell window' in the north aisle of York Minster. This window is of three lights, and in the lower compartment of the centre one is a representation of Richard Tunnock, bell-founder, on his knees, making an offering of the window to the Archbishop of York, who is seated in front of him. A label bears the founder's name, and his craft is designated by a bell upon his pouch, and he carries a bell in his right hand.

"As a set off to the disappointment alluded to, I am able to say that through the civility of Mr. Ferry, of Eastgate street, I saw, about ten years ago, a portion of William Henshawe's house, in which, if it still exist, there is a large room with a panelled ceiling of the 15th century, and also his coat of arms in a window of the same room. I expected to meet with a disappointment at that period, for I was told not to put any faith in Counsell's statement (see his *History of Gloucester*) that the bell-founder's arms are still preserved in two windows there. One shield, however, remains in a window as stated above, and the other I found in a dark cellar, somewhat mutilated, but in sufficiently good preservation to show what it was, viz., *azure* on a chevron between three lozenges *argent*, the same number of bells *sable*, and above them a laver pot.[*] It is probable that the shield remaining in the window is a model of the original one which I found in the cellar, and that the remnant is one of the two alluded to by Counsell. At a comparatively recent period the shield seems to have been repaired, and the tincture of the field, perhaps, changed from *gules* to *azure*, *gules* being the tincture given by Burke as belonging to Henshawe's arms."

Though the effigy of the husband has disappeared, yet the effigies of his two wives still remain. They are dressed very similarly with the exception of the belt. They wear the kennel headdress:—then it was the custom to hide as far as practicable all the hair on a woman's head, not even a stray curl was allowed to betray the natural wealth, so that brown locks and golden were equally out of fashion, artificial adornments were in vogue, not to aid the natural ones, but even to conceal them altogether. The lappets of their headdresses are richly embroidered with a diaper pattern and are long. A close-fitting gown with a high bodice and tight sleeves encases each, and falls in folds from the waist to the ground. Its lower edge is adorned with fur, and the cuffs are also purfled with the same. Beneath the gown emerge just the tips of their wide square-toed shoes. A broad embroidered band hangs loosely round the hips of each. On the lady to the left it is short and terminates in three rosettes, from

---

[*] Mr. Lukis says in a foot-note that he "had these shields releaded, and returned them to Mr. Ferry and I trust," he adds, "that they have been treated with proper respect."

which hangs a short chain to which is fastened an ornament. On the lady to the right the girdle is long, the tongue passes behind the front of the buckle and reaches nearly to the feet and finishes in a long pendant. The ladies are both erect and looking towards each other with hands in the supplicating attitude so usual.

Inscription.—On the plate of brass beneath them is the following legend :

𝔓ray for the soull of Will'm henshawe Belfounder, and late maire of this Towne, and Alys | and Agnes his wyfes, the whiche Will'm decessed the   day of   in the yer | of our lord God a thousand CCCCC   & the seid Alys decessed the seconde day of | ffebruary, the yere of or lord ml vc xix for whose soules of yor charite say a pater nost' & a ave.

Illustrations.—I know of none.

Portions Lost.—The effigies of husband and children. The Rev. H. Haines, M.A. (Manual i. cxxx.) records that "the device of a bell and melting pot on three legs" was on this brass.

Memoir.—William Henshawe was a bell-founder, but in *Church Bells of Gloucestershire*, by Rev. H. T. Ellacombe, M.A., there is no mention of any bells cast by him. Henshawe was Sheriff of Gloucester in 1496 and 1501, and Mayor in 1503, 1508, and 1509.

The Rev. W. C. Lukis is of an opinion that the fifth and sixth bells in the cathedral, and the curfew bell of St. Nicholas Church were cast by him.

In the Letters of Henry VIII. vol. i, p. 191, the recognisance of William Henshawe of Gloucester, bell-founder to appear before the Council is cancelled, 25 Oct., 1510.

LI.—Minchinhampton.

Edward Halyday, 1519, and wife Margery, with merchant's mark.—*Haines.*

Position.—On the north wall in the tower.

Size.—3 ft. 9 in. × 1 ft. 8 in. Husband, 3 ft. high. Wife, 2 ft. 6 in. high.

Description.—Edward Halyday has long clubbed hair covering the ears with a fringe, and he is clean shaven. His outer garment consists of a long loose gown reaching to his ankles; it is thrown open both above and below the waist, exposing to view the fur lining. The sleeves of the gown are loose, and hanging round the cuffs is a broad band of fur. Beneath this gown the underdress is seen fitting closely to the neck, and the tight-fitting sleeves of the same are to be seen at the wrists. He wears broad toed shoes which are fastened across the instep. Margery Halyday is represented in the then fashionable kennel or pedimental headdress, the left hand front lappet is the only one shown and this is embroidered. She wears a tight-fitting dress, with a narrow collar, the lower portion is so arranged in folds as to show the toes of her round shoes. The sleeves have large reflex cuffs lined with fur. The broad loose hip-girdle instead of being buckled, terminates in three rosettes, from these hangs a metal chain to which is fastened a metal pendant.

The figures are disproportionate in size, the effigy of the wife hardly reaching to her husband's shoulder. They are both erect, with hands together in supplication. Edward Halyday is full face, whilst Margery is turned to her right so as to look towards her husband.

The merchant's mark (90) is engraved on a disk, and consists of a double cross on a globe with E. H. on the sides.

Fig. 90.
Merchant's Mark.
1519
Minchinhampton.

When the brass was relaid this disk was turned upside down. Probably at the same time the scrolls proceeding from the mouths of both of the figures disappeared. When Mr. J. D. T. Niblett rubbed this brass in 1868 the labels had not then disappeared, and he very kindly told me that on the man's were these words:—*Misere mei de scdm magna m'cordia tua*. On his wife's were:—*Illuiet vultu suu sup' nos & mis'eatr n'ri.*, *i.e.*, Let his countenance lighten upon us and pity us.

Inscription.—Beneath the figures is a brass plate on which is engraved the following two-line inscription:—

Off yor charite pray for the soule of Edward Halydaye and Margery |
his wyf which Edwarde decessid the vj day of Aprill A° dni M°CCCCC xix.

Illustrations.—None known.

Portions Lost.—The scrolls mentioned above.

Memoir.—The wills of both Edward and Margery Halyday

are in the P.C.C., the former being 20 Ayloffe (1519) and the latter 32 Fetiplace (1514.)

LII.—Deerhurst.

A lady *circa* 1520, not recorded by Rev. H. Haines.
Position.—On the floor at the east end of the North Aisle.
Size.—2 ft. 5 in. × 8 in.
Description.—She is wearing the kennel, pedimental or diamond shaped headdress, in all its wonted stiffness and angularity; the lappets are adorned with a check pattern. The body is clothed in the tight-fitting dress of the period fastened in front, at the fastening from the waist upward is a narrow edge of fur, which is continued round the neck. The sleeves are tight-fitting, with deep reflex cuffs lined with fur. At the neck is seen the plaited top of her underdress. Round the hips hangs a broad loose girdle fastened by two rosettes in front from them depends a long chain at the end of which is a pomander (91). The figure is full-faced with hands in prayer.

Fig. 91.
Pendant. c 1520.
Deerhurst.

Illustrations.— None known.

Portions Lost.—All that remains is a three-quarter length of a female figure; of what the original memorial consisted is unknown. This portion was found during the restoration of the church by the rector, Rev. G. Butterworth, M.A.

LIII.—Dowdeswell.

A priest *circa* 1520, in cope with two evangelistic symbols, inscription lost, relaid.—*Haines.*
Position.—On a ledger stone in the chancel.
Size.—3 ft. 8 in. × 1 ft. 7 in.
Description.—His hair is long, covering the ears and clubbed, it is cut straight across the forehead, and the tonsure, though slight, is clearly shown. The priest is habited in processional vestments, viz., a long flowing cassock reaching to the ground and entirely concealing the feet, a full plaited surplice rather shorter with immense sleeves, around the neck the almuce, and over all a cope fastened across the breast by a square morse (92).

The cope is very slightly longer than the surplice and is richly diapered with fleur de lys in lozenges; the orphrey is adorned with a zigzag pattern. Rudder in his History says "the figure is not represented in the dress of an ecclesiastic, but in a robe semée with mullets and fleur de lis, which denote him to be of the family of Rogers;" whilst Bigland asserts that the "robe is diapered with roses and fleur de lis inserted in the interstices, but no mullets as has been said." He adds that "the ingenious Mr. Gough [Sepulchral Mon. p. 157] asserts it to be the exact counterpart of Robert Eglesfield,* founder of Queen's College, Oxford, only smaller, who died in xiv. century." The morse (92) or brooch is engraved with a rose en soleil. Beneath the sleeves of the cassock are visible at the wrists the tightly fitting sleeves of an under vestment, fastened underneath.

Fig 92   Morse.
c 1520.
Dowdeswell.

The priest is full face with hands in prayer.

Below are two panels with a margin of quatrefoils containing the evangelistic symbols† of St. Matthew and St. Luke.

Illustration.—None.

Portions Lost.—Inscription and the two symbols of St. Mark and St. John.

Memoir.—Atkyns calls it "an effigies, in brass of an abbot of Hayles," which is denied by Rudder, who, as may be seen above, thinks it belongs to a civilian of the Rogers family.

The late Rev. T. P. Wadley, very kindly sent me the following notes with respect to this brass.

A subsidy roll in the Bishop's Registry at Worcester, dated 1513, gives under Dowdeswell:—

"*Sir William Woodwarde*, *rector* (taxed) xxs.

Sir Gervaze Can'ton chaplain vjs. viijd.
Canton-Canerton? or Caverton?"

In the library at Lambeth Mr. Wadley found in Archbishop Morton's register, folio 12, that Sir John Choo is mentioned as rector of the church or curate of the chapel of Dowdeswell in the year 1487, so that this brass may commemorate one of the foregoing priests.

---

* This is an error of Gough's.   The figure at Queen's College represents Dr. Robert Langton, c. 1518.
† Vide No. XI, *Quinton*.

LIV.—Kempsford.

Walter Hichman, 1521, and wife Cristyan, with four sons, Thomas, John (both lost), Robert, John. Marginal inscription, Chancel.—*Haines.*

Position.—On a ledger stone on the south side of the Communion Table.

Size.—7 ft. 11 in. x 3 ft. 3 in.

Description.—Walter Hichman wears his hair long, and so cut as if to form a square border for the face. In accordance with the custom of that century he is clean shaven.

The outer garment consists of a long gown lined with fur: thrown open across the shoulders and also open down the front, the sleeves are long and wide, turned back at the wrists where the fur lining is shown. The gown is loose and unconfined by a girdle. The underdress has embroidered collar and sleeves; the skirt reaches nearly to the knees, and a narrow band keeps it in place at the waist; the rest is hidden by the gown. Tight-fitting stockings encase the legs, and low shoes with wide toes complete his attire. The figure is bareheaded, erect, and slightly inclined to his left to look towards his wife.

Cristyan Hichman wears the widow's cap, over which is thrown the veil headdress, so that very probably she survived her husband. Her dress is tight-fitting with a narrow collar. It is long but so arranged as to show the tips of her wide-toed shoes. She has a hip girdle fastened in front by three rosettes, from which no pendant hangs, as was usually the custom. Like her husband she is erect with hands upraised in prayer. Beneath were the effigies of four sons, but two have disappeared; the remaining two are dressed similar to their father, but without the fur lining to the gown.

Fig. 93.
Merchant's Mark.
1521. Kempsford.

Above the representations of husband and wife is a plate containing the merchant's mark (93):—a double tau cross on a triangle.

At each corner of the marginal inscription is a circular disk on which is engraved an evangelistic symbol.

Inscription.—

(*A winged eagle*) off youre charite pray for the soule of Walt, | (*an angel*) Richman here buryd which decessid the xxvijth day of September, the xiijth yere of the reign of Kyng Henry the viijth Anno dni—(*winged ox*) Millmo CCCCC₀ xxi° & for the soule of Cristyan—(*winged lion*) his wyffe which had to gedd' iiij sonnes viz., Thom's, John, Robert and John, on whois soules & all xren* | soul ihu have mercy.—Amen.

Illustration.—None.

Portions Lost.—The two effigies of the children under the husband, and his left toe; otherwise the brass is in splendid preservation.

Memoir.—His will is to be seen in the P.C.C. 20 Maynwaring.

LV.—Bristol. St. Mary Redcliff.

John Brook, sergeant-at-law and justice of assize in the West of England for Henry VIII., also chief steward of the Monastery of Glastonbury, 1522, and wife Joan, daughter and heiress of Richard Amerike. Chancel.—*Haines.*

Position.—On ledger stone in chancel.

Size.—3 ft. 6 in x 2 ft. 9 in.

Description.—His head is wholly covered by a cap or coif, which seems to be fastened beneath the chin. His hair is long and flowing, and is seen on his shoulders escaping from beneath the coif, and again it appears as a narrow fringe over the forehead. The face is clean shaven, and he is represented as an old man by the wrinkles shown. He wears his official robes as a sergeant-at-law, which were very similar to the judicial costume of the period; though sergeants-at-law were not allowed to wear the mantle or minever. Across his shoulders is a tippet, and over it a hood, from which depended two labels behind. His outer gown reaches below the knees, and is much plaited; the sleeves of it are very deep, but there is no fur lining shown. At the wrists are the closely buttoned sleeves of his underdress, the skirt of which comes below his gown and reaches his ankles. The feet are shod with the then fashionable round-toed shoes.

The dress of his wife is in the fashion which prevailed at the period of her death. She wears the kennel headdress, the

---

*Christian.

front lappets being embroidered. The tight-fitting gown sits close up to the neck, with a turn-down pointed collar: the fur cuffs are pointed and long, reaching to the elbows. The gown is arranged in folds over her feet, so as to show the toes of her wide shoes. Round her hips hangs loosely an embroidered girdle, the fastening in front is concealed by two rosettes; from these depends a chain, to which is attached a metal pomander. Both husband and wife are erect with hands joined in prayer, the husband being slightly turned to his left looking towards his wife, who is doing the same.

Inscription.—The figures stand on a plate of brass bearing this inscription :—

Hic iacet Corpus Venerabilis viri Job'is Brook quondam se'uient' ad legem Illustrissimi | principis felicis memorie Regis Henrici Octaui et Justiciam eiusdem Regis ad assisas in | p'tib3 occidentalib3 anglic ac Capitalis Senescalli illius honorrabilis domus et monas | tarij Beate Marie de Glasconia in Com' Som'cett qui quidem Johes obijt xxv° die Men | sis Decembris anno d'ni millesimo quingentesimo xxij° et iuxta cum Requiescit Johanna | uxor eius una filiaru et heredu Richardi Amerike quo3 aiab3 p'picietur deus. Amen.

It may be rendered into English thus :—

"Here lies the body of that venerable man John Brook, sergeant-at-law of that most illustrious prince of happy memory King Henry VIII., and Justice of Assize for the same King in the western parts of England, and Chief Steward of the honorable house and monastery of the Blessed Mary of Glastonbury, in the County of Somerset, which John died on the 25th day of the month of December, in the year of our Lord one thousand five hundred and twenty-two. And near him rests Johanna his wife, one of the daughters and heirs of Richard Amerike, on whose souls may God have mercy. Amen.'

Heraldry.—The arms are stated by Barrett to be "gules, on a chevron wavy argent three fleur-de-lis."

Illustrations.—None.

Portions Lost.—Seemingly none, and the brass is in excellent condition; yet Mr. Justin Simpson says that there was "at the lower dexter corner—Baron and femme the first of two coats per pale, COBHAM of Cobham, a crescent for difference, and the second gules on a chevron argent a lion rampant sable crowned or, armed and langued of the first BROOK impaling quarterly, COBHAM, second and third argent seven mascles conjoined 3, 3 and 1 gules BRAYBROOK. fourth BROOK."

Memoir.—The inscription gives a short account of John Brook, whose son David was a judge; David was born at Glastonbury, so that very probably John had settled there. In 1500 John Brook's father lived at Canynge House in Redcliff street, Bristol.

LVI.—Newent (also Quedgeley and Hempstead.)

Roger Porter, Esq., 1523, small, South Chancel.—*Haines.*

Position.—On a ledger stone of Purbeck marble at the east end of the south chancel.

Size.—The height of the figure is 17¼ inches.

Description.—Roger Porter is represented bare headed with long hair and in the armour of the period. His face is clean shaven. His armour consists almost wholly of plate, though mail is shown at the armpits and insteps, in addition he wears a skirt of mail below his tuiles. A steel gorget encircles his throat, while over each shoulder the upper edges of the paldrons are curved outwards in such a degree as to prevent the head from being struck off by a sweeping horizontal blow. The breast-plate has a tapul, and to it is fastened a short skirt of taces to which are buckled four ornamental tuiles, three of which are shown. The arms are encased in plate with large coudières, but the hands are left bare. The cuisses and jambarts are plain but the genouillières are large. In the heels of his broad-toed steel sabbatons are screwed his rowelled spurs; straight by his left side hangs his sword whilst a dagger is fixed to his right side.

The figure is erect slightly turned to his left and with hands raised in prayer.

Inscription.—Beneath his feet is a long narrow plate of brass bearing these words:—

Of your charity pray for the soull of Roger Porter Esquyer wh | ych Roger discasyd ithe xv day of Aprill the yere of our lord | God MVcxxiii on whose soull ihu have mercy. Amen.

Fig. 94. Shield. 1523. Newent.

Heraldry.—At the four corners of the stone were four shields, those on his left have disappeared, the ones on his right (94) are thus charged :—

"Quarterly 1st and 4th, Gules five merlions in saltire

argent, Porter. 2nd and 3rd, Argent three bars sable all over all as many ropes coiled, or, ALBANY."

The late Mr. J. D. T. Niblett. F.S.A.. of Haresfield Court furnished the above particulars of the Porter coat of arms.

Illustrations.—None.

Portions Lost.—Two shields.

Memoir.—Roger Porter was one of the Commissioners for Gaol Delivery at Gloucester Castle, 29 Oct., 1511. His will is in P.C.C. 7 Bodfelde.

QUEDGELEY.

This memorial consists of a shield with an inscription beneath in black letter.

Inscription.—The inscription beneath the shield is:

Here this place lyeth buryed ye bodies of Fredeswid Porter & Mary Porter doughters to Arthur Porter Esquyer and Alys his Wyffe Ano MlVcxxxij on whose soules and all cristen Jhu have mercy ame. |

Heraldry.—The shield (95) is PORTER impaling ARNOLD: 1. PORTER Gules, five merlions wings in saltire Argent. 2. HAYWARD, Argent three helmets close Sable. 3. ALBANY, Argent three bars Sable over all as many ropes coiled Or. 4. PORTER, as before. 1. ARNOLD, Gules a chevron Ermine between three pheons Or. 2. MADOC-AP-RYN, Gules, a chevron between three hawks lures Argent. 3. MADOC-AP-RYN, as before. 4 ARNOLD, as before.

Fig. 95. Shield. 1532 Quedgeley.

HEMPSTEAD.

A similar shield on the memorial to Nicholas Porter; the legend being:

Here this place lyeth buryed the bodyes of Nicholas Porter, Henry, Roger, and Nicholas, junr. Cecilly and Bridgid sonns and daughters to Arthur Porter, Esquyr and Alys his wife AD. MlVcxliij on whose soules Jhu have m'cy.

The Porters attended the Visitations of Gloucestershire in 1583 and 1623.

LVII.—Deerhurst.

Elizabeth, daughter of Thomas Bruges, Esq., of Coverle', and wife of William Cassey, of Whyghtfylde, and then of Walter Rowdon, Esq., 1525, inscription lost. North aisle.— *Haines.*

Position.—On the floor at the east end of the north aisle.

Size.—The height of the figure is 2 ft. 11 in.

Description.—This brass affords a good illustration of the changes (though slight) which were made in ladies' attire about the year 1525. The front angular lappets of the formal kennel headdress still remain, in this example they are much shorter than the last ones described, and they are adorned with a diamond pattern. The hair appears to have been kept in place by a roll or caul which was also "penthouse" shaped and a narrow frill was worn down each side of the face. She wears a necklet fastened in front and from which hangs a square pendant. Her gown is cut at the neck, the sleeves are wide at the wrist, and very probably stiffened to keep them in the constrained position shown. Beneath are close-fitting sleeves striped longitudinally, and often richly embroidered, while graceful frills encircle the wrist. Mr. Haines remarks that "it is perhaps uncertain whether these sleeves were added to the partlet, or to an undergarment termed a waistcoat." The skirts are long enough to conceal her feet. A highly adorned girdle, fitting more tightly than the last examples, keeps the gown in place; the fastening consists of a single rosette from which dangles a long chain with a pomander at the end.

> "A bob of gold
> Which a pomander ball does hold
> This to her side she does attach
> By a gold crochet of French pennache."
>
> *Mundus Muliebris.*

The pomanders were used for containing scent or preservation against infection and even a metal ball for warming the hands. In a church in Normandy is still shown the "pomander" which was used by the priest officiating in the early morning in winter to keep his hands warm. It consisted of a hollow sphere of perforated metal work in which a heated iron or even brick ball was inserted. In the volumes of the

Archæological Journal there occur several notices of pomanders, e.g., vol. vii., p. 98, xi., pp. 79, 80, &c., and they are often to be seen in collections of archæological objects.

She is represented erect, full-face, with hands upraised in prayer.

Inscription.—This is preserved by Bigland :—

Here lyethe Elyzabeth Rowdon, sumtyme Wyffe to Wyll'm Cassey, of Whyghtfylde, Esquyer, after the Dethe of the sayde Wyll'm was married to Walter Rowden, Esquyer which Elyzabethe dyed the xxvi Day of Januarie, Anno D'ni MDXXV for whose Sowle of your Charite say a Pater Noster.

Heraldry.—In Bigland's time the brass was more perfect, and he records (*History of Gloucestershire*, vol. I. p. 465) that there were "four corner escutcheons, one only remaining :—

Quarterly 1 and 4 Argent a cross Sable, charged with leopard's face in the centre Or. BRUGES. 2 DE CHANDOS. 3 BERKELEY of Coberley."

The DE CHANDOS coat was "Or, a pile, Gules," and the BERKELEYS of *Coberley* bore "Argent, a fess between martlets Sable."

Illustrations.—None.

Portions Lost.—Of the complete composition, only the figure remains.

Memoir.—"William Cassey was son of John and Elizabeth Cassey. He was of Cassey Compton, Wightfield and Stratton, and died 1517; he was succeeded by his son Robert, who married Elizabeth Poole and died 1547." *Deerhurst, by G. Butterworth.* Rev. W. Bazeley's paper on the Cassey Family in Trans. of the Bristol and Gloucestershire Archæological Society vol. xi, pp. 2-5 (1886-7), gives the date of William's death as 1509, leaving Leonard, son and heir, aged three and a half years.

In 1514 pardon was granted to Henry Kemys and Elizabeth, formerly the wife of William Cassy, deceased, for marrying without the king's licence. In P.C.C. is the will of "Walter Rouudon, gent., monast. of St. Peter, Gloucester" (1514)
1 Hodder.

LVIII.—Berkeley.

[William Freme, feodary of the Berkeley estates under Henry VII., and escheator of the Hundred of Berkeley, 1526,] head and feet gone, marginal inscription mutilated, now South Aisle.—*Haines*.

Position.—On a ledger-stone now in the chancel on the South side of the Communion Table.

Size.—6 ft. 7 in. × 2 ft, 6½ in.

Description.—This brass affords a very pleasing illustration of the costume of a well-to-do yeoman of the reign of Henry VIII.

Following the prevailing fashion William Freme is clean shaven, whilst his hair is long and clubbed.

His outer garment is a long tunic or gown lined and faced with fur, open down the front and reaching to his ankles. Over his shoulders he wears a fur cape, which Mr. Haines says "is very rarely seen on brasses."* The sleeves are ample and have fur cuffs. Beneath the tunic is shown the waistband of his doublet, and the tight-fitting sleeves of the same appear at the wrists.

On his breast he holds a heart (96) inscribed with "M'cy." Hearts are usually found on Pre-Reformation Brasses, and it is said "that such memorials indicate the deceased was enabled to perform a vow which he had made; but more probably they have different meanings, according to the inscriptions attached to them; and are generally intended to indicate sincere trust in the promises of God." † In Boutell's *Christian Monuments* there is more than one instance of "Heart-memorials" pourtrayed.

Fig. 96. Heart. 1526. Berkeley.

Inscription.—Around the margin of the stone was a fillet of brass bearing an inscription. Unfortunately most of it has disappeared, but the words in brackets have been supplied from Rudder's *Gloucestershire*, who with Bigland gives the

---

* *Monumental Brasses*, I. p. ccxxxii.
† *Monumental Brasses*, vol. I., p. cvi

inscription, but in their time a few of the words had vanished :—

[Hic iacet corpus Willielmi Freme] . . . . . o cuius Anime propicietur deus et Animarum omnium fidelium defunctorum parentum et . . . . [suorum Amen. Contende] intrare per [angusta] m portam.

Which may be rendered into English :

"Here lies the body of William Freme . . . . on whose soul may God have mercy, and on the souls of all the faithful departed his relatives and (? friends). Amen. Strive to enter by the narrow gate."

Below the inscription is cut on the stone " Ob. 1526."

Heraldry.—Above the figure are the matrices of two shields : Bigland gives his arms as : Two chevronels between three cronels, for FREME, impaling a bend componé on a chief three escallops for . . . .

Illustrations.—None.

Portions Lost.—The head (now restored) and feet, two shields above the figure and portions of the marginal inscription. The late Mr. J. H. Cooke, F.S.A., of Berkeley, preserved the head, and in February, 1884, he had it securely fastened in its proper place, so that the memorial is more complete, and not a mere headless trunk as heretofore.

Biographical Account.—In Fisher's *History of Berkeley*, p. 25, is to be found " A sepulchral brass on the floor on the south side of the font marks the resting place of a Romish priest." Mr. Cooke gave the following account of the brass:—
"The Fremes were for many generations freehold tenants under the Lords Berkeley, for lands in the manors of Hinton, Alkington, and Canonbury, in the parish of Berkeley and in Berkeley Borough, by Knight's Service and the rent of twenty horseshoes, and their nails, annually. The first of the family who appeared in this neighbourhood married the heiress of John Usher, *temp.* Edward IV. The name was originally spelt Reme or Reom. William Freme, Esq., died, as stated on his tombstone, in 18 Henry VIII., but his death was presented at the Halimote Courts of Hinton and Alkington as happening in 17 Henry VIII. His widow afterwards married Richard Walsh, and died 31 Henry VIII., leaving her son and heir, Thomas Freme, then 23 years of age. Thomas Freme, of Lyppiatt, the great grandson of the last named Thomas, held the lands in 1639."

His name appears in the Commission for the County of Gloucester in the early part of Henry VIII's reign.

LIX.—Northleach.

Thomas Bushe, woolman and merchant of the Staple of Calais, 1525, and wife Joan, 1526, with canopy and marginal inscription, three or four sons, and two or three daughters lost. Nave.—*Haines*.

Position.—On a ledger stone in the Nave.

Size.—6 ft. 9 in. x 3 ft. 8 in.

Description.—In its original state this memorial must have been extremely interesting. Under a double canopy are the figures of husband and wife.

Thomas Bushe has long clubbed hair cut straight across the forehead, and parted down the middle. His face is clean shaven, and by the wrinkles shown on it, he is represented to be well advanced in years. His outer garment consists of a tunic scarcely reaching the ankles. It is open down the front and faced as well as lined with fur. The sleeves are ample, the cuffs are made of fur. Beneath the gown appears the doublet, which was a kind of frock coat with close fitting sleeves and a short skirt, the waist is encircled by a narrow belt adorned with studs. The legs are clothed with hose, and on his feet are broad-toed low shoes fastened in front by a buckle (97). The supporters of his feet are a horned sheep and a woolpack, the former being under his left foot and the latter under his right.

Fig. 97. Feet. 1526. Northleach.

Rings are shown on the first and last fingers of his right hand and on the last finger of his left.

Joan Bushe wears the pedimental headdress, the front and

the back lappets are hanging down in front of her. Her attire is in the fashion of the commencement of the 16th century, viz., a long close fitting dress with tight sleeves and fur cuffs. A loose hip girdle fastened by three rosettes, from which hangs a chain terminating in a metal pendant completes her costume. The skirt of her robe is gracefully arranged in folds to allow the toes of her wide shoes to be seen resting on a woolpack and horned sheep, the former being under her left foot and the latter under her right (98). She is wearing rings on the first, second, and last fingers of her right hand, and on the two last fingers of her left hand.

Fig. 98. Feet. 1526. Northleach.

Both are erect, full face, with hands upraised in prayer.

Beneath the figures and above the fillet bearing the inscription are the matrices of two groups of children, and between is a brass-plate on which is Thomas Bushe's merchant's mark (99):—A Latin cross standing on XX and T, B on either side.

The figures of Thomas and Joan Bushe are beneath a fine double canopy, with circular heads and crocketted ogee gables. Each pediment is filled with a rural scene representing a tree under which are three

Fig. 99. Merchant's Mark. 1526. Northleach.

horned sheep with long tails, the sheep in the middle is lying down, the other two are standing and are looking towards each other. (100) On either side of the gables and from

Fig. 100. Canopy. 1526. Northleach.

between them rise pinnacles terminating in crocketted finials, the outer ones are continued downwards, and are panelled.

Inscription.—Between their bases is a fillet of brass bearing this inscription :—

"Off your charite pray for ye Soull of Thomas Busbe, m'chaute of ye Staple of Calis | and Johan, his wife, which Thomas deccssed the   day of   An Dn MCCCCCXXV3."

Around the margin of the stone is a narrow band of brass with an evangelistic symbol at each corner, and on it is this inscription, which commences over the husband's head :

(*Eagle*) * Off yor charite pray for the soule of Thomas (*Angel*) Busbe, suntyme m'chunt of the staple of Caleys, which decessyde the   day of   in the yere of or lorde God (*winged ox*) M⁰ V⁵ xxv. And for the soule of Johan, his wife (*winged* lion), which decessyde the [portion lost] pere of or lorde God M̄· v̄ xxvj., for who' soull of yo' charite say a p'r noster & a ave

Heraldry.—Above the tree suspended by a hook is a shield charged with the arms of the *Merchants of the Staple of Calais*:—Barry nebulée of 6, Argent and Azure, on a chief Gules, a lion passant guardant, Or.

Illustration.—None.

Portions Lost.—The plates on which were engraved the children, the whole of the central pinnacle, except the extreme end of the finial, the upper half of the pinnacle on Joan's left side, the finial of the gable over her head, and a portion of the marginal inscription.

Memoir.—Thomas Bushe was one of the wealthy wool merchants of the Cotteswolds, and in addition he was a merchant of the staple of Calais, which at that time belonged to the English. The will of Thomas Bushe is in P.C.C., 38 Bodfelde, and that of his wife is 15 Porch.

LX.—Cirencester.

Two female effigies c. 1530, husband (?) and inscription lost.—*Haines.*

Position.—On the floor of the Lady Chapel.

Size.—2 ft. 9 in. x 1 ft. 5 in.

Description.—Here "are two female figures—small but well executed—(the male one in the centre is lost), with some children at the feet. The two wives are represented as wearing a close-fitting kirtle to the feet, with tight sleeves, furred at the wrist, and a square cut collar; the dress is secured at the waist by a massive embroidered cincture, which, slung loosely round the person, and passing through an embroidered loop (the figure on the left hand having the larger loop of the two), falls down with a long pendant end in front of the figure nearly to the feet; on their heads they wear the *kennel* or angular head dress so generally worn during the latter part of the reign of Henry VII., and which continued in fashion some time after the accession of Henry VIII. It was made of velvet or embroidered cloth, sometimes of lighter materials and being pointed somewhat stiffly over the forehead descended in lappets on the shoulders and back. A similar head dress is worn to the present day in some of the valleys of the Pyrenees.

From the style of costume, therefore, in this brass we may fix the date as being of the end of the 15th or early in the 16th century.

On this slab remain the indents and nails of the two figures, male and female, both somewhat larger than the existing effigies. The Rev. W. Dyke is disposed to consider the present effigies are those of the children of the persons represented by the missing brasses, but in this opinion I do not concur, as I never remember an instance of children being delineated otherwise than as very young, and in a diminishing scale. Probably the slab was used for an earlier memorial, which, being lost, some members of the same family made use of it as a foundation of their own brasses." † This group has no connection with this brass, but will be described and illustrated later on.

Illustration.—The girdle of the wife on the left hand of the husband is figured in *Haines' Introduction*, p. ccxli.

Portions Lost.—The effigy of the husband and the inscription have disappeared, a quatrefoil over the husband's head, a single child below between husband and each wife.

Memoir.—The Rev. H. Haines, M.A., in his private copy of *Monumental Brasses*, had added this marginal note:—" possibly Thomas Neele," whose will is in P.C.C., 29 Vox.

LXI.—Northleach.

William Lawnder, priest *circa* 1530, in surplice (?), kneeling, marginal inscription mutilated, Holy Trinity and Blessed Virgin Mary lost. Chancel.

Position.—On a ledger stone at the base of the Altar steps.

Size.—5 ft. 9 in. x 2 ft. 5 in.

Description.—William Lawnder is represented with hair reaching to the shoulders, but cut so as to form a fringe across the forehead. He is clean shaven and has a tonsure.

William Lawnder is vested in a surplice plaited round the neck, the sleeves are very deep and beneath are seen the sleeves of his cassock. To the surplice is fastened a hood. Mr. Haines (*Mon. Brasses*, i. p. lxviii.) says that "a kneeling figure painted on glass, and now in the large west window of

---

† The Reverend W. E. Hadow, M.A., in the *Transactions of the Bristol and Gloucestershire Archæological Society* for 1877-8. Part I., p. 154.

Cirencester church, represents an ecclesiastic in similar costume; both the cassock and hood are of a red colour." The hood must not be confounded with the *amice* of which an account was given in No. xxii. of this series.* The hood is fastened on the left shoulder by a rosette.

William Lawnder is kneeling in front of a fald stool and is turned to his left. His hands are uplifted in prayer, and from them proceeds a scroll with these words: "𝕺 regina poli mediatrix esto Lawnder Will'i" (O Queen of Heaven be the Mediator of William Lawnder).

Above his head is the matrix of the Virgin Mary holding the infant Saviour on her right arm, and by the side of this vacant place is another scroll also containing an invocation to the Blessed Virgin: "𝕺 Hymen celi Lawnder miserere Will'i" (O Deity of the Sky have pity on William Lawnder).

Above this matrix was another plate, but, unfortunately, there is no record of what was engraved on it. Mr. Haines suggests that it was "a large representation of the Holy Trinity."

Inscription.—Around the margin is the following quaint inscription :—

† [Man in what] (102) state that euer
  thow be Timor Mortis (1) shulde truble the ffor when thow
    leest Wenyst (2) veniet te
mors sup'are (3) [And]
so thy grave greuyst (4) Ergo Mortis memorare. (5) (101)

Fig. 101. At End of Inscription. C 1530. Northleach.

This inscription is to be found at Witney, Oxfordshire, 1510, and Luton, Bedfordshire 1513, and it was on a brass at

* Robert Lond, St. Peter's, Bristol.
† 1 Fear of Death. 2 Thinkest. 3 Death will come to overtake thee. 4 Diggest. 5 Therefore remember death.

Great Tew, Oxfordshire, 1513. The admixture of Latin and English in the inscription is very curious.

Before the word "*state*" is a shield containing the well-known verbal emblem of the Holy Trinity. (102)

Other examples may be seen at St. Cross, Hampshire, 1382, Cowfold, Sussex, 1433, and in S. Mary Magdalene, Reigate, is an instance (painted) 1476.

Illustration.—None known.

Portions Lost.—Four words of the marginal inscription, and two plates over his head.

Fig. 102. "Holy Trinity."
C 1530 Northleach.

LXII.—Fairford.

Sir Edmond Tame, 1534, and two wives, Agnes [daughter of Sir Richard Greville] with two sons and three daughters, and Elizabeth [Tyringham] in heraldic dresses, North Chancel.—*Haines.*

Position.—On a ledger stone in the Chapel at the East end of the North Aisle.

Size.—7 ft. 6 in. x 3 ft. 6 in.

Description.—Sir Edmond is represented bare headed (103) as was then the custom, his hair is parted in the middle of the forehead, and is long, the face is beardless. His head rests on helmet adorned with a lambrequin and surmounted by his crest—a colt's head with mane erect couped. He wears a armour somewhat similar to that in which his father (John Tame) * is represented though the body is concealed by a richly embroidered *surcoat* or *tabard* † on which are emblazoned his arms, yet the following armour is discernible. Around his neck is the collar of mail; small coudiéres and plain brassarts protect the arms, whilst the hands are not gauntletted. Below the tabard is the skirt of mail, over which are shown four pointed and scalloped tuiles. Hanging perpendicularly from

---

* Vide No. xl. of this series.
† The *tabard* was described in No xxvii of this series.

his left side is a sword, and below his right elbow is seen the handle of his dagger. The legs are encased in massive plate armour and broad-toed sabbatons guard his feet; in his heels are screwed rowelled spurs. He wears a neckchain, from which hangs a T cross.

Fig. 103. Sir Edmond Tame. 1554. Fairford.

On each side of Sir Edmond is the effigy of a wife, the one on his left being a daughter of Sir Richard Greville. She wears the kennel or diamond shaped head dress, the front lappets being richly embroidered and hanging in graceful curves not in the stiff formal fashion which was so prevalent. Over her shoulders is thrown a mantle on which are embroidered the Greville coat of arms—Sable, on a cross engrailed, or, five pellets within a bordure engrailed of the second. The same arms, with a mullet for difference, are on

the brass of William Grevel, 1401, Chipping Campden. §
The mantle shews no method of fastening. Around her neck
is a chain to which is attached a cross similar to her husband's.
Her gown is like the one worn by her mother-in-law, Alice
Tame. It is long and tight-fitting, the sleeves terminate at the
wrists in embroidered cuffs. She has a loose hip girdle
fastened in front by three rosettes, from which hangs a chain
terminating in a pomander.

Sir Edmond's second wife is on his right hand. She wears a
modified form of the kennel head-dress, but the lappets are not
so long as those worn by Lady Agnes. Her mantle bears the
Tyringham arms—Or, a saltire engrailed, sable. It is
fastened by a cord stretching across the breast, the two ends of
which pass through a slide and reach to her feet terminating in
large tassels. Over her mantle she wears a chain. Her gown
seems to be of a different make to that of Lady Agnes. It is
gathered in neat folds and fastened by a brooch at the neck,
and it is so long as to require to be tucked up. The sleeves
fit closely with plain broad cuffs and a narrow frill at the wrists.
She wears over her gown a short jacket. Like the other two
she wears a cross hanging from a neck chain.

All three are erect full face and with hands joined in prayer,
Lady Agnes being on Sir Edmond's left, and Lady Elizabeth
on his right. Sir Edmond is represented as being of less
stature than either of his two wives.

Beneath Sir Edmond are two sons in long tunics with wide
sleeves and broad-toed shoes.

Beneath Lady Agnes a group of three daughters in kennel
headdresses and tight-fitting gowns.

Fig. 104. Inscription. 1534. Fairford.

Inscription.—The marginal inscription is :—

Of youre charite pray [for the soul of Edmond Tame (104) Knyght here under buried which decessid the fyrst day of October in the yere of oure lorde god a thousand CCCCCxxxiiij and

§ Vide No. VII.

for the soule of Æres (?) | his first wife which decessid the xxvj day of July an. | [Dn'i Milesimo cccccvi] the prosperite of Dame Elizabeth his last wife . . . . s & all xren soules ihu haue mercy, amen. (105)

This inscription has been repaired but unskilfully, the words "*soul of Edmond Tame*" (104) being evidently the work of a much later period, for the rest of the inscription is in black letter, and these words are engraved in a clumsy imitation of Roman letter; the piece on which is the portion "*the prosperite of Dame Elizabeth his last wife*" has been inserted reversed, and at the end is a skull. (105)

Fig. 105. Inscription. 1534. Fairford.

Heraldry.—At each corner of the slab is a shield but they are not so well engraved as the figures are. At the upper dexter corner above Lady Elizabeth appears the Tame arms, which are repeated at the lower sinister corner; at the sinister upper corner above Lady Agnes is Tame impaling Greville, and at the lower dexter corner is Tame impaling Tyringham. The Tame arms are mentioned in No. XL. of this series: King Henry VIII. granted Sir Edmond Tame " as his armorial bearings the supporters of the Royal Arms of England—a crowned lion and a griffin—combatant and respectant—the lion being azure crowned and clawed gules, and the griffin vert clawed gules in a field argent."‡ On the brasses to Sir Edmond the arms bear a crescent for difference. Illustrations are given in the next description.

Portions Lost.—The lower portion of Sir Edmond's sword and portions of the marginal inscription.

Illustration.—*Bigland's Gloucestershire*, vol. I. p. 571.

Memoir.—See the next description.

LXIII.—Fairford.

The same individuals as last, in heraldic dresses, but with one son only, mural, North Chancel.—*Haines.*

‡ H. F. Holt, Esq., in *Archæological Journal*, 1871.

Position.—On the north wall of the chapel at the end of the North Aisle.

Size.—2 ft. 10 in. × 2ft. 6 in.

Description.—This is the only instance we have in Gloucestershire of two brasses in the same church commemorating the same individuals.

In the brass now under consideration Sir Edmond is kneeling to a faldstool on which lies an open book. He faces his two wives who also kneel at faldstools, one behind the other.

Sir Edmond wears armour very similar to the suit already described, the following being the chief points of difference—neither tuiles nor dagger appear, and between his brassarts and jambarts are shewn gussets of mail.

Behind him is only one son who wears an ample gown faced with fur.

Lady Agnes wears a heraldic mantle—her husband's arms being on the right hand side and her own (Greville) on the left hand; her mantle is fastened by a chain; otherwise she is dressed as described in the last account. Behind her are kneeling her three daughters in Queen Mary bonnets and long veils; their dresses are low with wide bell sleeves whilst the tight fitting sleeves of the underdress reach the wrists.

Lady Elizabeth is habited similarly to Lady Agnes, but impaling the Tyringham arms instead of the Greville.

From Sir Edmond proceeds a label, **Jesu, lord that made vs**; from Lady Agnes, **wt thy blod vs bought**; and from Lady Elizabeth, **for give vs ovr trespass**.

Fig. 106. "Holy Trinity" 1534. Fairford.

In the centre under the middle of the arch at the top of the memorial is the pictorial symbol of the Holy Trinity (106) on a separate brass plate beautifully incised. The Almighty Father, the "Ancient of Days," is represented as an aged monarch seated on a throne. He wears the long flowing regal robe. His hair and beard are long, and He is crowned; the two first fingers of His right hand are held up in the attitude of benediction, whilst His left hand holds a cross tau-shaped to which is nailed God the Son, whilst above the head of the crucified Son hovers the dove-emblem of the Holy Spirit : all three of the figures are nimbed.

Inscription.—Beneath the figures is a plate of brass on which is the following inscription in raised characters :—

𝔥𝔦𝔠 𝔦𝔞𝔠𝔢𝔫𝔱 𝔈𝔡𝔪𝔲𝔫𝔡𝔲𝔰 𝔗𝔞𝔪𝔢 𝔪𝔦𝔩𝔢𝔰 𝔢𝔱 𝔄𝔤𝔫𝔢𝔰 𝔢𝔱 𝔈𝔩𝔦𝔷𝔞𝔟𝔢𝔱𝔥 𝔳𝔵𝔬𝔯𝔢𝔰 𝔢𝔦𝔲𝔰 | 𝔮𝔲𝔦 𝔮𝔲𝔦𝔡𝔢 𝔈𝔡𝔪𝔲𝔫𝔡𝔲𝔰 𝔬𝔟𝔦𝔧𝔱 𝔭𝔯𝔦𝔪𝔬 𝔡𝔦𝔢 𝔒𝔠𝔱𝔬𝔟𝔯𝔦𝔰 𝔄'𝔫° 𝔡'𝔫𝔦 𝔐 𝔙𝔠 𝔵𝔵𝔵𝔦𝔦𝔦𝔦 𝔢𝔱 𝔄'𝔫𝔬 𝔯𝔢𝔤𝔫𝔦 | 𝔎𝔢𝔤𝔦𝔰 𝔥𝔢𝔫𝔯𝔦𝔠𝔦 𝔬𝔠𝔱𝔞𝔳𝔦 𝔳𝔦𝔠𝔢𝔰𝔦𝔪𝔬 𝔰𝔢𝔵𝔱𝔬 𝔮𝔲𝔬𝔯𝔲𝔪 𝔞'𝔦'𝔪𝔞𝔯𝔲𝔪 𝔭'𝔭𝔦𝔠𝔦𝔢𝔱𝔲𝔯 𝔇𝔢𝔲𝔰. 𝔄𝔪𝔢𝔫.

This may be thus translated—" Here lie Edmund Tame, knight, and Agnes and Elizabeth, his wives, which Edmund died on the first day of October, 1534, and in the 26th year of the reign of King Henry VIII., on whose souls may God have mercy. Amen."

It is worthy of notice that the regnal year of the sovereign is mentioned, which was often the case if the person commemorated was connected with the Court.

Heraldry.—Above Sir Edmond is a shield, Tame impaling Greville (107), and over Lady Elizabeth is Tame impaling Tyringham (108). See *Heraldry* in last description.

Fig. 107.   Shield.   Fig. 108.   Shield.
1534. Fairford.   1534. Fairford.

Portions Lost.—None; the whole composition is in excellent condition.

Illustration.—I have not met with any.

Biographical Account.— Edmund Tame's mother had been snatched away in his infancy, a circumstance of itself likely to endear him greatly to John Tame, and there is no doubt that he proved himself fully worthy of the love his father gave. That he never married whilst John Tame was alive, and that he found a wife in a lady of distinction among the county families, almost as soon as the period of mourning for his father ended, is a proof that he devoted himself to cheer the failing years of the old man as the pulses of life began to chill and slacken. At the time of his father's decease, Edmund Tame was in his thirty-sixth year, an age which enabled him to thoroughly appreciate the value and importance of the large properties, both personal and landed, which he then inherited—those in Gloucestershire, alone including (among others) Harnhill, Nimpsfield, Notgrove, Rendcombe, Tetbury, and Fairford, at which last mentioned place he took up his residence, in the mansion then in course of completion. John Tame's remains having been duly laid in the spot selected by him, Edmund's first duty was to give effect to his father's will by founding the chantry and erecting the tomb.

That the religious zeal of Edmund Tame, and his interest in Fairford church is beyond all question, is evident from the following extract from his will:—in P.C.C., 17 Hoger. " I, Edmund Tame, the elder, being of hole mynde, thanked be Allmighty God, make my testament in fourme following. *Firste,* I bequeathe my soule to Allmighty God, and to our blessed lady, and to all the holly cumpany of Heaven, and my body to be buried in our lady chappell in the Churche of Faireford. *Item.* I bequethe to the Vicar of Faireford iijli. vjs. viijd (£3 6s. 8d.). *Also* I will, that my Feoffees of my lande in Castleton to stande, and to be seased to this only use, that is to find a Priest for ever to sing for the soules of my Father and mother, and for the soules of me and of my wife, and other my friends, according to the feoffament thereof made."

That Edmund in every respect fulfilled his father's wishes, and maintained to the full the dignity of the family name, may be readily imagined by his adding to the family estates the manors of Dowdeswell, Barnsley, and Eastleach Turville, in Gloucestershire. In 1505, he was "Sheriff of

Gloucestershire," on the 26th of July in the following year lost his wife Agnes (a daughter of Sir Edward Greville), by whom he had four children—a son, Edmund, and three daughters, Alice, Margaret, and Elizabeth, all of whom afterwards married and survived him.

After remaining a widower for a few years, Edmund married a second time, his bride being Elizabeth Tyringham. No issue, however, resulted from this marriage, which appears to have been a very happy one. Indeed, as time progressed, Edmund Tame developed as much ambition and determination as had ever distinguished his father, very shortly after whose demise Edmund was included in the Commission of the Peace for Gloucestershire, in which he was confirmed by Henry VIII. on the 1st March, 1510. On the 17th November, 1513, Edmund's name was returned a *second* time in the sheriff's roll of his native county, and in 1515 he was also inserted in the Commission of the Peace for Wiltshire, where as already stated, he possessed considerable property. At this time he had abandoned all active interference in business, although he still embarked an extensive capital in the breeding of enormous flocks of sheep. His ambition was, however, rather with the Court than the counting-house and so successfully did he play his cards as to receive the honour of knighthood from Henry VIII. in 1516, in which year he was attached to the Royal Household, as appears from the " list of names of the king's officers and servants sworn to attend in his chamber;" and wherein the name of Sir Edmund Tame appears as a knight of the body, and that of his son, Edmund Tame, as an esquire for the body extraordinary.

During the last few years of his life, Sir Edmund the elder appears to have lived in retirement at Fairford, at which place he died on the 1st October, 1534; and in accordance with his before mentioned wish, was buried in the Lady Chapel there, beside his first wife Agnes. By the care of his widow, the Lady Elizabeth Tame, a blue marble slab in the floor of the chantry founded by his father, marked his resting-place. As Sir Edmund made provision in his will for barring the dower of his widow, his extensive landed property was inherited by his son Edmund, who had livery of the manor of Fairford the same year in which his father died. Notwithstanding, however, Sir Edmund's succession to Fairford, he did not attempt to take up his residence there; but in deference to his step-mother, the Lady Elizabeth Tame, he permitted her to occupy the Manor House, which she continued to do for some time after her step son's (Sir Edmund) decease. His will is in P.C.C., 17 Pennyng.

His pedigree is to be found in the Visitation of Gloucestershire, p. 260 *(Harleian Society)*.

Though Lady Katherine Tame, widow of Sir Edmund the younger, was entitled to Fairford as her jointure, she never appears to have disturbed Lady Elizabeth in the tenancy of the Manor House. In November, 1550, Lady Elizabeth made her will which commences thus:—" I bequeth my soul to Almightie God, Father, Sonne, and Holy Ghost, three persons and one God in Trinity, to our blessed lady Saint Mary the Virgin and Mother inviolate of our Saviour Jesus Christe, and to all the Holy Company of Heaven, and my body to be buried in North Chapell of our Lady in Faireford aforesaide, by my late husbande, Sir Edmund Tame the elder, Knight, deceased, whose soule God pardon, yf it fortune me, the said Dame Elizabeth, to departe out of this present lyfe in Faireford aforesaid, etc." P.C.C., f. 45 Pennyng.

The foregoing is taken chiefly from "The Fairford Windows," by Rev. J. G. Joyce; and "The Tames of Fairford," by H. F. Holt.

LXIIIA.—St. John Baptist, Gloucester.

Chronicled as lost.—*Haines*.

Position.—North Wall.

Size.—Length of husband 18½ in.; of the wife 17½ in.

Description.—John Semys wears long straight hair not parted in front where it is cut to form a fringe and reaching to the shoulders concealing the ears, in accordance with the usual custom of the period he is clean shaven. He is represented as wearing the official mantle fastened on the right shoulder leaving his right arm free, and hanging gracefully over his left. The mantle is both lined and faced with fur, is gathered in at the neck and covers all the doublet, except the little collar and the sleeves, the latter being moderately wide at the wrist and revealing beneath the tight fitting sleeves of his underdress (109).

His wife displays the pedimental headdress so characteristic of the period, the left lappet shows the ornamentation very plainly, it consists of a quatrefoil in a diamond, the back lappets are longer and reach nearly to the elbow. She wears a

Fig. 109. John Semys. 1450. St. John Baptist, Gloucester.

tight fitting dress cut square at the neck thus showing the upper portion of her under-dress and fastened down the front, it is encircled at the waist by a loose hip girdle also ornamented with a diamond pattern: the buckle through which the end of the girdle passes is large, and the tang does not pass through the girdle. The sleeves are narrow, tight fitting at the wrist with deep reflexed cuffs purfled with fur (110).

Fig. 110. Margaret Semys. 1540. St. John Baptist, Gloucester.

The figures are both erect, the husband being full-face and the wife turned to her right to look towards him. The hands are uplifted in prayer, the tips of the fingers just touching.

In the original memorial this wife's effigy stood to the left of the husband and was his first wife Elizabeth, beneath were their eleven children.

Rudder also gives the following account of the brass:—

"Upon a large grave-stone in grey marble, which was in the chancel before the old church was demolished, but now altered, or taken away, was a plate of brass, on which the effigy of a man at full length between two wives and several children, was engraven, and the following inscription in old black character:—

>   Here under buried John Semys lyeth,
>   Which had two wives, the first Elizabeth
>   And by her vj. soonnes, and daughters five;
>   Then after by Agnes, his secund wive,
>   Eight soonnes, seven daughters, goddes plente,
>   The full numbre in all of six and twentie.
>   He passed to God in the moneth of August,
>   The thousand five hundred and fortie yere just.
>   (24 Aug.)

Round the verge of the stone on the south side:—
>   Plaude poli patria, plaude et paradise colonum
>   Astri chorus plaudat, plaudat, hic astra peteno;
>   Plausus culmen opes; p'cul ite valete mag'ri
>   Laus et fama, vale decor: caro puireat opto.

On the west side:—
>   Scripta legas tumuli moritus nunc reperat hic qui
>   Laudis erat dignus, prudens, sapiensque benignus.

On the north side:—
>   Mitis, item lenis, discretus, largus egenis
>   Hic quasi fundator, miseris fuit et miserator.
>   Plangit conventus pastorem Religionis,
>   Regula tutorem: plangito, plange domus.

On the east side:—
>   Patra plange patrem, dominum vos plangite sui
>   Plange potens paup............natis plange sua.

On each of the four corners, without the inscription, was a scroll with writing on it, but one of the brasses long since torn off. On the other it is thus written:—
>   Siste gradus, Ora, Congita, Remiscere, Plora.
>   Sic redis in cineres, hujus es, et ejus es.
>   Gloria divicie fugiunt te, mors, manet et te.

Within the verge at the south-west corner are the old arms of the city, and no other arms are upon it.

In Fosbroke's time the inscriptions in Latin appear to have been lost.

Illustrations.—*Gloucestershire Notes and Queries,* Vol. V. (here reprinted).

Portions Lost.—During the restoration of this church in 1882 two plates of brass, of which an illustration is given, were found amongst some rubbish in a vault in the church. On them are engraved the three-quarters effigies of a male and a female figure. I am of the opinion that these are the fragments of the memorial to John Semys described by Rudder. No other portions have been as yet discovered, but I am glad to record that the plates just described have been affixed to the north wall of the church and are thus preserved for posterity.

Biographical Account.—A few words on the life of John Semys may possibly not be devoid of interest, for even the barest details are worth preservation—though in the present case, unfortunately, they are but too meagre.

John Semys was one of the two Sheriffs of Gloucester in 1525 and Mayor in 1528 and 1535. During his official life he had the honour twice of assisting at the reception of royalty visiting the city of Gloucester. The inaugural address of Mr. R. V. Vassar-Smith, president of the Bristol and Gloucestershire Archæological Society for 1889, gives a description of these visits.

In 1529 the name of John Semes, mayor, occurs in the list of justices for the gaol-delivery at Gloucester in June of that year.

On the 11 Nov. 1534, John Semys, maire, the recorder, and nine aldermen subscribe a letter to Thos. Cromwell to beg that he will have a commission directed to them of the same import as those directed to the shire of Gloucester for the due search and view of corn, as the town and county of Gloucester is distinct from the shire.

In June, 1535, his name again occurs on a Commission to make enquiry respecting Tenths of Spiritualities for Gloucestershire and the town of Gloucester.

Undoubtedly a careful search of the archives of the city of Gloucester would reveal more particulars, and I hope that my description of the brass in its mutilated state may induce others to make that inquiry which I myself am unable to effect.

LXIV.—Gloucester, St. Mary de Crypt.

John Cooke, alderman, 1529, and his wife dame Joan, 1544, triple canopy with St. John Baptist, all lost but two pediments (a third lately stolen), inscription lost, now fastened to a board in north transept, slab buried in chancel.—*Haines*.

Position.—On a large slab erected against the north wall of the north transept.

Size.—5 ft. 1 in. x 2 ft. 10 in.

Description.—John Cooke wears long hair and is clean shaven. His outer garment is a gown or mantle only used at this period as a sign of office. It is fastened by a single button on the right shoulder, and is thrown over the left arm in a somewhat clumsy manner (111). Beneath is a long tunic

Fig. 111. John and Joan Cooke, 1544. St. Mary de Crypt, Gloucester.

reaching to the feet; this is open above and below the waist, and faced with fur. The sleeves are of moderate and uniform breadth, and have wide fur cuffs. At the neck is seen the embroidered collar of the doublet, and the tight-fitting sleeves of the same appear at the wrist. From his girdle, which is concealed by his mantle and arms, hangs a gypcière or external purse. The toes of his wide shoes show beneath the gown.

His wife Joan is attired in widow's weeds. Mourning costumes varied little during the XV. and XVI. centuries,

She wears the veil headdress and the stiffly-plaited barbe—the distinctive tokens of widowhood (111). From her shoulders hangs a long and ample mantle which is looped up under the right arm, thence falling in graceful folds. Her dress is confined by a narrow girdle: the sleeves are also narrow with wide plain cuffs. On the first finger of her left hand is the widow's jewelled ring. The tops of her wide-toed shoes are just visible below the dress.

Fig. 112. Canopy. 1544. St. Mary de Crypt, Gloucester.

Both the figures are erect, with hands raised in prayer; John Cooke has his wife on his left hand and is turned a little to his left to look towards her, and Joan is turned a little to her right.

Above them was an elaborate triple canopy, but the

pediment over Joan's head has disappeared. Fosbroke* says that "over her head was a merchant's mark, viz., a sort of fret, or rather two squares interlaced, one a lozenge-wise ; in the centre a rose" (112). I am much indebted to Mr. Mill Stephenson, F.S.A., who has kindly lent me a rubbing of the portion of the canopy which has now disappeared. Over John's head is an exceedingly interesting pediment—it has a round cusped head surmounted by a crocketted ogee gable, and terminated in a floriated finial. The tympanum contains a circular panel in which is a rose with five petals and five barbs ; the spandrils are filled with trefoils. The cusps also have trefoils, and terminate in a cluster of three berries. The central pediment consists of a canopy between two pannelled pinnacles with crocketted finials and flowered pendants. In the pediment is a figure of St. John Baptist : in his left hand is a book on which is the Lamb of God holding a cross, from the stem of which is floating a flag with two streamers. Both the Lamb and St. John are nimbed. St. John is pointing to the Lamb with the index finger of his right hand—"Behold the Lamb." St. John is represented with long straggling hair, but smooth faced. The gown seems coarse, but not so realistic as is shewn on the brass at Deerhurst commemorating Sir John Cassy, 1400.† His right arm may be noticed as being covered by the sleeve of some under vestment, whereas the feet are bare, as is also the left leg, which is exposed nearly to the knee. St. John is on a corbel, and two smaller pinnacles rise on either side of him (113). The background consists of a lozenge-shaped diaper, with a sexfoil in the centre of each lozenge. Above him, stretching from side to side, is a branch forming a triple-headed arch over him, and under its centre he stands. This gable has straight sides, not ogee like the one above John Cooke's head. The groining of the canopy is also shown (113).

Inscription.—Above this elegant canopy the following words have been cut in the stone :—

Johannes Cooke, fundator scholæ juxta hanc ecclesiam obijt | Anno Domini M°CCCCC°xxix° | Johanna uxor eius obijt Anno Domini M°CCCCC°xl·iv°.

"John Cooke, founder of the school near this church died A.D. 1529. Joan his wife died A.D. 1544."

---

* *Gloucester*, p. 323. † See page 13.

Monumental Brasses.

Fig. 113.   Canopy   1544.   St. Mary de Crypt, Gloucester.

Heraldry.—In the Wantnar MS. his arms are given—Or, a chevron chequie, Gules and Azure, betweene three Cinque foiles of y⁰ first.

Illustrations.—I know of none.

Portions Lost.—The inscription, the pediment over Joan's head, of which an illustration is given (112), and the finials of the central pediment and the side pinnacles.

Memoir.—The following is taken from Atkyn's *Gloucestershire*, p. 978 :—" Here is a free school erected by Joan Cook, widow of John Cook, alderman, 31 Henry VIII. She, in performance of her husband's will, vested several manors and lands in the mayor and burgesses of Gloucester for divers charitable uses, and ordered £10 a year to be paid to a schoolmaster, if a priest, and but £9 a year, if a layman; which schoolmaster is to be nominated by the mayor, recorder, and two senior aldermen. There is now a salary of £30 a year allowed to the head master, and £16 to the usher." He was four times mayor, 1501—1519. The will of John is in P.C.C., f. 4, Allen; and that of Joan, f. 38, Porch.

LXV.—Weston-upon-Avon.

Sir John Greville. lord of the Manor of Milcot, 1546, chancel.—*Haines.*

Position.—On the Chancel floor.

Size.—4 ft. x 2 ft. 1 in.

Description.—We have now arrived at the period when the bold characteristic outlines of the earlier brasses have yielded to the finer lines and shades of the copper-plate engraver; one consequence of this is that the rubbings of these later brasses are not at all so clear and well defined as those of former centuries.

Sir John is bare-headed, revealing his hair closely cropped, but his moustaches are long and drooping, and his beard is trimmed to a point long enough to touch the tips of his fingers. The face is represented wrinkled, as he is an old man. His head rests upon his helmet, which is surmounted by a dog's head couped and collared (114). Sir John wears a tabard, a garment worn by knights in the Tudor era. Before 1400 a jupon was worn over plate armour. During the first half of the fifteenth century the polished armour of the warriors was uncovered and reflected the bright rays of the sun. After 1450 was introduced the tabard. It was a kind of jacket, short, closely fitting the form of the wearer, and had wide sleeves reaching to the elbows. On the

Fig. 114. Sir John Greville. 1546. Weston-upon-Avon.

front and the back of it, as well as on each sleeve, were displayed the arms of the wearer. This coat is to be seen at Chipping Campden, on the brass of William Grevel, 1401. At the neck is a small frill, the commencement of the fashion which in Queen Elizabeth's reign became so excessively large and unwieldly. Brassarts protect the arms but the hands are bare. Below the tabart is the skirt of mail reaching nearly to the knees. The skirt of taces is divided by an arched opening in front, the lower ends are seen extending below the tabard over each thigh, and to them are hinged small vandyked and pointed tuiles. Plate armour encases the legs, and broad-toed laminated sabbatons complete his defensive attire. In the lower part of his jambarts are screwed long-shanked spurs with large rowels. Beneath his right arm projects the pommel of his dagger and by his left side hangs perpendicularly his sword. Between his feet is a conventional flower — emblem of the resurrection. The artist has filled the portions of the memorial not occupied by the figure with a dotted background.

Inscription.—On a plate of brass beneath his feet is the following four-lined inscription :—

Hic situs est Joannes Grevillus eques auratus Milcoti | olim dominus qui fatu' implevit An° redemptionis humanæ | supra Millesimu' quingentesimu' quadragisimo Sexto Edvardj uero sexti Angloru' regis Secundo Calendas Decembric.

"Here was buried John Greville '*eques auratus*,' formerly lord of Milcote, who died on the calends of December, in the forty-sixth year of the redemption of mankind above one thousand five hundred in the second year of the reign of Edward the sixth, King of the English."

Heraldry.—"Crest, upon a wreath a grey-hound's head coupt collared, and on his surtout are repeated the following arms, viz. :—Quarterly 1 & 4, on a cross within a border engrailed nine balls . . . . * 2 . . . . a fess compony . . . . 3 . . . . per pale and per fess dancette . . . . in the first quarter a cressant."—*Bigland*.

Illustrations.—None known.

Portions lost.—Two shields above his head.

Memoir.—In the "*Visitation of Warwickshire*, 1619," published by the Harleian Society, the pedigree of Grevill is to be found. William Grevill of Campden had a son Ludovicus, whose son was William Grevill of Drayton, his son was Rad'us Grevill sepultus apud Moxton in Com' Oxon, and he was the father of John Grevill of Milcote, who had a son, Edw.

* The Greville Arms, *see* No. vii., p. 23.

Grevill of Milcote, knight a distinguished military character in the reign of Henry VIII., particularly at the battle of Spurs. He married Anne, daughter of John Denton, of Amersham, co. Bucks, by whom he had four sons, John, the subject of this memoir, Fulke, Thomas, and Edward, so says Burke in his *Peerage*, but the *Visitations of Warwickshire and Gloucestershire* only give John and Fulke; possibly Thomas and Edward died without issue.

Edward Greville, so Dugdale relates, obtained the wardship of Elizabeth, eldest daughter and afterwards sole heiress of Edward Willoughby, only son of Rd. Willoughby, Lord Brooke, by Elizabeth, his wife. He intended to marry her to John, his son and heir, "but she better affecting Fouke, the younger, became his wife." John Greville seemingly did not break his heart over the loss of Elizabeth Willoughby and her manors, for he married Eleanor, daughter of Ralph Verney, and when she died he espoused Elizabeth, daughter of John Spencer, of Hodnet, by whom he had issue an only son, Edward, who is commemorated by the "brass" next described.

Sir John Greville was lord of the manors of Milcote and Drayton. He represented the county of Warwick as one of the knights of the shire in the Parliament of 30 Henry VIII., "so fatall to the Religious Houses." On the coronation of King Edward VI. he was knighted, but he did not long enjoy this honour, for he died on the 25th of November in the next year, leaving Edward his son and heir aged 30 years. Following the example of his father he was buried in "St. Anne's Chappell in the Church of Weston *super* Avon." His will is in P.C.C., 16 Populwell.

Of the manor of Milcote it may be stated that William Greville, of Campden (see No. 7 of this series), bought it of Sir Walter Beauchamp in 1398, and entailed it upon his heir male. He was succeeded by his son John, whose grandson, Sir Thomas Greville, assumed the name Cocksey on succeeding to the estates from his grandmother's family. Sir Thomas died 14 Henry VII. without issue, when the lands of the Cockseys passed to heirs of that family, but Milcote reverted to the representative of Ludovic Greville, second son of the William Greville, of Campden, mentioned above.

LXVI.—Weston-upon-Avon.

Sir Edward Greville, lord of the Manor of Milcot, 1559, in armour, chancel.—*Haines.*

Position.—On the Chancel floor.

Size.—4 ft. 3 in. × 1 ft. 9 in.

Description.—The armour of Sir Edward is similar to that worn by his father, Sir John (see above). The following are

Fig 115. Sir Edward Greville. 1559. Weston-upon-Avon.

the chief points of difference:—There are no tassels to his helmet beneath his head, at the wrists are small frills, the lower edge of his skirt of mail is vandyked, the tabard covers all the skirt of taces and only the tuiles are shown, his sword hangs diagonally behind his left leg (115).

Inscription.—On a plate of brass beneath his feet are engraved the following words:—

Ibic situs est Edvardus Greuillus eques auratus | Milcoti olim dominus qui fatu' cocessit pridie natalis | Christi An'o Salutis humanæ quinquagesimo nono supra millesimu' et quingetesimu' imperante tum Anglis | serenissima Regina Elysabetha annu' iam alterum.

"Here was buried Edward Greville '*eques auratus*' erst lord of Milcot, who yielded to his destiny on the eve of Christmas day, in the fifty ninth year of human safety above one thousand five hundred, Elizabeth then being the most serene ruler over the English, already in her second year."

Illustrations.—None known.

Heraldry.—As his father, see last account (page 160).

Portions lost.—Two shields above his head.

Memoir.—Sir Edward Greville was 30 years of age at his father's death (recorded in the last account). He was a knight and married Margaret, daughter of William Wellington, of Burleston or Brakston or Barcheston in Warwickshire. He had an only son Lodowick, who was 22 years of age when his father died. Of Sir Edward, there does not appear to have been much information preserved. His son Lodowick seems to have been very unscrupulous, and Dugdale (*Warwickshire* pp. 534-5) gives a circumstantial account of how he murdered a tenant named *Web* to obtain his property, but that the affair was found out and Lodowick was pressed to death at Warwick. Amongst the Domestic State Papers *temp.* Elizabeth is a bond of William Porter, of Aston Underedge, to Lodovic Grevile, of Milcote, Warwickshire, in £2,000, dated April 1, 1564. Lodowick's son (by his wife Thomasine, daughter of Sir William Petre), Sir Edward, married Joan, daughter of Sir Thomas Bromley, and had several daughters, but an only son John, who died in his father's time *sine prole*, and Sir Edward then sold the whole estate to Lionel Cranfield, Earl of Middlesex, to pay his debts. At Sir Edward's death the elder branch of the Grevilles became extinct.

LXVII.—Whittington.

Richard Coton, Esq., 1536, and wife Margaret, 1560, between them a child in swaddling clothes, a son (in cloak above) lost.—*Haines.*

Position.—On the Chancel floor.

Size.—2 ft. 11 in. × 2 ft. 1 in.

Description.—Richard Coton has his hair moderately long, but he is clean shaven.

His gown reaches to his ankles, not girded, but thrown open in front. The arms pass through openings in the sides of the gown with very short sleeves over the arm, but with long strips pendant from behind the openings. The top of the gown is not turned down, but stands up round his neck. Of his doublet is seen a portion of the row of buttons down the front, and above it is a neat frill encircling the throat. Low shoes complete the visible portion of his attire.

Margaret Cotton wears a modified form of the kennel or pedimental headdress, the outward casing of which is still cumbrous and stiff, but it is relieved by a caul or frill-work over the forehead. The large frontal lappets have vanished, and instead the sides of the headdress turn up at the ends, so that this shape was fast merging into a bonnet. The top of her gown stands up round her neck something after the fashion of her husband's gown, and above it a small frill shows itself. The sleeves only reach as far as the elbows, where they hang down. Her forearms are covered with sleeves, generally richly adorned, but here represented plain, and puffed beneath, whilst at the waist are small frills. Her gown is confined at the waist by a sash tied in a bow in front. The tips of her shoes just emerge from beneath her dress, and it may be noticed that both husband and wife wear shoes with thick soles.

The figures are standing erect with hands in a prayerful attitude, the husband has his wife on his left hand, and they are both slightly turned to face each other.

Inscription.—Beneath them is a plate of brass on which is engraved in Roman characters the following :—

HERE LYETH THE BODDYES OF RICHARD COTON, ESQVIER | AND MARGARET COTON HIS WIEFE. HE DECESSED THE NINE AND TWENTYTH DAYE OF MAYE, IN THE THYRD AND | FOWRTH YEARE OF THE REYGNE OF KINGE PHILLYPP AND | QVEENE MARYE ANNO DOMINI 1556, AND THE SAYD | MARGARET DECES. SED THE   DAY OF MAY IN | THE FYRST YEARE OF THE REYGNE OF OVRE SOVERAIGNE LADYE QUEENE ELIZABETH ANNO DOMINI 1560.

Portions Lost.—Rudder records that there were "two children between them," and adds, "note the arms are torn off this stone." The indents of the foregoing are still visible. One of the children has disappeared since the Rev. H. Haines's time. The illustration of the child in swath-bands is reproduced from a rubbing in the late Mr. Haines's collection (116).

Illustration.—In the continuation of Bigland's *Gloucestershire*, s.v. *Whittington*, will be found an illustration.

Memoir.—In the parish registers of Whittington are the following entries :—

[1555] *Richard Cotton, Lord and Patron of the p'ishe of Whittington was buried the xviijth day of May. Mrs. Margarett Cotton, the wief of Mr. Richard Cotton, Esquire, was buried the 9th day of April,* 1559.

Fig. 116. Child. 1560. Whittington.

King Henry VIII., in the 36th year of his reign, granted the Manor and Advowson of Whittington to Thomas Stroud, etc., who alienated it to Richard Cotton (*Patent*, 36 Henry VIII.)

Tradition says that this Richard Cotton was killed in a duel. During his lordship of the manor he commenced to erect the manor-house, a fine specimen of the then prevailing style of domestic architecture. But his premature death put a stop to building operations, and the house still remains in an unfinished state.

His son John succeeded him and died seized of the manor and advowson of Whittington in 1600.—*Inquis. P. M.*, 42 Elizabeth.

LXVIII.—Grammar School, Bristol.

Nicholas Thorne, merchant and mayor [in 1544] founder [together with his brother] of a school, 1546, æt. 50, and 2 wives and children: by his first wife he had Bridget and John, by his second wife, Jane, John, Francis, Robert, Mary, Joan, Nicholas, Edward ; 18 Latin verses, engraved c. 1570, mural.—*Haines.*

Position.—On the wall of the large upper room in the new buildings of the Bristol Grammar School, removed there by a faculty from the walls of St. Werburgh's Church, when the latter was pulled down.

Size.— 2 ft. 9 in. x 2 ft. 3 in.

Description.—About the year 1570 it became fashionable to sport beards and moustaches, but Nicholas Thorne is represented with a clean shaven face.

His gown is long, with strips or false sleeves hanging behind the elbows. It is faced with fur and thrown open. Above his hands can be seen the buttons of his doublet. Around his neck and wrists are narrow frills. Low shoes complete all the visible portion of his costume.

On either side of him is represented a wife, both of whom are similarly attired (127). A close-fitting cap with lappets curling over each ear and a veil pendent behind formed the headdress, known by the name of "*Paris Head,*" or "*Paris Hood.*" The collar of the gown is thrown back to reveal a tight-fitting partlet surmounted by a slight ruff, the whole seeming so stiff and formal that the lady's head appears to be in "the stocks." The sleeves are adorned with a stripe wound round them, and they terminate in slight frills. The gown is encircled at the waist by a girdle, tied in a bow in front. Like their husband they wear low shoes.

Fig. 127. Mary Thorne. c. 1570. Bristol.

The sons are dressed similarly to their father ; the daughters wear a square bodice, instead of a collar.

Nicholas Thorne and both his wives are shown kneeling at faldstools, on which are lying open books. He is slightly turned to his left ; facing him is his first wife, Mary, with five sons and three daughters kneeling behind her ; their names (Jane, John, Francis, Robart, Mary, Johane, Nycholas, and Edward) are engraved on a brass plate over their heads. Behind Nicholas Thorne is kneeling his second wife, Bridget, with a son and daughter kneeling behind her, whose names (Bridgett and John) are recorded on a plate over their heads. Haines has chronicled the first wife as being the mother of two children and the second as mother of eight children. But an examination of his will shews that Mary was first wife and

Bridget his second. Above are three shields which are painted and not engraved.

Inscription.—Beneath are 18 lines of Latin verse in black letter:—

> Hac Nicolaus humo Thornus iacet, optime lector
> Olim mercator nobilis atque probus :
> Cuius dicta fides, constantia facta regebat
> Et virtute vacans actio nulla fuit
> Bristoliæ natus fato queque functus ibidem
> Qui magis æternum vivere dignus erat
> Hanc etenim prætor rexitque scholaque superba
> Ornauit, fratris su(m)ptibus atque suis
> Munificu(m)que patre(m) sensit respublica tota
> Bristolia, cuius, iam bonitate viget
> Huncque, senes, iuvenes, pueri, innupteque puellæ
> Totaque plebs deflet tam cecidisse cito
> Coniuge que gemina et bis quina prole beatu(m)
> Sedibus his miseris sustulit omnipotens
> Cuius in æthereas animus penetravit in auras
> Relliquias tantum corporis archa tenet
> Uxoremque eadem fidam tenet archa prior m
> Atque hunc qui primus natus vtrique fuit
> Qui obijt 19 Augusti A., Dni 1546 ætatis suæ 50

Low in this earth here Nicholas named Thorn, good reader see,
A Merchant rich and trustworthy within these walls was he,
Whose words and deeds alike by truth and faith were ever swayed.
And destitute of honour's stamp no action which he made,
In Bristol born, he here by fate his life laid down,
Who rather seemed worthy to be of an eternal crown.
This City well he ruled as Mayor, and with a school full large
And stately did adorn, at his own and brother's charge.
The City's whole community a grateful sense retains
Of her too liberal father while his benefit remains.
Old men and young, boys, dowerless girls, the mass of Bristol's poor,
Weep his removal from their midst, who spent so full a store.
By double wedlock he was blessed with children numbering ten
When power divine his soul conveyed from wretched haunts of men,
While his freed sprite with ready joy roams o'er the heavenly plains
This tomb you see his body's baser part alone retains,
The while it also holds in trust his first and faithful wife
And him on whom their mutual love bestowed his firstborn life.

Portions lost.—None.   *Illustration.*—None.

Heraldry.—By the kindness of Mr. R. L. Leighton, Head Master of the Grammar School, Bristol, I am enabled to give the following:—*Blazon of middle chief of brass*, quarterly : 1 and 4 arg : 2 lions pass : reg : sa : (?) in chief above fess : or :

below one lion : sa : (?) pass : reg : mid : base. 2 and 3 arg : rebute : sa : fess : above lion az : pass : reg : mid : chief. loz : gu : dex : and sin : chief. below : loz : gu : mid : base. *Blazon of dexter chief and sinister chief of brass,* 6 quarterings paity per tierce in pale party per fess. 1.3.5. ar : *bear; or : muzzled : erect : unchained : chain crossing bend sinr : ring of chain in nombril dexter. 2.4.6. or. (?) fox's head erased : gu.

Memoir.—The following is taken from various histories of Bristol :—"Buried in St. Nicholas crypt are Robert Thorne and his wife, the parents of Robert and Nicholas Thorne, the founders of the Bristol Grammar School, a species of thorn that Fuller wishes ' God may send us many coppices of.' " Robert Thorne, senr., made among others the following bequests :—". . . Also I bequete to Robert Thorne my son lx *li* in redie monney and lx ounces of plate. Also to Nicholas Thorne my son lx *li* in redie monnez and lx ounces of plate. . . . ."

In 1542-3, Nicholas Thorne was Mayor that year. The plague at this time was sore in Bristol throughout the whole year, so that Nicholas Thorne, then Mayor, held his Court of Admiralty in Clevedon. In an old ledger book in the custody of Mr. Hackluit written about 1526, by Mr. N. Thorne, the elder, principal merchant of Bristol, it was noted that before that year one T. Tyson, an Englishman, had found the way to the West Indies, and resided there, and to him the said Mr. N. Thorne, then a merchant in Bristol, sent armour and merchandise, whereby it appears there was an established trade there very early, and from the city of Bristol. He left his geographical and nautical instruments to the Grammar School. He died August 19th, 1546, aged 50 years, and was buried at the east end of St. Werburgh's church, now demolished, and his ashes, if they have not been disturbed now lie under the middle of Small Street at the Corn Street end.

The portraits of the brothers Robert and Nicholas Thorne may still be seen in the office of the Charity Trustees, and copies are also hung in the small committee-room of the Council House. Robert would seem from his likeness to have much resembled his bluff contemporary, Henry VIII., while Nicholas has a hungry ascetic look. With that pedantic punning on names which characterised the period, Nicholas

---

*Bear as per Earl of Warwick erect but unchained and no staff.

has had placed over his head, in a corner of the canvas, the words, *Ex spinis uvas colligimus*—"We gather grapes of thorns." The quaint conceit is repeated, but not so epigrammatically, in the portrait of Robert, who is made to say, in the same learned tongue, "I am called a thorn; the glory be given to God who giveth the good things which the Thorne dispenses to the poor." "Nicholas Thorne by his will, dated 4th August, 1546, did give and bequeath towards the reparation of the Bridge, Back and Key, and the banks on the Marsh, £20; towards making a yard for corn, for provision of the Commons, £30; towards the making of the dock at the Key for the better repairing of their ships there, £25; to the poor housekeepers in Bristol, one hundred marks; towards repairing of the Free School and making a library there, £30; and [illegible] investments towards retaining learned council to ensure the lands of the Bartholomews: to the Mayor and Commonalty towards the maintenance of the Free School, £20; to the Chamber of Bristol, £4, for the use of cloth-making and helping of young men; whereof £2 of the money of one Mr. Thos. Howell, towards the reparation of highways and maintaining the conduits of water, the Pithay Well and S. Peter's."

The Visitation of Gloucestershire (Harl. Soc.) gives Nicholas married first Bridget, daughter of — Milles, of Hampton, and by her he had John; Bridget, wife of Richard Bowser, of Dursley; and Richard. The memorial shews only two children: Richard probably died in infancy. His second wife was Mary, daughter of Roger Wigston, of Wolverton, Warwickshire. Their children were Edward, who married — Thorne; Frances, wife of Hugh Patridge; Mary, wife of Robert Owgan, Suffolk; Nicholas, married Mary, daughter of Sir Richard Waker, or Walker, of Hartwell, Northants, and widow of Francis Catesby, by her he had three daughters; Robert, married Mary, daughter of John Bulbeck, of Clevedon, Somerset, who died without issue.

LXIX.—Thornbury.

Thos. Tyndall, 1571 (effigy lost), and wife [Avice, daughter of John Bodie], 12 English verses, once on Altar Tomb, Chancel.—*Haines*.

Position.—On the floor of the chancel.

Size.—3 ft. 5 in. × 1 ft. 5½ in.

Description.—All that is left of this fine memorial are two plates of brass; on the upper is engraved the representation of Avice Tyndall (128), while the lower one contains the epitaph.

Fig. 128. Avice Tyndall. 1571, Thornbury.

Avice Tyndall is habited in costume very similar to that worn by the wives of Nicholas Thorne previously described, but as she is represented standing, and nearly full face, her richly embroidered petticoat is displayed to advantage. The gown is confined by a sash tied at the waist, below which it is thrown open to reveal the gorgeous petticoat, beneath which are seen the tips of her thickly soled shoes. Her head is slightly turned to her right, to look towards her husband (128).

Inscription.—The inscription is as follows:—

Thomas Tyndall Dyed the xxviii of Aprill, 1571.
Ye se how deathe dothe spare no age no kynd
How I am lapt in claye and dedd you fynde
My wyfe and Children lye here with me
No gould no Frende no Strenthe could ransome bie

The end of care and matter to repent
The end of vayne delightc and ill intente
The end of facre for frynde and worldly wo
By deathe we haue and of lyke thovsand mo

And deathe of synes in vs bathe made an end
So that nothinge can ouer estate amend
Who would not be content suche change to make
For worldly thinges etarnall lyfe to take.

Heraldry.—Argent, a fess gules between three garbs, sable, a crescent for difference.—*Harl. MS.* 1543, *fol.* 43.

Illustrations.—None.

Portions lost.—Rudder says: "At the foot of the altar there formerly stood a large raised tomb of black marble, inlaid with brass. But when the chancel was afterwards repaired, the tomb was taken down, and the upper slab fixed in the floor." Evidently the husband's effigy had then disappeared. A rubbing of this slab made by the late Rev. H. Haines, shews that the husband stood to the right of the wife. Over her head was a label. Beneath the inscription are the matrices of one son and one daughter, with a label over each. Bigland reports: "At the four corners were coats of arms, the only one remaining is on the right hand corner at the bottom, viz.:- argent on a fess gules, between three garbs sable, a martlet."

Memoir.—"Thomas Tyndale was elder son of Edward Tyndale, of Pull-Court, Worcestershire, who was fourth son of Sir William Tyndale, of Hockwold, in Norfolk. Thomas settled at Eastwood, in the parish of Thornbury, of which he had a grant, 7 Eliz., 1565, after the attainder of Edward, Duke of Buckingham; and by Avice, his wife, daughter of John Bodie, of London, had Edward and Elizabeth, who both died before their father. By his will he gave the estate at Eastwood to his cousin, Thomas Tyndale."—*Rudder.*

In *Gloucestershire Notes and Queries*, vol. ii, *pp.* 201, *etc.*, is an interesting account of the *Trotman Family*, and on p. 203 is the following allusion to Thomas Tyndall:—

"Thomas Tyndale, of Eastwood, 'gentilman,' who died at 'Master Pennes house in London,' 28th April, 1571, and was buried in Fanchurch (Fenchurch) in that city 7th May, and on the 31st of the same month re-interred, according to the direction in his will, at Thornbury." Richard Trotman, of Cam, was one of his executors. Will in P.C.C., 19, Holney.

LXX.—Clifford Chambers.

Hercules Raynsford, Esq., Lord of the Manor, 1583, æt. 39, in armour, and wife Elizabeth, daughter of Robert Parry, Esq., with two sons and one daughter. Altar Tomb, Chancel. —*Haines.*

Position.—Before the restoration in 1887, this brass was on an altar tomb at the east end of the nave; the pulpit partially rested upon it. Now the slab, in which are inlaid the brasses, will be found erected against the north wall of the chancel, near the mural memorial to another member of the Raynsford family. The altar tomb before referred to, had some sandstone panelling divided with pilasters on one side and at one end, but the stone was in a broken and crumbling condition, too far gone for a satisfactory retention.

Size.—4 ft. 6 in. x 1 ft. 10 in.

Description. Hercules Raynsford is bare headed, his hair is cut short, and his head rests on his helmet. His moustache and beard are of moderate length. Around his neck and wrists are slight frills. A gorget of plate reaches to the chin, the paldrons have their upright edges scroll-shaped, brassarts of plate, with plain coudières, protect the arms, and a cuirass covers the body. At this period, civilians wore trunkhose; this was also adopted by the men in armour, so we may notice that the skirt of mail (*vide* Sir John Greville's brass at

Weston-on-Avon*) has disappeared, and instead, Hercules Raynsford is wearing trunkhose. Trunkhose were large breeches well padded, puffed and slashed. As the stuffing was not of sufficient firmness to protect the thighs, to the projecting rim of the breastplate or cuirass were hinged tassets which somewhat filled the functions of the tuiles so conspicuous in earlier armour. These tassets consisted of a series of small plates rivetted together, and may be considered to be the last remnant of the skirt of taces. In this example, the plates of the tassets are of a rectangular form. Steel armour encases the remainder of the legs, and his genouillères have elegant rosettes. Large rowelled spurs are screwed into the heels, whilst sollerets with very wide toes complete the suit of armour (129). Around his waist is a narrow strap, from which hangs obliquely another, to which is attached a long sword on his left side. On his right side is affixed a short dagger.

Fig. 129. Feet. 1583. Clifford Chambers.

Elizabeth Raynsford is in dress very similar to Avice Tyndall described in the last.

Hercules and his wife are erect, she being on her husband's left hand, they are mutually turned a little towards one another. Two sons are shewn lower down the slab, but in my rubbing the pulpit covers all but their closely cropped heads, the little frill round their necks, and the jackets or cloaks on their shoulders; they look towards their sister, who is dressed somewhat like her mother, but no ornament or embroidery is shewn, the girdle is buttoned in front.

Inscription.—On the plate of brass beneath their feet is engraved the following inscription :—

* No. LXV. of this series, p. 158.

𝕳ere lyeth 𝕭uryed the 𝕭oddy of 𝕳ercules 𝕽aynsford, esquier | 𝕷ord of this 𝕸annor of Clifford, who marryed 𝕰lizabethe | 𝕻arry, daughter of 𝕽obert 𝕻arry, esquier, by whome havyng | 𝕵ssue too sonnes and on daughter, died the second daye of | 𝕬ugust, 𝕬no 𝕯ni 1583, and in the yeare of his age 39.

Heraldry.—Over the head of Hercules Raynsford is an elaborate shield (130), the crest, a stag's head, surmounts an esquire's helmet, from which depends an elegant mantling: the shield is blazoned by Bigland:—

Fig. 130. Arms 1583. Clifford Chambers.

1. Argent a cross sable for *Raynsford*. 2. Azure an eagle, displayed argent gorged with a coronet and beaked and membred or, for *Wylcotts* of Wylcotts. 3. Azure an eagle displayed argent, beaked and membered or, for *Wyllycotes* of Gt. Tew, co. Oxon. 4. Sable on a chief argent three lozenges, gules *Mollins*. 5. Argent an eagle displayed gules for *Hall*. 6. Azure a chevron ermine between three bucks trippant or, for *Greene*. 7. Argent a chief indented azure, for *Glanvile*. 8. Per Pale or, and azure a chevron ermine, for *Lions*. 9. Gules on a chevron argent a cinquefoil between three garbs or, for *Scocathe*. 10. Argent a chevron between three cinquefoils gules, for *Wakested*. 11. Argent a chevron engrailed between three escallops sable, for *Arderburgh*, or *Arderboughe*. 12. Vairè argent and gules on a bend sable three boars' heads erased or, for *Purscell*. 13. Or, three bears' heads erased sable muzzled of the first, for *Berwicke*. 14. Argent three bendlets azure on a canton sable a lion passant or, for *Shersal*. 15. Or, three chevronells braced in base sable on chief gules, three plates, for *Prattell*.

Over the wife's head is a shield bearing these arms, "Argent a cross sable, differenced with a crescent, for *Raynsford*, impaling, Argent, three boars' heads caboshed sable for *Parry*.

Illustrations.—Bristol and Gloucestershire Archæological Soc. Transactions, vol. XIV., plate VI.

Portions lost.—None; and the whole composition is in good condition.

Memoir.—Charles Raynsford of Clifford, co. Gloucester, was twice married, first to Jane, daughter of John Morgan, of Camberton, co. Worcester, and secondly to Frances, daughter of Henry Wyndsore, who was living at the date of her husband's will, 26th April, 1578. The said will was proved 10th May, 1581. By his first wife he had issue :—

1. Thomas. 2. Hercules. 3. Anthony, executor of his father's will 1581. 4. Morgan, who was living in 1578. 5. Jane, wife of John Prouse, of Slaughter, co. Gloucester. 6. Elizabeth, wife of Robert Wincott, of Kensham, co. Oxford, both living 1578. 7. Eleanor. 8. Margaret, living unmarried 1578.

The second son Hercules, bapt. 3 Dec., 1544, was of Clifford, and married Elizabeth, daughter of Robert Parry, and died 2nd August, 1583. Administration of his effects was granted 3rd August, 1583, to Elizabeth his relict (Inquis. P.M. 26 Eliz., No. 198.) Elizabeth his widow afterwards married Willam Barnes, of Clifford.

By her he had issue :—

1. Sir Henry. 2. Elizabeth, his daughter, named after her mother Elizabeth, has her memory perpetuated by another "brass" in Clifford Chambers Church; her memorial will be described after, it being LXXVI. of this series. 3. Another son, who is represented on the brass and mentioned but not by name in the inscription.

The authority for the foregoing statements is *The Genealogist*, vol. II, 1878, which contains an exhaustive pedigree of the Raynsford family.

The manor of Clifford Chambers formerly belonged to the abbey of Gloucester, but was granted to Charles Raynsford, 4 Eliz., the father of Hercules. Henry, son of Sir Henry, mentioned above, had his estate sequestered in the civil war because he was a partisan of King Charles, but he compounded for £900; the Manor of Clifford Chambers soon after passed away from the Raynsford family, for this same Henry sold it to Job Dighton, Esq., in 1649.

LXXI.—Bristol; St. Werburgh.

William Gyttyns, merchant, and one of the common council, 1586, and wife Mary (who erected brass) with six sons and four daughters. Quadrangular plate, mural.—*Haines*.

Position.—On the wall of the vestry of the recently erected church of St. Werburgh.

Size.—1 ft. 10 in. × 1 ft. 10 in.

Description.—In the figure of William Gyttyns we have a capital representation of a well-to-do citizen of the latter portion of the sixteenth century.

He wears a long robe with a broad band around the hem, behind the arm holes depend sleeves, of no real use to protect the arms, but being banded with lateral bars, very probably of velvet, they served as ornaments to his robe, and were possibly insignia of his dignity as a "common councilman." As he kneels to the desk, this long robe conceals most of his other garments, though the doublet with frills at neck and wrists is shown with skirt fastened by a sash tied in front.

Behind him kneel six sons, in long robes and doublets, the eldest has his name—John—cut on the lower part of his robe.

Mary Gyttyns wears a long robe which, like her husband's, has a broad band but it has no sleeves, a sash tied in a bow in front keeps all in place; she, too, has frills at neck and wrists, her petticoat is plain. Behind her kneel four daughters dressed like their mother, except that there is no veil to their headdress, nor any band to their robe.

* Fig. 131. Circular Plate. 1586, Bristol. ? Monogram.

In the earlier memorials, it was customary to commence the inscriptions to the departed with *Orate pro anima*, or some similar pious ejaculation, but at this period, the effigies of the deceased are often represented as praying for themselves, and in accordance with this custom, William and Mary are shewn kneeling at a low desk, on which lie two open books. The background is covered with small oblong panels, and between them hangs a circular plate, on which are the initials, M.G., probably the monogram Mary Gyttyns (131). The floor is tiled with square and round tiles.

* Figs. 131, 133, 134, are ¼ scale, and not ½ as the remaining illustrations.

Inscription.—Beneath is the following long inscription :—

My frend who so this place of myne thow be that shall be boulde,
With patiences pause and beare a frind his minde to the unfould;
Seacke not with heapes of worldly toyes to furnishe thy delighte
Nor let him fancie highe degres that hopes to liue arighte ;
If thow haue wealthe supply thic want that languishe in decaye ;
And linger not thy good Intent vntill thy latter daye ;
If pouertye opresse thy mind let pacience be thy guyde,
Let rigoure sarlie bould faist thy faithe what bap so the betide :
Ffor as from deathe no waye that is they selfe for to deffend,
So happye may no creature be before the finall end ;
Wherefore of God his mercye craue who hath of mercye store,
And vnto him comend my soule, my frend, I craue no more.
Heare lithe buried the body of William Cystyns, late of the Cittie of Bristoll.
Marchaunte & one of the Common Counsell of the same, who had one only wife,
Named Marye, by whom he had yssbue vi. sonns and iiij daughters, who departed
This trancitory lief the xxv. day of Ffebruary ano dm, 1586.
In and for whose memory the said Marye his louinge wife hath made this monement.

Illustrations.—I know of none.

Portions lost.—None, but the plate is not in a very good condition.

Memoir.—In Wadley's *Bristol Wills*, his Will occurs on pp. 249, 250.

LXXII.—Cirencester.

Philip Marner (clothier), 1587, standing. He left a noble yearly for a sermon in Lent, and gave the interest (?) on £80 to 16 men in Cirencester, Burford, Abingdon, and Tetbury. Mural S.A.—*Haines.*

Position.—On the wall between the Trinity Chapel and nave.

Size.—1 ft. 6 in. x 1 ft. 2½ in.

Description.—Philip Marner is represented as an old man, standing and supported himself by a knotted staff, shod with iron. His hair and beard are cut close, and his face shews the furrows graven by age. He is clad in the usual long gown of the period with false sleeves pendant from the shoulders. This gown is slightly open over the breast and shews the closely buttoned doublet tied with a sash at the waist.

Beneath the gown are shewn his feet in thick soled shoes. He is erect, slightly turned to his left, with a staff in his left hand and a flower in his right. Near his right foot is seated a dog, and this forms one of the latest instances where dogs are represented on brasses. In the upper left-hand corner is represented a pair of shears—emblem of his trade (132).*

Fig. 132. Philip Marner. 1587. Cirencester.

Inscription—The rhyming epitaph is as follows:—

In Lent by will a Sermon be deuised,
and perely Drecher with a noble prised.
Seuen Nobles he did geue ye poore for to defend,

---
* See No. XVII. of this series, p. 49. Thos. Fortey, etc., 1447. Northleach.

and soli. to xvi. men did lend,
In Cicester, Burford, Abington, and Tetburic,
ever to be to them a stocke yerly.

Phillip Marner, who died in the yere 1587.

Illustrations.—None known.

Portions lost.—None, and the whole monument is in a good state of preservation.

Memoir.—The will of this benefactor to Cirencester is in the Probate Court at Gloucester, and was made on the 14th September, 29 Eliz.

LXXIII.—Weston-sub-Edge.

William Hodges, 1590, he married the daughter of Sir George Throgmorton, of Kaughton [Coughton], and widow of John Gifford, Esq., of Weston-under-Edge.—*Haines.*

Position.—Formerly on floor of centre of chancel, now placed upright against the north wall of chancel just west of altar step.—*A. W. F.,* June 26th, 1871.

Size.—3 ft. 1 in. × 1 ft. $9\frac{1}{2}$ in.

Description.—His short curly head seems to rise out of an immense plaited wheel-ruff: his beard is trimmed, but the moustache gracefully curls. The body is clothed in a close fitting doublet, girt about the waist by a narrow belt, from which hangs a long sword. Over the doublet is worn a short loose cloak, the cape of which was buckled in windy weather. The arrangement of buttons on the cloak presents marked peculiarities. He wears knee-breeches and long hose with low shoes on his feet. He is represented standing on a tiled pavement, slightly turned to the right, with hands clasped in prayer.

Inscription.—On the brass plate beneath is the following inscription:—

HERE LYETH THE BODYE OF WILLIAM HODGES, WHO | MARIED YE DAUGHTER OF SIR GEORGE THROGMORTON | OF KAUGHTON KNYGHT, AND WAS THE WYDDOWE OF | JOHN GYFFORD, OF WESTON UNDEREDGE, ESQUIRE, WHO | DEPARTED THIS LYFE THE XXIII OF AUGUSTE, A.D. 1590. |

Illustrations.—None.

Portions lost.—None, and the whole memorial is in good condition.

Biographical Account.—In the *Visitation of Gloucestershire* 1623 (Harl. Soc.), John Gifford, of Weston under Edg, in

Com. Gloc., married Elizabeth, second d. of Sir George Throgmorton, Knt., by whom she had twelve children. She married secondly Will'm Hodges, and they had issue Anna and Adrina. In volume V. of *Bristol and Gloucestershire Archæological Transactions*, p. 234 is

Weston } Mrs. Elizabeth Hodgs, the wyffe of Mr.
Subedge } William Hodgs, Esquor.

LXXIV.—Yate.

Alexander Staples, 1590, and two wives, Avis, with two sons and three daughters, and Elizabeth (who erected brass), with four sons and two daughters, eight elegiac verses, quadrangular plate.—*Haines*.

Situation.—On the chancel floor, but when the church was restored, the choir-screen on the south side was built over this memorial, and only a portion is now visible.

Size.—1 ft. 8 in. x 2 ft. 2 in.

Description.—As mentioned above, only a portion of this brass is now to be seen, but the late Mr. J. D. T. Niblett, F.S.A., of Haresfield Court, kindly gave me a rubbing of the whole memorial, which he had made before the church was restored.

* Fig. 133. Child. 1890. Yate.

In the centre stands Alexander Staples, vested in a long gown which nearly covers his feet. His hair and whiskers are cut short, around his neck and wrist are frills. The gown is faced with fur, and being slightly open in front, it reveals the buttons of the closely-fitting doublet. From his shoulders hang the then fashionable short sleeves, which are adorned with bars, probably of velvet.

On either side, slightly turned towards their husband, stands a wife. On his left is Avis, his first wife. She wears a French hood, or bonnet, with a ruff round her neck. Over

---

* Figs. 131, 133, 134, are ½ scale and not ¼ as the remaining illustrations.

her shoulders is a cape with an escalloped edge, a long dress thrown open to show her embroidered stomacher and richly-adorned petticoat, completes her outward attire.

The second wife, Elizabeth, is somewhat similarly dressed, but she wears no cape.

The sons are in close-fitting gowns with small lappets (133): the daughters resemble their mothers.

Inscription.—Beneath is the following inscription :—

"Corpus Alexandri Staples lapis iste tuetur :
    Spiritus ætherea sede beatus erit.,
Rursus supremum tuba cum taratantara clanget
    Spiritui junget mortua membra Deus.
Tercentum lustris octodenoque fluente,
    Bernardi, a Christo, concidit, ipse die,
Saxum hoc moesta suo ponebat Eliza marito,
    Conjugii signum quod pietatis erit.
            22° Augusti, 1591."

" The corpse of Alexander this stone shall safely keep,
His spirit in the heavenly realms its blessedness shall reap,
When the last trump with clangour loud the universe shall fill,
God shall his soul and body join at His own holy will,
Three hundred lustres fleeted by, years ninety-one beside,
From Christ, His birth, on Bernard's feast when this our Staples died,
With tears this stone to her loved lord has sad Eliza laid,
Thus sign alike of wedlock's tie, and of her lord she made."

Portions lost.—None.

Illustrations.—None known.

Memoir.—Thos. Staples, Esq., of the Middle Temple, 5th son of Alexander Staples, Esq., of Yate Court, Gloucestershire, was created a baronet of Ireland, 18th July, 1628.

LXXV.—Leckhampton.

William Norwood, Esq., and wife Elizabeth [daughter of William Lygon, of Madresfield, Worcestershire], 1598, æt. 50, with nine sons and two daughters, six elegiac verses, quadrangular plate mural.—*Haines.*

Situation.—On the south wall of the south aisle, near the east end.

Size.—1 ft. 10 in. x 1 ft. 11 in.

Description.—This interesting brass affords a good example of the costume of a gentleman and a lady towards the end of the reign of Queen Elizabeth,

William Norwood has his hair and beard closely cropped, but his moustache is allowed to grow. A stiff ruff encircles his neck, a fashion often noticed sarcastically by the writers of the period. His cloak covers the rest of his attire, except the top of his doublet and its tight-fitting sleeves. From the shoulders hang long false sleeves unadorned.

Behind him kneel nine sons. Their hair is cut short, and they wear ruffs. Their cloaks appear to be sleeveless, and consequently we see more of the long-breasted doublet: on the three elder sons, this doublet is represented as fastened by a row of buttons, but the mode of fastening is not shown on the others. Their cloaks are short, so that the long hose from the knee are shown. Their feet are protected by low shoes. By the left side of the eldest son hangs a sword.

Elizabeth Norwood wears a French hood with a hanging veil, a large ruff like her husband. The over-gown is thrown back a little, to show the plaited partlet. Her costume is marked by extreme simplicity and lack of embroidery work, which so lavishly bedecked the dresses at this period.

Behind her kneel two daughters somewhat similarly attired, but with no veils to their head-dresses.

*Fig. 134. Shield. c. 1598. Leckhampton.

The husband and wife are kneeling to a low fald-stool with a flat desk, on which two open books are lying. The book in front of William Norwood has leather thongs for fastenings, and the one before his wife has clasps.

Heraldry—Over the fald-stool is their coat of arms (134): Ermine a cross gules, NORWOOD, impaling Argent, 2 lions passant gules LYGON. Above the wife and daughters is a scroll on which is engraved, EXPECTO DONEC VENIAT INVITATIO MEA, "I wait until my summons may come."

Inscription.—Below is the following inscription :—

" ELIZABETHA NORWOODD, VXOR GVLIELMI NORWOODD ARMIGERI, CVI PEPERIT NOVEM FILIOS, FILIAS DVAS,

*Figs. 131. 133. 134 are ½ scale, and not ¼ as the remaining illustrations.

ANOS NATA 50: APRILIS 16, ANO DNI 1598, PIE
ET FELICITER EXPIRAVIT IN CHRISTO.
SCILICET VNDENA VIXI QVÆ PROLE BEATA
VNO NON POTVI FVNERE TOTA MORI
LIBERIOR TOTV MIHI VITA EXCVRRIT IN ORBEM
CÆLV ANIMA TENEO POSTERITATE SOLV
SI TELLVRE PO LOQ. FRVOR DEVISA, NECESSE EST
DEFVNCTA NVLLO ME PERIISSE LOCO.

"Elizabeth Norwood, wife of William Norwood, Esq., to whom she bore nine sons, two daughters, having lived fifty years, she piously and peacefully died in Christ, on April 16, A.D. 1598.

"I, who eleven times did multiply
Myself on earth, cannot in one death die;
Rather my lively sprite both world's shall roam,
Heaven is my soul's—earth is my offspring's home;
If then I freely range both spheres of space
I perish not in any resting place."

Portions lost.—None, and the whole composition is in a good state of preservation.

Illustrations.—None.

Memoir.—The family of Norwood is of high antiquity and consequence, and is regularly traced from John de Northwode, of Northwood Chasteners, in the Isle of Sheppey, Co. Kent. John de Northwode was summoned as a Baron of Parliament in 1294, which Barony became extinct in 1375. A descendant of a brother of the first Baron migrated into this country, and in consequence of his marriage with Eleanor Giffard became possessed of the manorial estate at Leckhampton. From him descended William Norwood, who married Elizabeth Lygon. The epitaphs of William and of his son Richard are thus given by Bigland:—

"Here was buryed the body of William Norwood, Esq., who died September the 23, 1632.

Here lyeth the body of Richard Norwood, the eldest son of William Norwood, Esqvyer, who deceased the xii. day of January, Anno Domini, 1630."

The following interesting particulars are taken from *Miscellanea Genealogica et Heraldica*, edited by Dr. Howard, N.S., vol. ii, p. 43. The representation of the seal and autograph of William Norwood here given (135), are copied from a deed in the possession of the late Rev. C. B. Trye, of Leckhampton Court. The indenture is dated 21 November, Jac. I., between Thomas Fogge, of Clerkenwell, in the county of Middlesex, Esq., William Norwood, of Leckhampton, in the county of Gloucester, Esquire, and Anne, his wife, mother of the said Thomas Fogge, John Sackville, of Sedlescombe in the county of Sussex, gentlemen, on the one part; and Sir Samuel

*Fig. 135.
Seal and Autograph of William Norwood.

Peyton, of Knolton, in the County of Kent, Knight and Baronet, and Sir Robert Darrell, of Calehill, in the County of Kent, Knight, and Thomas Hales, of the City of Canterbury, Esq., on the other part, relating to the manor of Southcombe, Kent.

Anne (born 1555) daughter of Christopher Sackville, Esq., married Richard Fogge. of Tilmanshort, county Kent, Esq. He died 1598, October, leaving three daughters and Thomas Fogge, born 28 August, 1585, mentioned above.

This *Anne Sackwel* appears from this deed to have married William Norwood, although in the pedigree entered by him in the *Visitation of Gloucestershire*, 1623, such fact is not mentioned. The only wife ascribed him there is Elizabeth Lygon, by whom he had many children. He survived till 23 September, 1632. Elizabeth Norwood was a daughter of Wm. Lygon by Eleanor, daughter of Sir Wm. Dennes, Knt. She was granddaughter of Sir Richard Lygon, Knt., who married Margaret, sole daughter and heiress of Sir William Greville,† of Arle Court, near Cheltenham, and by her the Lygons became possessed of that manor.

* Kindly lent by Messrs. Mitchell & Hughes, Ye Wardour Press, London.
† *Vide* No. XLVII. of this series, p. 113. *Cheltenham*, Sir William Greville, 1513

Feet of Fines, 36 Eliz. Trinity. Betw. William Lygon, Esq., George Blunte, Esq., John Stywarde, Esq., and Augustin Stywarde, Esq., Q., and William Norwoode, Esq., and Elizabeth, his wife, def., of the Manor of Leckhampton, with app'ces and 60 mess., &c., and £24 rent in Leckhampton, in co. Glouc. And of the Manor of Uphatherley with app'ces and 2 mess., &c., and 2 shillings rent in Uphatherley, in the County of the City of Gloucester. Whereupon, &c. Warranty to William Lygon, George, John, and Augustin, and the heirs of William, against William Norwood and Elizabeth, and the heirs of William. And for this, &c., they have given to William Norwood and Elizabeth, £800.

LXXVI.—Clifford Chambers.

Elizabeth, daughter of Hercules Raynsford and wife of Edward Marrowe, Esq., of Barkswell, Warwickshire, 1601, loose.—*Haines.*

Position.—When I rubbed this brass in 1882, the two pieces forming this memorial were lying loose in the church, but I have much pleasure in adding that at the restoration in 1887, they were let into a stone slab, and erected over the door between the chancel and vestry, on the north wall with the other monuments of the Raynsfords. The original position of these fragments could not be ascertained, so it was thought by the rector and the architect (Mr. John Cotton, Birmingham) desirable to place them with the other Raynsford memorials altogether on the north side of the chancel.

Size.—2 ft. 7 in. × 10 in. and 1 ft. 9 in. × 6½ in.

Description.—Elizabeth Marrowe has her hair well brushed back from the temples, she wears a French hood of the shape popularly appropriated to Mary, Queen of Scots, but this is nearly wholly hidden by a huge calash which covers the head and shoulders, and falls down behind the back nearly to the ground. A stiff ruff encircles her neck, but none are worn at the wrists; instead neat cuffs appear. An embroidered stomacher peaked in front relieves the plainness of the rest of her costume. A slight farthingale supports the weight of her skirts, which barely reach her ankles. Low thick-soled shoes with a rosette in front encase her feet (136).

In her arms she carries a little babe wrapped in swaddling clothes. Over its head is thrown a small hood, a little ruff is round its throat, and on its breast is a plaited bib.

Fig. 136.   Elizabeth Marrowe.   1601.
Clifford Chambers.

She is represented erect, slightly turned to her right, and holding her babe on her right arm.

Inscription.—Beneath is this inscription :—
VNDER THIS STONE LYETH THE BODY OF ELIZABETH | DAVGHTER OF HERCVLES RAINSFORD OF CLIFFORD IN YE | COVNTY OF GLOC : ESQVIRE, MARRIED TO EDWARD MAR | ROWE SONNE AND HEIRE OF SAMVELL MARROWE | OF BARKSWELL IN THE COVNTIE OF WARWICK ESQ | WII ELIZABETH DECEASED THE 29 OF OCTOB' 1601.

Fig. 137. Shield. 1601.
Clifford Chambers.
See p. 174.

Heraldry.—In Rudder, mention is made of another piece of "brass" on which was "a scutcheon, Baron and femme. 1. *Argent, a fesse engrailed sable between* 3 *boars' heads couped proper* for *Marrowe.* 2.—*Rainsford* as above,"* which is *Argent, a cross sable* (137). This at the restoration in 1887 was placed over the head of Eliz. Marrowe.

Illustrations.—Bristol and Gloucestershire Archæological Society Trans. Vol. XIV. plate 7.

Portions lost.—A part of the shield.

Memoir.—Edward Marrowe, of Berkswell, Warwickshire, son and heir of Samuel Marrowe, is represented in Dugdale's *Warwickshire*, p. 718, as having married Ursula, daughter of Rich. Fienes, Lord Say and Sele : by her he had Samuel his heir, Thomas, Edward, Franciscus, Georgius, Johannes: he died anno 1632. In Camden's Visitation, 1619 (*Harleian Society Publications*), "Sir Edw. Marowe, of Barkswell, Kt." is shown as having been married twice, 1st to " Elizb. Da., of — Barnes, of Gainsfford, of Gloucest., by whom he had one child, Elizabeth, and secondly to Ursula, as given above. " Barnes, of Gainsfford, of Gloucest.," was very probably Hercules Rainsford, of Clifford Chambers. In the Raynsford pedigree in the *Genealogist*, vol. II, it is stated that Elizabeth, daughter of Hercules Raynsford, married Edward, son of Samuel Marrowe, of Berkswell.

LXXVII.—Wormington.

Anne, eldest daughter of Richard Daston, and wife of John Savage, Esq., of Nobury, Worcestershire, 1605, Æ. 25, in childbed, with infant, marginal inscription.—*Haines.*

---
* See p. 174.

Position.—Affixed to the south wall of the chancel.
Size.—2 ft. 9 in. × 2 ft. 4 in.
Description.—Anne Savage is represented in bed with her babe lying on the coverlid near her. The bed is one of the old-fashioned " four-posters." The curtains are looped back to the posts. She lies propped up by a high pillow, the coverlid is neatly turned down, and a fringed rug is thrown

Fig. 138.   Anne Savage.   1605.   Wormington.

over her. She wears a close cap, and a close fitting dress with an embroidered front. Her arms rest on the coverlid, and her hands are clasped in prayer. Her babe is swathed in long bands round its under clothes and over its head (138).

Inscription.—Beneath is this inscription :—
FILIOLVS, CONIVX, PATER EFFERA FATA QVERVTVR
QVÆ DILECTAM Annam Sauage ERIPVERE MARITO
ET PRIMOGENITAM Daston VELVT ALTERA PHÆNIX
DVM PARIT ILLA PERIT, DVM PARTVRIT, INTERIT Anna
Anna ANIMA E CŒLO LVSTRIS IAM QVINQVE PERACTIS
IN CŒLVM REDIJT SED TERRA HUIC OSSA RELIQVIT.

This may be rendered :—
Child, spouse, and sire the cruel fate lament
Which tore their Anna from their husband's love
Her father's firstborn offspring—but she went,
E'en as a Phœnix seeks to rise above.
Dying, new life she gave, she passed away
Leaving the promise of a longer day.
Five lustres from heaven's court her soul had strayed
Now thither mounts—in earth her bones are laid.

Around the margin is :—
HERE LYETH BVRIED THE BODYE OF ANNE | SAVAGE THE
WIFE OF IOHN SAVAGE | OF NOBVRY IN THE COVNTY OF
WORCESTER | XVII. DAY OF JUNE, 1605, BEINGE OF |

This inscription is not now complete.

Fig. 139.   Shields.   1605.   Wormington.

Heraldry.—Fixed on either side of the brass are two shields :—Argent, six lions rampant sable—SAVAGE, and Quarterly, one and four, Gules on a bend or three mullets sable. DASTON. Two and three, or a fess wavy between six billets sable, DUMBLETON. (139). These arms also appear on the brass to Anthony Daston, 1572, in Broadway Church.

Illustrations.—I know of none.

Portions lost.—A part of the marginal inscription.

Memoir.—The inscription tells of her being the eldest daughter of Richard Daston: he died seized of property in Wormington held of Corpus Christi College, Oxford, and left by Ann his wife two sons, Anthony and Edward. In the Parish Registers of Broadway occurs this entry:—Baptisms, 1580, May 22, Anne, daughter of Mr. Richard Daston.

LXXVIII.—Abbenhall.

Richard Pyrke, of Micheldean, 1609, *æt.* 60, and wife Joan, daughter of John Ayleway, Gent., with their sons, Thomas and Robert. Chancel.—*Haines.*

Position.—On the floor in the middle of the chancel.

Size.—5 ft. 8in. x 2 ft. 2 in.

Description.—In accordance with the prevailing custom of this period, Richard Pyrke has his beard and hair closely trimmed, but the moustache is not so closely cut.

He wears a long gown with false sleeves, beneath is seen the peascod doublet, above which is a stiffly plaited ruff. Trunk hose and low shoes complete his outward apparel.

Joan has her hair well brushed back into a hood, above which is a broad-rimmed hat, wreathed round the crown; this headdress was generally worn by persons living in the country. A stiff ruff is round her neck. She wears a long bodied stomacher with rounded point at the waist, and plainly plaited. A slight hoop supports her dress, which barely reaches her insteps. Her low shoes have thick soles and are fastened by a little rosette.

On a plate of brass beneath are engraved the figures of their two sons. The one wears a long gown reaching to his heels, above is a broad collar instead of the ruff. The gown conceals the rest of his clothing except the sleeves of the doublet. The other son wears a short cloak with a broad collar. The doublet is fastened at the waist by a buckle, but the characteristic buttons down the front are not shewn. He wears trunk hose, tight stockings, and low shoes (140).

All are erect, with hands uplifted in the attitude of prayer. The husband has his wife on his left, and is slightly turned towards her, and she is slightly turned towards him. The sons are both slightly turned to their left.

Fig. 140.   Thomas and Robert Pyrke.   1609.
Abbenhall.

Inscription.—Between the figures of the husband and wife and those of their sons is the following inscription :—
HERE LYETH THE BODY OF RICHARD PYRKE OF MICHELL DEANE | IN THE COVNTYE OF GLOVR & IOHAN' HIS WIFE YE DAUGHTER OF IOHN AYLEWAY GENT: WCH RICHARD DIED THE 23 DAYE OF OCTOBER ANNO DNI 1609 AGED LX YEARES.

On another plate of brass below the sons is :—
HERE LYETH THE BODIES OF THOMAS PYRKE & | ROBT PYRKE SONNES OF THE SAID RICHARD & IOHAN' WCH THOMAS DIED THE   DAY OF   ANNO DNI   AGED   ROBT DIED YE | DAY OF   ANNO DNI   AGED

The blank spaces in this inscription have not been filled up.

On the stone below this inscription are cut the following words :—
HERE LYETH THE BODYE OF | DUNCOMBE PYRKE 2D SON OF NATH. PYRKE, ESQR., WH DEPARTED | THIS LIFE OCTR 9TH ANO DNI 1725 | ÆTATIS SUÆ 34

Between the heads of husband and wife is :—

    CHRISTVS MIHI VITA
    MORS MIHI LVCRVM.

which may be rendered
  "Christ is my life, Death to me is gain."

Illustrations.—None.

Portions Lost.—A piece of the wife's head-dress.

LXXIX.—Todenham.

William Molton, Esq., 1614, and wife Millicent, daughter of Gilse Spencer, Esq., of Nurthen, Warwickshire, 1604. Out of 12 children he left 3 married. 12 English verses, mural, chancel.—*Haines.*

Position.—Over the vestry door on the north wall of the chancel.

Size.—2 ft. 6 in. x 1 ft. 10½ in.

Description.—William Molton is dressed in the ordinary costume of the period. His hair and beard are cut close. He wears doublet with broad cuffs, trunk hose, and low shoes, over all he wears a short sleeveless cloak. The stiff ruff is still sported.

His wife has her hair well brushed back into a small hood, from her shoulders spring an enormous projection—the calash headdress; within is a large stiff ruff, much like that of her companion. Her peaked stomacher is braided horizontally. Over her shoulders is a small cape, her long dress covers her feet.

Both are shown nearly facing each other, kneeling on hassocks with tassels at each corner on a tiled pavement. Between them is an altar on which is a double reading desk, and a book lies open before each of them. Above the desk is a coat of arms. (141).

The whole brass plate has a twisted cable ornament for border.

Inscription.—Beneath is a long inscription:—

    Stay Passenger this tvmb doth hovld
    A coffin fvll of holy movld
    If vertve have a grave lo heer
    Religiovs care and love syncere,
    Wise goverment and zeale wel led
    A davntlese covrage hvmble dread
    Bovnty of hand and chere of face
    Good natvre perfected by grace
    And which gave lyfe to all the rest
    A trve harte in a fravde lese brest
    If these on earth were lately mist
    Lo whear they ly in Movltone chist.

* * * * *

HEERE LYETHE BODYES OF WILLIAM MOLTON, OF TODDENHAM, ESQ., AND MILLICENT HIS WYFE, DAVGHTER OF GILSE SPENCER, OF NVRTHEN OF WARWICKSHIRE, ESQ., WHICH MILLICENT DYED THE 10 OF DESEMBER, 1604 AND WILLIAM AFTER LOVNG SIKNES DYED THE VI. OF IANUARY, 1614, HAVING BEFORE HIS DEATH MARIED 3 DAVGHTERS THE ONLY CHILDREN THEN REMAYNING OF 12, WHERE OF THE I WAS MARYED TO THOMAS BAVFOV, ESQ., SONNE AND HEIER TO SER THOMAS BAVFOV, KNIGHT, THE 2 TO RICHARD SAVADGE, SONNE AND HEYER OF WALTER SAVADGE, ESQ., THE 3 TO WILLIAM WILLOVGHBY, OF NORMANTON, ESQ.

Fig. 141. Shield. 1604.
      Todenham.

Heraldry.—Argent, three bars gules charged with seven escallops, three, two and two, MOLTON, impaling azure, six sea-mews' heads erased argent, SPENCER.

Illustrations.—None.

Portions lost.—None.

LXXX.—Minety.

[Nich Poulett, Esq.] in arm, and wife [Marg. daughter of Thos. Hungerford] c. 1620, with 4 children, Amyes, Elizth, Mary, Edight, inscription covered (?) quadrangular plate, mural, North Aisle.—*Haines*.

Position.—On North wall of North Aisle.

Size.—1 ft. 8 in. x 1 ft.

Description.—The husband is represented bare-headed, the beard trimmed to a point which rests on the stiff ruff round his neck; the paldrons have an escalloped edge, the cuirass is plain with a projecting edge, to it are attached tasses buckled over his trunk hose. The arms and legs are encased in plate armour and the hinges and rivets are plainly shewn; spurs with rowels not clearly defined are fastened to the jambs, a broad sword belt hangs loosely, on his right side a dagger, on his left a sword. One son, AMES, kneels behind him, of whose dress only the ruff and long cloak with false sleeves are shown.

Mary Powlett has a French hood with a pendent veil. Like her husband she wears the cumbrous ruff, the sleeves of her dress are of moderate size, with ornamental wings on the shoulder. Her peaked stomacher is fastened by a sash, the gown is thrown back to show the petticoat ornamented by scales. Behind her kneel three daughters, ELIZABETH, MARY and EDIGHT, who are dressed similarly to their mother, except the shoulders have no ornaments and their petticoats are plain.

The husband and wife are kneeling with hands clasped in prayer on tasselled cushions facing each other, the wife being on the husband's left hand; the family kneel on the tiled pavement. Behind is a pillar in the middle, thus dividing the wall into two compartments. Over the heads of the figures are the names of those commemorated; starting on the left they read as follows:—

AMES POWLETT, NICOLAS POWLETT, MARY POWLETT, ELIZABETH, MARY, EDIGHT.

Heraldry.—On the wall at the back of the father and son is a shield:—Sable, three swords in pile, the points in base, argent, pomels and hilts *or*, POWLETT. On the left of the shield is a dexter arm in armour, gauntletted, brandishing a sword, and on the right, a dexter hand, bare, holding a sword bearing the label, GARDES LA FOY (Keep the faith)—the Powlett crest. Above the wife is a shield:—Sable, two bars ermine, in chief three plates, a crescent for difference, HUNGERFORD. On the left is a garb between two sickles proper, rising from a crown, on the right three sickles braced in a triangle with a mullet in the centre. On the wall beneath OF SVFFERANS COMES EASE. (142).

Fig. 142. Crests. 1620. Minety.

Illustrations.—None.

Portions Lost.—There is no inscription.

Memoir.—Rudder says: "I take this Nich's Powlett to be second son of Sir Hugh Powlett, who died in the reign of Queen Elizabeth, and was ancester to the present Earl Poulet."

He married Mary, daughter of Thomas Hungerford, of the Lea, Wiltshire. In the Visitation of Gloucestershire only one son is mentioned, Amyas, of Thornbury, who married Christian, daughter of . . . . . Purnell, of Wooton. They had one son, William, "4 yere old, 1623." There are no Paulet entries in the Minety Parish Registers, and no inscription, so the Rev. W. W. A. Butt, M.A., informs me.

LXXXI.—Cirencester.

Mr. John Gunter, 1624, æt. 89, buried at Kintbury, Berks, and wife, Alice, 1626, æt. 86. Jo. Plat, their son-in-law, and executor pos. St. Catherine's Chapel.—*Haines.*

Position.—Lady Chapel.

Size.—1 ft. 10 in. x 1 ft. 8½ in.

Description.—For the following account of this brass I am indebted to a paper "On the Monumental Brasses at Cirencester," by the Rev. W. E. Hadow, M.A., and published in the Transactions of the Bristol and Gloucestershire Archæological Society for 1877.

"John Gunter and his wife are represented in the stiff dresses of the latter part of the sixteenth and early part of the seventeenth century, from Elizabeth's later years to the beginning of Charles I.'s reign. The man wears a long furred robe, the sleeves of which are ornamented with velvet and shewing the sleeves of the doublet beneath. Around his neck is a ruff, and frills round his wrists, the head is bare and the beard is cut in the quaint and formed way not uncommon in the time of James I. The woman wears a broad brimmed hat (143), a ruff round the neck, and a stiff-bodied full-buttoned dress with tight sleeves. The inferiority of the execution of this brass to those of earlier date is very apparent, and the attempt to give the effect of shading by means of hatched lines is very poor. It is, however, very usual in brasses of this and subsequent periods."

Fig. 143. Alice Gunter. 1624. Cirencester.

The brass at Kintbury is an exact copy of this brass, with the exception of the inscription.

Inscription.—The inscription is in capitals :—

MR. JOHN GUNTER AND ALICE HIS WIFE BEING FULL AS OF YEARS SO OF BOUNTY AND CHARITY ARE GATHERED | TO THEIR FATHERS IN PEACE. SHEE WAS HERE BURYED | 18" MARTII AO. DNI, 1626, AGED 86 YEARES. HEE WAS | BURYED AT KYNTBURY IN THE COUNTY OF BERKS | WITH THE LIKE MONUMENT 2D JANVARII, AO. DNI | 1624, AGED 89 YEARS. | JOS. PLAT AR. EORONDM. GENER ET EXECR HOC POSUIT.

Fig. 144. Shield. 1624. Kintbury.

Heraldry.—The shield is lost at Cirencester, but fortunately it still remains at Kintbury, where it is charged:— Sable, three sinister gauntlets argent, with a crescent for difference. GUNTER. (144).

Illustrations.—None.

Portions lost.—Shield.

Memoir.—By the kindness of the Rev. A. W. H. Edwards, M.A., Vicar of Kintbury, I copied the following from the Kintbury Registers:—" 1624, John Gunter, gent' was buried the second day of January." Tradition says his brother was slain in trying to save John Hampden, at the Battle of Chalgrave Field, June, 1643.

LXXXII.—Bristol, St James.

Henry Gibbes and wife Ann, *not recorded by* Haines.

Size.—1 ft. 7 in. x 2 ft. 2 in.

Description.—Henry Gibbes has short hair, beard, and moustache. Around his neck is a widely plaited frill. His gown is long with fur edged and short full sleeves also edged with fur. The sleeve of the doublet is seen from the elbow, at the wrist is a frill. His shoes are low with high heels. Behind him kneel four sons with curly hair, beard and moustache. One son has a collar with a frilled edge both at neck and wrists, and others have plain collars. They wear loose cloaks with wide lappets. The doublet is shewn, also the shoes with high heels.

Ann Gibbes is wearing a low hat with a wide brim depressed before and behind. A wide frill is round her neck and on her shoulders a cape. The sleeves of her dress are moderately full with turned down cuffs with escalloped edges at the wrist. Her dress is long and flowing. The four daughters kneeling behind her are dressed like their mother except that one wears a cap with brim turned back, thus showing her face.

The husband is represented much larger in size than his wife. They were all kneeling with hands upraised in prayer. Between husband and wife, who kneel on cushions, is a table draped, and on it a reading desk with a book before each. Over the desk is a winged skull bearing an hour-glass (145).

Inscription.—Beneath is this inscription :—

HERE LYETH YE BODY OF HENRY GIBBES SOME TIME MAYER & | ALLDERMAN OF THIS CITTY WHO HAD ISSVE BY ANN HIS WIFE 4 | SONNES & 4 DAVGHTERS HEE DEPARTED THIS LIFE THE 19TH DAY | OF MAY ANNO D'NI : 1636: AGED 73 |

ALSO HERE LYETH YE BODY OF ANN GIBBES WIFE VNTO YE | ABOVE NAMED HENRY GIBBES WHO DEPARTED THIS LIFE— THE 15TH DAY OF DECEMB' : ANNO DNI 1631. AGED 70.

Illustrations.—None.

Portions lost.—None.

Memoir.—Henry Gibbs, brewer, resided in St. James' Back, at that time a very different neighbourhood to the present, as the remains of mediæval mansions testify. He was a son of W. Gibbes. Bedminster. He married Anne, the sister of Matthew Warren, and was Mayor in 1624 His third son Philip went to Barbadoes and was ancestor of Sir Philip Gibbs, Bart. During his official year it was ordered that "no burgess of this city should buy any merchandise from strangers within the liberties of this city on pain to lose 12 pence on every pound." His daughter Elizabeth married Thomas Lloyd, Mary married Richard Neathaway, Margaret married William Bird, and the fourth daughter married Walter Stevens, the leader of the iconoclastic mob who, in 1642, destroyed the Virgin Mary Chapel on Bristol Bridge.

"On his route from Plymouth to London, Galigha, a Turkish Pasha, arrived in Bristol, March 31st, and was royally entertained by the Mayor. Henry Gibbes."—*Bristol Past and Present.*

Summary.

The Monumental Brasses are scattered all over the county of Gloucester, from Clifford Chambers in the north to Bristol in the south, from Lechlade in the east to Micheldean in the west. As may be anticipated, the parish churches of the Woolstaplers at Chipping Campden, Cirencester and Northleach, contain many more Brasses than occur in other parts of the county. The city of Gloucester, with its magnificent cathedral, is not well represented on the list—matrices tell the sad tale of spoliation.

The Brasses may be divided into the following classes:—

I. ECCLESIASTICAL.

Nameless Priest (21), *c.* 1460, Temple Church, Bristol, p. 58; Robert Lond (22), 1461, St. Peter's, Bristol, p. 58; Ralph Parsons (29), 1478, Cirencester, p. 75; Priest (31), *c.* 1480, Cirencester, p. 81; eldest son of John and Elyn Hampton (46) *c.* 1510, Minchinhampton, whilst their eldest daughter, Dame Alice, is habited as a nun, p. 110; Priest (53), *c.* 1520, Dowdeswell, p. 124; William Lawnder (61), *c.* 1530, Northleach, p. 139; These call for no special comment with the exception of Priest (31), *c.* 1480, Cirencester, who is in a cassock.

II. MILITARY.

Thomas, 4th Lord Berkeley (2), 1392, Wotton-under-Edge, p. 2; Sir Morys Russel (8), 1401, Dyrham, p. 25; Richard Dixton (12), 1438, Cirencester, p. 33; Man in Armour (16), *c.* 1445, Newland, p. 44; William Prelatte (24), 1462, Cirencester, p. 62; Philip Mede (27), 1475, St. Mary Redcliff, Bristol, p. 69; John Tame (40), 1500, Fairford, p. 98; Morys and Sir Walter Denys (44), 1505, Olveston, p. 106; Roger Porter, (56), 1523, Newent, p. 129; Sir

Edmond Tame (62 & 63), 1534, Fairford, p. 141; Sir John Greville (65), 1546, Weston-upon-Avon, p. 158; Sir Edward Greville, (66), 1559, Weston-upon-Avon, p. 162; Hercules Raynsford (70), 1583, Clifford Chambers, p. 172; Nicholas Poulett (80), c. 1620, Minety, p. 194.

III. JUDICIAL.

Sir John Cassey (4), 1400, Deerhurst, p. 10; Sir John Juyn (13), 1439, St. Mary Redcliff, Bristol, p. 37; Sir William Greville (47), 1513, Cheltenham, p. 113; John Brook (55), 1522, St. Mary Redcliff, Bristol, p. 127.

John Edward (23), 1461, Rodmarton, is termed *in lege peritus*.

IV. CIVILIAN (excluding children).

Civilian (3), 1396, Temple Church, Bristol, p. 9; Wine Merchant (?), (5), c. 1400, Cirencester, p. 16; Wool Merchant (6), c. 1400, Northleach, p. 19; William Grevel (7), 1401, Chipping Campden, p. 21; John Barstaple (9), 1411, Trinity Almshouses, Bristol, p. 28; Robert Page (14), 1440, Cirencester, p. 39; Reginald Spycer (15), 1442, Cirencester, p. 42; Thomas Fortey, William Scors (17), 1447, Northleach, p. 48; William Welley (18), 1450, Chipping Campden, p. 51; John Townsend (19), c. 1450, Lechlade, p. 52; John Fortey (20), 1458, Northleach, p. 54; John Lethenard (25), 1467, Chipping Campden, p. 66; William Notyngham (26), c. 1470. Cirencester, p. 68; Thomas Rowley (28), 1478, St. John, Bristol, p. 73; John Jay (30), c. 1480, St. Mary Redcliff, Bristol, p. 76; Civilian (32), c. 1480, Cirencester, p. 81; William Gybbys (33), 1484, Chipping Campden, p. 82; Woolman (35), c. 1485, Northleach, p. 87; John Taylour (36), c. 1490, Northleach, p. 89; John Ceysyll (37), 1493, Tormarton, p. 91; John Benet (38), 1497, Cirencester, p. 94; John Camber (39), 1497, Sevenhampton, p. 95; Civilian (42), c. 1500, Minchinhampton, p. 103; Robert Serche (43), 1501, Northleach, p. 105; John Twinyhow (45), c. 1510, Lechlade, p. 109; Edward Halyday (51), 1519, Minchinhampton, p. 122; Walter Hichman (54), 1521, Kempsford, p. 126; William Freme (58), 1526, Berkeley, p. 132; Thomas Bushe (59), 1526, Northleach, p. 135; John Seames (63a), 1540, St. John, Gloucester, p. 149; John Cook

(64), 1544, Crypt Church, Gloucester, p. 154; Richard Coton (67), 1560, Whittington, p. 163; Nicholas Thorne (68), 1570, Grammar School, Bristol, p. 165; William Gyttyns (71), 1586, St. Werburgh, Bristol. p. 176; Philip Marner (72), 1587, Cirencester, p. 177; William Hodges (73), 1590, Weston-sub-Edge, p. 179; Alexander Staples (74), 1590, Yate, p. 180; William Norwoodd (75), c. 1598, Leckhampton, p. 181; Richard Pyrke (78), 1609, Abbenhall, p. 190; William Molton (79), 1614, Todenham, p. 192; John Gunter (81), 1624, Cirencester, p. 195; Henry Gibbes (82), 1636, St. James, Bristol, p. 197.

V. LADIES (excluding children).

These may be divided into two classes: (*a*) those who are represented by themselves; (*b*) those who are with their husbands.

(*a*) Lady (1) c. 1370, Winterbourne, p. 1; Isabella Barstaple (10), c. 1411, Trinity Almshouses, Bristol, p. 28; Joan Clopton (11), c. 1430, Quinton, p. 30; Lady, Palimpsest (21), c. 1460, Temple Church, Bristol, p. 58; Mary and Alice, wives of Thomas Baynham (34), c. 1485, Micheldean, p. 83; Katharine Sewell (48), 1515, Bisley, p. 115; Elizabeth Knevet (49), 1518, Eastington. p. 117; Alys and Agnes, wives of William Henshawe (50), 1519, St. Michael, Gloucester, p. 119; Lady (52), c. 1520, Deerhurst, p. 124; Elizabeth Rowdon (57), 1525, Deerhurst, p. 131; Two Ladies (60), c. 1530, Cirencester, p. 138; Avice Tyndall (69), 1571, Thornbury, p. 169; Elizabeth Marrowe (76), 1601, Clifford Chambers. p. 185; Anne Savage (77), 1605, Wormington, p. 187.

(*b*) Margaret, wife of Lord Berkeley (2), 1392, Wotton-under-Edge, p. 2; Alice Cassy (4), 1400, Deerhurst, p. 10; Margaret............(5), c. 1400, Cirencester, p. 16; Wife (6), c. 1400, Northleach. p. 19; Marion Grevel (7), 1401, Chipping Campden, p. 21; Isabel Russel (8), 1401, Dyrham. p. 25; Margaret Page (14). 1440, Cirencester, p. 39; Margaret Juliana, Margaret, Joan Spycer (15), 1442, Cirencester, p. 42; Wife (16), c. 1445, Newland, p. 44; Agnes Scors (17), 1447, Northleach, p. 48; Alice Welley (18), 1450, Chipping Campden, p. 51; ....Townsend (19), c. 1450, Lechlade, p. 52; Agnes and Joan Prelatte (24), 1462, Cirencester, p. 62; Joan Lethenard (25), 1467, Chipping Campden, p. 66; Cristina

Nottingham (26), *c.* 1470, Cirencester, p. 68;............and
Isabel Mede (27), 1475, St. Mary Redcliff, Bristol, p. 69;
Margaret Rowley (28), 1478, St. John, Bristol, p. 28; Joan
Jay (30), *c.* 1480, St. Mary Redcliff, Bristol, p. 76; Wife (32),
c. 1480, Cirencester, p. 81; Alice, Margaret and Marion
Gybbys (33), 1484, Chipping Campden, p. 82; Wife (35), *c.*
1485, Northleach, p. 87; Joan Taylour (36), *c.* 1490, Northleach, p. 89; Agnes Benet (38), 1497, Cirencester, p. 94;
Alice Tame (40), 1500, Fairford, p. 98; Wife (42), *c.* 1500,
Minchinhampton, p. 103; Anne Serche (43), 1501, Northleach,
p. 105; Elyn Hampton (46), *c.* 1510, Minchinhampton, p.
110; ....Greville (47), 1513, Cheltenham, p. 113; Margery Halyday (51), 1519, Minchinhampton, p. 122; Crestyan
Hichman (54), 1521, Kempsford, p. 126; Joan Brook (55),
1522, St. Mary Redcliff, Bristol, p. 127; Joan Bushe (59),
1526, Northleach, p. 135; Agnes and Elizabeth Tame (62,
63), 1534, Fairford, p. 141; Elizabeth and Agnes Seames
63A), 1540, St. John, Gloucester, p. 149; Joan Cook (64),
1544, Crypt Church, Gloucester, p. 154; Margaret Coton
(67), 1560, Whittington, p. 163; Mary and Bridget Thorne
(68), 1570, Grammar School, Bristol, p. 165; Elizabeth
Raynsford (70), 1583, Clifford Chambers, p. 172; Mary
Gyttyns (71), 1586, St. Werburgh, Bristol, p. 176; Avis and
Elizabeth Staples (74), 1590, Yate, p. 180; Elizabeth Norwoodd (75), *c.* 1598, Leckhampton, p. 181; Joan Pyrke (78),
1609, Abbenhall, p. 190; Millicent Molton (79), 1614, Todenham, p. 192; Mary Poulett (80), *c.* 1620, Minety, p. 194;
Alice Gunter (81), 1626, Cirencester, p. 195; Ann Gibbes
(82), 1636, Bristol, St. James, p. 197.

VI. CHILDREN.

Robert Page (14) has fourteen children, p. 39; On Thomas
Fortey's brass (17) are eight children, p. 48; John Jay (30) has
fourteen children, p. 76; William Gybbys (33) has thirteen
children, p. 82; Woolman (35) has four children, p. 87; John
Taylour (36) has fifteen children, p. 89; Robert Serche (43)
has four children, p. 105; John Hampton (46) has nine
children, p. 110; Sir William Greville (47) has eleven children,
p. 113; Katherine Sewell (48) has twelve children, p. 115;
Walter Hichman (54) has four children, p. 126; Sir Edmond

Tame (62) has five children, p. 141 ; Nicholas Thorne (68) has ten children, p. 165; Hercules Raynsford (70) has three children, p. 172; William Gyttyns (71) has ten children, p. 176; Alexander Staples (74) has eleven children, p. 180; William Norwoodd (75) has eleven children, p. 181 ; Elizabeth Marrowe (76) has one child, p. 185; Anne Savage (77) has one child, p. 187; Richard Pyrke (78) has two children, p. 190; Nicholas Poulett (80) has four children, p. 194; Henry Gibbes (82) has eight children, p. 197.

See the inscription to John Seames (63a), the father of six and twenty, p. 152.

VII. ECCENTRIC.

Two of the brasses may be recorded under this head : John and Elyn Hampton (46) are in shrouds, p. 110; and Anne Savage (77) is in bed, p. 187.

VIII. CANOPIES.

Groined canopies may be seen on Wine Merchant (5), p. 16, John Jay (30), p. 76 ; John Cook (64), p. 154. Canopies are also shewn on Sir John Cassy (4), p. 10 ; William Grevel (7), p. 21 ; Sir Morys Russel (8), p. 25 ; John Barstaple (9) and Isabella Barstaple (10), p. 28 ; Joan Clopton (11), p. 30 ; Richard Dixton (12), p. 33 ; Robert Page (14), p. 39 ; Thomas Fortey (17), p. 48 ; John Fortey (20), p. 54 ; John Jay (30). p. 76 ; Thomas Bushe (59), p. 135. This last is a very interesting example.

IX. COATS OF ARMS.

Sir John Cassy (4), p. 10 ; Wine Merchant (5), p. 16 ; Willlam Grevel (7), a merchant's mark appears on the same memorial, p. 21 ; Sir Morys Russel (8), p. 25 ; Isabella Barstaple (9), p. 28 ; Joan Clopton (11), p. 30 ; Richard Dixton (12), p. 33 ; Sir John Juyn (13), p. 37 ; Man in Armour (16), the crest is worthy of notice, it represents a "free-miner," p. 44 ; Philip Mede (27), p. 69; Thomas Rowley (28), also a merchant's mark, p. 73 ; John Tame (40), p. 98 ; Morys Denys (44), p. 106 ; Elizabeth Knevet (49), p. 117; Roger Porter (56) p. 129 ; Thomas Bushe (59), Arms of the Merchants of the Staple of Calais. p. 135 ; Sir Edmond

Tame (62 and 63), p. 141; Sir John Greville (65), p. 158; Sir Edward Greville (66), p. 162; Nicholas Thorne (68), p. 165, Hercules Raynsford (70), p. 172; William Norwoodd (75), p. 181; Elizabeth Marrowe (76), p. 185; Anne Savage (77), p. 187; William Molton (79), p. 192; Nicholas Poulett (80), p. 194.

For a list of those whose armorial bearings are blazoned see the Index s.v. Heraldry.

X. MERCHANTS' MARKS.

William Grevel (7), p. 21; John Barstaple (9), p. 28; Robert Page (14), p. 39; Reginald Spycer (15), p. 42; John Fortey (20), p. 54; Thomas Rowley (28), p. 73; John Jay (30), p. 76; Woolman (35), p. 87; John Taylour (36), p. 89; John Twinyhow (45), p. 109; Edward Halyday (51), p. 122, Walter Hichman (54), p. 126; Thomas Bushe (59), p. 135.

XI. BREAKS IN INSCRIPTIONS.

Sir John Cassy (4), p. 10; Joan Clopton (11), p. 30; Sir John Juyn (13), p. 37; Thomas Fortey (17), p. 48; John Ceysyll (37), p. 91.

LOST BRASSES.

Among one of the most painful duties which may fall to the chronicler is to deplore what is lost. With monumental brasses one has often the melancholy satisfaction of seeing the matrix, or indent, or casement of the brass; and one can from these indents call up vividly the shape of the brass, and oftentime fill in the blank space with the incised memento of the departed worthy.

The Rev. H. Haines records that the brasses have been "lost at Bishop's Cleeve, Churchdown, Painswick, and St. John the Baptist, Gloucester. At Churcham is the matrix of a large cross 14th Century." Fortunately portions of one of those lost at St. John the Baptist, Gloucester, have been found, and are described see p. 149.

MATRICES.

The following remarks are arranged under the names of the places where the brasses originally were. In some instances the matrices are left, and are noticed; in the remaining ones the descriptions taken from the County Histories are given.

Badminton.

"There is a grey marble flatstone, inlaid with brass, upon which are engraved the figures of two knights; in a scutcheon, a lion rampant, and round the edge, in old black letters, Radulphus Botiler, Miles dominus."—*Rudder*.

The Vicar, Rev. G. H. Ford, B.A., writes under date 4th January, 1898: "There is no trace of any brasses in Badminton Church."

Bishop's Cleeve.

Rudder says: "There is also the figure of a military person upon a brass plate fixt on a stone in the chancel, with

his arms, *three piles*, and this inscription in old character:—
...... armiger qui obiit undecimo die mensis Julij m,ccc·lxx, quinto cujus aic p'picietur deus amen."

Atkyns records: "There is an effigies, in the chancel, of a soldier in brass, who died 1370."

The Rev. Thos. Jesson, M.A., under date January 6th, 1898, informs me that he can find no traces of any old brass in Bishop's Cleeve Church.

Churcham.

Not mentioned by Rudder, but Haines chronicles a large XIV cent. cross.

The Rev. W. J. Selby, under date January 4th, 1898, writes: "I cannot find any trace of the cross; the church has, however, been twice restored since 1861 (once in consequence of fire), and consequently a great deal of the old work is gone."

Churchdown.

Not mentioned by Rudder.

Cirencester.

A.—An angel and lily pot, *c.* 1460, man, wife and children lost, north aisle.—*Haines.*

In the north aisle is a slab measuring 36in. x 30in., the lily pot is *in situ*, there are indents, one on each side, and below the indents of the heads of man and wife. Possibly when Mr. Haines saw the slab it was more perfect. On the pillar near is the Angel Gabriel, and careful measurement shews that it will fit the indent on the left of the lily pot, and most probably there was a representation of the Virgin Mary on the opposite side, the whole composition representing the Annunciation. The Angel nimbed is three-quarters face and turned to his right and holding a mace in his right hand and a book in his left. The lily pot much resembles a modern cream jug and three sprays of flowering lilies are in it (146).

Fig 146. Lily Pot, c. 1460. Cirencester.

B.—A civilian and wife, circa 1500, with four sons, one in academicals, and three daughters, between them a pot of lilies mutilated; the wife, daughters and lily pot (which is loose), are now on the same slab with two female effigies; inscription lost, mural. St. Catharine Chapel. Probably John Avenyng, 1501, and wife Alice, relations, of Bishop Ruthall, of Durham, born at Cirencester, whose mother's name was Avening."—*Haines.*

A rubbing of the brass when *in situ* has been kindly lent me by Mr. Mill Stephenson, F.S.A. (147). Unfortunately it is not known when it was rubbed, but it was at one time in the Rev. H. Haines's collection. It was not made by him, for when he chronicled the brasses the various portions had been dispersed. Kneeling at a prie-dieu is the husband, John Avenyng. His hair long, but cut across the forehead; the face is clean shaven. His gown is long and covers his feet, though he is kneeling; it is thrown open in front, but the usual fur facing does not appear. The sleeves are long and very open and deep at the wrists. The lappet on the left hand is thrown over the cushion and thus is shewn. His vest or undergarment appears both at the throat and wrists; his hands are uplift in prayer. On the prie-dieu lies an open book which nearly covers the desk, the supports are so arranged as to have Gothic arches. Four sons kneel behind him. They are similarly habited to the father, except one wears a hood over his shoulders. Their hands are not clasped in prayer, only the tips of the fingers meeting in two instances, the youngest simply raises his hands, and the one immediately behind the father is so much hidden by the son in academicals that only his head and shoulder appear.

Facing this group is another consisting of the mother and her three daughters. Like her husband she is kneeling to a prie-dieu, but of different construction, the arch is round and not Gothic. Near is a flower, emblem of the Resurrection. As the head is turned to the left the lappet hanging behind is clearly seen; all the lappets are plain. Her dress is long and plain; at the neck it is turned down to form a square collar. Its sleeves are tight fitting and the cuffs being reflexed shew the fur lining; it is tied at the waist by a long sash. Behind her kneel three daughters, with hair flowing freely below the waist. They wear loose gowns, with small collars; the

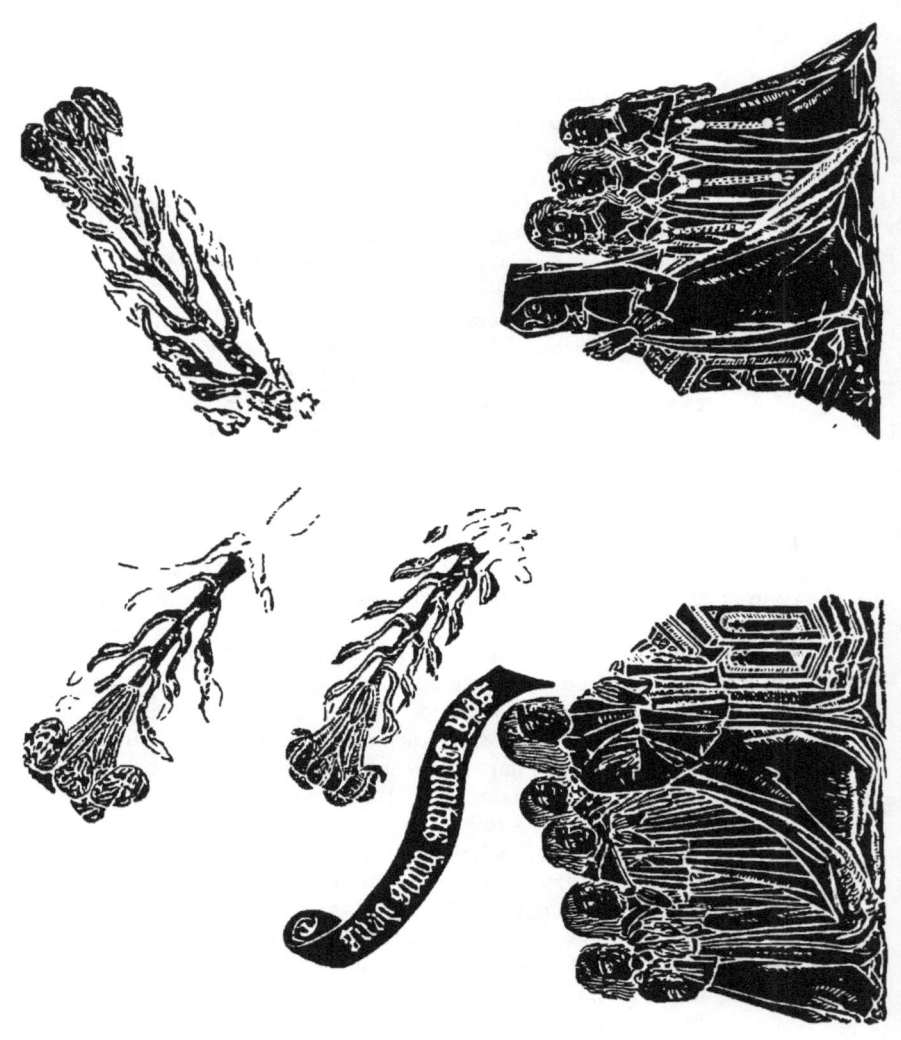

147. Civilian and Wife, c. 1500   Cirencester.

sleeves are narrow, with bell-shaped cuffs. They have each loose hip girdle fastened by three rosettes, from which hangs a chain with an ornamental pendant. Each wears a plain cap fastened by a rosette on the forehead. Both mother and daughters have their hands clasped in prayer.

From the husband proceeds a label inscribed:
S'cta Trinitas unus Deus.
No label is shewn over the wife.

Above the groups are three sprays of lilies which appear to have been rubbed as they were placed on the slab. It has been suggested that these originally sprang from a lily pot, but there is no trace of one on the rubbing (147).

We regret to say that this memorial has become separated from its original matrix; a part is on one of the pillars dividing the chancel, another piece is on the floor, and some is lost.

Memoir.—In 1673 "Mr. Thomas Carles, Minister of God's word in that place, *i.e.*, Cirencester, copied the epitaphs in the church. On his list appears:—

Sub hoc tumulo requiescunt Corpora Johannis Avenyng et Aliciæ uxo ejus qui obierunt xiiij die Aprilis A.D. 1501, and had viij children.

He records that this epitaph was in "St. Katherine's Chappell." In his will John directed that his body should be buried in the Chapel of St. Katherine. Leland says that Alice gave 100 marks towards the building of the south porch. Bishop Ruthall, of Durham, was her sister's son. Her name, in old English letters, is borne on a fess across her monumental shield with a woman's head between the words, and appears on the capital of one of the pillars on the north side of the south aisle.

C.—"On a flatstone, engraved on brass, in the South aisle, are the effigies of a man and woman. On labels proceeding from their mouths:—

Mercy God of my misdede.—Lady help at my most neede.

On a brass plate under their feet:

Ryse gracious Thee to endless lyfe
At thy grete dome where all schall apere
Hughe Horys Groc' and Johan hys wyf nowe dede in grave
  and beryed here
Do' p'yers desyring there souls for there the x day of July
  the yere our Lord God m°cccccxix.

The above verses are engraved on the plate in a continued form, like prose."—*Rudder.*

Fig 148. Vase, Cirencester.

Rev. Thos. Carles, in his "Short Notes," 1673, adds that he was buried July 10th, 1529, and had six children. Of this memorial the inscription only is left, and that has been torn from its slab and fixed on a pillar.

D.— Of this elegant vase (148) I have no information, and the brass has disappeared.

E.—The Rev. Thomas Carles reports: "At the upper end of the south ayle there was lately in brass this monkish distich:—

Munde vale, tibi ve, fugiens me, dum sequerer te
Tu sequeris modo me, Munde vale, tibi ve.

Stollen A.D. 1672°
Sacrilego poenam, poenitentiam
optat Thomas Carles

"I suppose" (sayeth Mr. Carles) "this following epitaph was intended as its translation on a brass in the middle ayle:—

Margaret Hooper, wife to Henry Hooper, was buried here March the 4th, 1601.
Oh! wretched world, vaine and unsure!
As I am fled from thee;
So, mayst thou die within an houre,
Then thou shalt follow mee."

Cubberley.

One shield, all that remains of the brass of Sir Giles Bruges, *c.* 1511, and wife Isabel, daughter of Thomas Baynham, with three sons and four (?) daughters. Mural, south chancel.—*Haines.*

On the south wall of the south aisle is the solitary remnant of the brass. It originally measured 27 ft. 9 in. x 2 ft. 3 in., but all has disappeared except a shield in upper sinister corner.

The husband had his wife on his left hand, his head was resting on a heaume, but I am unable to particularise any other details either of husband or wife. Beneath the figures was a fillet of brass which contained the inscription, below this are the matrices of two groups of children, seemingly three sons and three daughters. At each corner of the slab were shields, but only the one at the upper sinister corner, *i.e.*, above the wife, remains (149). This shield bears :—

Quarterly, 1st and 4th Argent, on a cross sable a leopard's head, or, BRIDGES, 2nd, Or, a pile, gules ; DE CHANDOS. 3rd Argent, a fess between martlets, sable ; BERKELEY of *Coberley* —impaling quarterly, 1st Gules, a chevron between three bulls' heads cabossed, argent ; BAYNHAM. 2nd Gules, on a bend ermine, a talbot passant guardant, or : WALWYN. 3rd Paly or and vert 9 goutes de sang ; GRENDOUR (*old*). 4th a fess between *three* (and not as in *Bigland six*) cross crosslets, gules, GRENDOUR (*new*). (149).

Fig 149.
Shield. c. 1511. Cubberley.

"The shield tells the history of the Bridges' family as far as it goes :—

Thomas Berkeley, the last male representative of the Coberley branch of the Berkeleys of Dursley, the tenant of the Berkeley Honor under William I., William II., Henry I. and Stephen, married Joan the daughter and heiress of Sir John de Chandos and had two daughters, co-heiresses, Margaret, wife of Nicholas de Mattesden (Matson) and Alice wife of Thomas de Bruges or Bridges. Giles, the great grandson of Thomas and Alice Bruges, married Isabella, daughter and heiress of Thomas Barynham, by Alice his wife, daughter and heiress of — Walwyn, and grand-daughter of Walwyn by his wife—daughter of John Grendour of Abbenhall."

For the above I acknowledge my indebtedness to the Rev. W. Bazeley, M.A., Rector of Matson.

For an account of the above mentioned Thomas and Alice Baynham, of Micheldean, see p. 86.

Sir Giles Bruges by his will in P.C.C. 21 Fetiplace, dated Nov. 20th, 1511, orders " his body to be buried in the Chapel of *Coberley*, and that a priest have ten marks for singing his Requiem." *Collins, Tit. Chandos,* Vol. II., p. 247. See also

Dumbleton.

"In the north cross aisle, upon a flat stone, under the figures of a man and woman in brass, is this inscription in old characters:—

Orate p'aiabus Willi Daston filii Jobis Daston et Annæ uxoris ejus qui quidem Willius obiit anno dni Millimo cccc°xiii° quor aiab' p'picietur deus."—*Rudder.*

The Rev. C. H. Fairfax, under date January 5th, 1898, writes: "I see some traces of what may be the matrix of a brass, but the piece of stone remaining is only about 18 inches square and very much broken."

Gloucester Cathedral.

"Before this alteration [to the Choir, in 1741] there were five other large grave-stones found, to which Brass plates were fixed, long since torn off, three of which belonged to some of the abbats."—*Rudder.*

A Guide to the Cathedral Church of Gloucester, by the Rev. H. Haines, M.A., p. 58, says:—"In the south transept are some brassless slabs—

One a figure in armour, two feet long, *c.* 1450. (*a*)

Another, two figures under canopies, *c.* 1500, with implements of trade (?), having handles inserted above, the lower parts of the slab chiselled down for an inscription, 1753. (*b*)

A third in St. John the Baptist's Chapel (7ft. 3in. x 3ft. 3 in.) with the figure of an Abbot (3ft. 8in. long) under a single canopy, with a marginal inscription, probably for John Brown, 1514, usually ascribed to Walter Froucester, but the style seems too late. (*c*)

A slab (7ft. 8in. x 4 ft.) with incised cross, the scroll on the stem probably bore the name of Thomas Goold, and is now obliterated.

In the north transept are three brassless slabs:—

One (8ft. x 3ft.), a priest or abbot, *c.* 1330, under a triple canopy, the Lombardic inscription around nearly obliterated. (*d*)

A second (8ft. 11in. x 3ft. 5in.), a priest in cope in the head of a long cross. (*e*)

A third, much worn, (9ft. 3in. x 3 ft. 10½in.) an abbot under a single canopy surrounded by an inscription. (*f*). From its position it would seem to be the memorial of Thos. Horton, 1377, or John Boyffield, 1381, precentor and "superior operis," or superintendent of the building of the north transept, under Horton, but the indent of the mitre shews it to be more likely that of Walter Froucester, 1412.

Other brassless slabs remain in the Lady Chapel and east walk of the cloister."

"In 1741 were destroyed part of the screen in the nave and chapels. Before these alterations there were 5 large gravestones, stripped of their Brasses, of which three at least belonged to abbot. (*Furney's MSS.* in the Bodleian Lib., pp. 582-3). Perhaps one of these gravestones commemorated Adam de Elmeleye, a monk of St. Peter's, who, on account of his sanctity, was buried at the request of the people in front of the altar of the Holy Cross, in 1273. Many miracles were said to have been afterwards wrought at his grave." (*Do.* p. 66).

"On Duke Robert's gravestone hath been a cross in brass now torn off which was lately taken away. *Furney's MSS.*, p. 582. (*Do*).

These are all the indents of Brasses representing persons I noticed on visiting the Cathedral in December, 1897. The other "brassless slabs" mentioned in Haines's *Guide* most probably contained inscription plates only.

South transept:

a. The figure was represented in complete plate armour with sword hanging perpendicularly and the inscription at foot. The slab is a very large one, the figure was 2ft. 3in. long.

b. Part only of the slab remains, and this measures 4ft. x 3ft. 6in. The heads of husband and wife are under a double canopy crocketted and cusped with pinnacles at sides and in centre. No marginal inscription shewn.

c. Chapel. The abbot was under a single canopy with pinnacles at the side, and a marginal inscription; the head of the crook is turned inwards.

North transept:

d. As far as I could make out, the slab being much perished, the abbot lay under a single canopy with pinnacles on each side. Marginal inscription. Slab is cracked, and measures 7ft. 9in. x 2ft. 7in.

e. This slab is in very fair condition, though cracked across the middle. The head of the floriated cross in which was a priest, measures 3ft. in diameter. The inscription was at foot. There were seven crockets round the head and three pairs on the stem. The cross is 6ft. long.

f. Slab partly under railing. ? Abbot under canopy, pinnacles marginal inscription. Very much perished.

Gloucester—St. John Baptist.

"Upon an ancient stone, with a large engraving on brass, are the effigies of a man in armour, and a woman attired in her proper habit. The man has a sword by his side, his spurs on, and at his feet a greyhound couchant.

Here lies John Briggs and Agnes his wife,
He died 19th April, 1483, and she a little time after.
God give them joy and everlasting life,
That pray for John Briggs and Agnes his wife."—*Counsel.*

Gloucester—St. Mary de Crypt.

"In the south chancel against the south wall a mural monument, the inscription and crosses on brass torn off, supposed to be for the founder of this chapel."—*Rudder.*

Hawkesbury.

During the restoration of the church in 1882, the matrix of a priest was discovered, and is now in the sacrarium. I regret to say that I have not seen a rubbing of it, nor is the brass mentioned in the county histories.

Iron Acton.

The Rev. G. H. Browne writes under date, January 8th, 1898:—"There are one or two flat tombstones in this church, which have once had Brasses let into them; one a Poyntz memorial and another, that of a former rector or priest." Unfortunately I have not been able to find time to go to Iron Acton and have not any rubbings of these indents.

Minchinhampton.

* Upper half of female effigy, *c.* 1530, loose.—*Haines.*

No trace of this was left when I rubbed the other Brasses in this church.

---

* This signified that Haines had not seen this Brass.

Newland.

Not in Rudder. A figure in full armour, head resting on a helmet; a child on each side. 34½in. x 20in.

Northleach.

Wm. Bicknell, 1500 and wife Margaret, 1493, founders of chancel in 1489; all lost but 2 sons and 2 daughters. South chancel. *Haines.*

Fig. 150. Children. 1500. Northleach.

William Bicknell built the south chapel in the year 1489; he and his wife lie buried therein.—*Atkyns.*

Painswick.

Against the north wall of the Chantry Chapel is a large altar tomb of Purbeck marble. On the wall were the kneeling effigies in brass of Sir William Kingston and Elizabeth his wife, with scrolls proceeding from their mouths to a Trinity. Above Sir William's head a shield surrounded by the garter, and above his wife's also a shield. On the canopy of the tomb four shields, round the verge was the inscription, the front of the base of the tomb has three panels, in each of which was a shield, also a shield in the panel at each end. The slab of the tomb has been utilised as the resting place of the effigies of Dr. Seaman and his wife; he died in 1623, aged 59, and had originally a monument at the east end of the chancel.

The following account is taken from the Ashmole MS. (1118, fol. 97) in the Bodleian Library:

"In ye church of Painswick in Glouc. shire.
In ye north Isle.
On a tumbe there was y^r proportion of a man in brasse kneeling, habited in ye Garment of a Kt. of ye Garter, hauing

yᵉ crosse of St. Georg on his right shoulder with yᵉ garter about it and this inscription vnder him :—

Vnder this . . . . tumbe lyeth buryed yᵉ bodye of Sir Wyllyam Kyngston, Knight of yᵉ Order of the Garter, one of yᵉ Kynges Maiesties priuye councell Vice-Chamberlayne to the Kynges Highnes, Comptroller of yᵉ Kyng's most honourable Household, Constable of yᵉ tower, Captayne of yᵉ Gard, who departed this present world yᵉ XIII. of [May] in yᵉ yeare of our Lord God MDXL., and in yᵉ XXXII. year of yᵉ dread soueraigne lord Kyng Henry yᵉ VIII., and also Dame Elizabeth his wife, on whose soules God have mercye.

This inscription with yᵉ proportion, being tore off from yᵉ Tumbe, 1644 or thereabouts by soldiers, Mr. Joh. Theyer, of Cooper's hill, near Glouc. (whose wife is descended from yᵉ said Sr. Will.) obtained it and keepeth it to this day."

His will is in P.C.C., F. 32, Alenger. "My body to be buried in the next church to the place where I die." The widow in her will desires to be buried at Painswick, with my late husband, Sir William Kingston, Knight of the Honourable Order of the Garter. Dame Mary Kingston's will is in P.C.C., F. 23, Populwell.

Possibly Elizabeth is a mistake for Dame Mary Kingston, who was formerly Jernyngham.

Ashmole is in his History of the Order of the Garter (1715), describes the arms thus :—Azure, a fesse between 3 leopards' faces, or.

Quinton.

Thos. de Rous, Esq., of Ragley, 1499, and wife of Matilda; worn, effigies lost, chancel.—*Haines*.

The late Mr. J. D. T. Niblett, F.S.A., kindly gave me a rubbing of the inscription, which reads thus :—

"Orate s'palit' p aiabz . . . . nup' de Ragley armigeri et | matilde uxoris . . . . an' d'ni m | cccc nonagesi' nono. Sit r͞o laus & gl' | ia . . . vita eterna."

which may be translated :—

Pray specially for the souls of [Thomas de Rous] late of Ragley, Esq., and of Margaret, his wife . . . . A.D., 1499. May praise and glory be to Christ . . . life eternal,

In P.C.C., 39, Horne is the will of Thomas Rowse, gent., Qwynton, Gloucester, and dated 1499.

Siddington St. Peter.

Rudder: "There is a large grey stone in the chancel, which had once the effigy of a man in armour upon it, said to have been intended for one of the Langleys, but the brass is now torn off."

Bigland: "In the North Wall of this Chapel [Langley's] are three Niches that have had brass figures and Inscriptions, but now entirely gone."

The wills of the following members of the Langley family are in the P.C.C. :—

1490. Langley, Edmond, squier, Sudington Petre, Gloucester . . . . 33 Milles.

1459. Langley, John, Sudington St. Peter, Gloucester, Sheppewassh, Devon . . . . 18 Stokton.

1462. Langley, Walter, esquire, Sudyngton St. Peter, Gloucester . . . . 30 Godyn.

Tewkesbury.

Rudder: "Robert Fitz-Haimon was buried in the Chapter-house in the year 1107, but removed into the presbytery in 1241, and thence in 1397. to the north side of the choir, where his bones, wrapt in fine diaper, were laid in a tomb of grey marble, which had brasses at top, with his figure and ornaments, long since torn off.

"In the middle space under the tower, is a large grey marble, which had brass plates affixed to it, and is said to have been for the unfortunate Prince Edward, only son to King Henry the Sixth."

Dingley thus wrote in 1680 :—

"This fair tombstone of grey marble, the brass whereof has bin pickt out by sacrilegious hands, is directly underneath the tower of this church, at the entrance into the quire, and sayed to be layd over Prince Edward, who lost his life in cool blood, in the dispute between York and Lancaster, at wch time ye Lancastrians had the overthrow."

"Monuments to be consider'd under this magnificent pile are first that of the Founder hereof Robert Fitzhamon this is within a fair chappell on the north side of the quire or chancell erected to his memory both which I have touched off in the two following sides or pages, his arms and figure of brass plate inlayd were stol'n away in the time of the late civil war." Illustrations of the two tombs are given.

The Editor of Bigland's Collections, *sub* Tewkesbury, alludes to the lack of brasses in Tewkesbury Abbey, and explains that the Parish Church was of old in another part of the town, and was afterwards pulled down or suffered to fall into decay. "It is noted that the brasses on what was supposed to have been the flat tombstone of Prince Edward are gone; a loss which Vicar Knight supplied by a small plate fixed in the stone."

The following is taken from "*Historical Memories of Tewkesbury Abbey*, by Rev. H. Hayman, D.D., which appeared in *The Antiquary*, Vol. I, 1880:—

"The wife of the gallant Earl, Gilbert de Clare, the third, who fell at Bannockburn, was a lady whose family connections touched all the three component parts of our present United Kingdom. We might strew the rose, the shamrock, and the thistle together on her grave. She was Maud, daughter of John de Burgh, Earl of Ulster, her eldest sister being the wife of King Robert Bruce. That grave has been identified together with that of her husband, close on the north side of it. Cut short perhaps by grief at her bereavement, the young widow was laid there in the first year of her widowhood. It was marked by 'a fine and large slab, from which a magnificent brass had been ruthlessly taken.' How touching is the pathos which these shattered memorials of bereavement and blighted hopes bespeak. The shadow of sorrow fell upon her life, its gloom deepened, and she died without a son to keep in remembrance the name of her dead lord's illustrious house."

Tormarton.

Sir John de la Rivière, c. 1350, lost, chancel.—*Haines*.

Leland says:—"*There lyeth buried in the Body of the Paroche Churche of Thormerton one Petrine de la Ryvers, with a Frenche Epitaphie. He was owner of the Lordshippe of Tormerton.* And Sir Robert Atkyns observes that in his time the effigies of Sir John de la Rivière, with the model of the church in his hand remained in the chancel; but the brasses of both these monuments are now torn off and lost."—*Rudder*.

The stone has now a plate inscribed:—

"The tomb of John de la Rivers, founder of this Church."

The late Sir A. W. Franks thus describes the memorial:—
"It consists of a floriated cross, within the head of which is the knight holding up the model of the Church which he had founded; on the stem of the cross appears to have been a helmet, at the base probably an Agnus Dei, and in the angles shields of arms surmounted by helmets and crests." An illustration appears in *Haines's Manual*, p. cxxiv.

Wotton-under-Edge.

Richard de Wotton, rector, c. 1320, kneeling at a cross with Lombardic inscription lost, matrix. Chancel.—*Haines.*

"In the chancel is the following:—Round the verge of a grey marble flatstone, which had a brass plate fixed on it, with the figure of a man, now torn off, are these lines in Saxon characters:—

"Ratus in hac villa cognomine dictus ab illa
 Qui Rector fuit hic, aptum nomenq; sibi sic
 R. de Wottona jacet hic, cui cælica dona,
 Impetret ipsa pia pulcherrima virgo Maria. Amen."

In the middle of the stone:—

'Es mihi vergo pia, Dux et Lux, sancta Maria.'"—*Rudder.*

The slab measures 7 ft. 6 in. × 2 ft. 11 in. In the lower part is the kneeling figure of R. de Wotton, rector of this church, under a small canopy with slender shafts; a long scroll proceeds from his hands to the figure of the Virgin (*see inscription*), seated and enclosed in a fine large floriated cross. A marginal inscription in Lombardic letters surrounds the whole, and reads as given above. *Rudder* has incorrectly transcribed the first two words on the scroll, which should read **Sis michi.**

The slab was originally in the chancel, but is now lying loose, near Lord Berkeley's tomb (see p. 2), and has been cracked. An illustration is given in the Portfolio of the Monumental Brass Society, VIII, December, 1897.

The inscription might be thus translated:—

"Born in this town, after which he was named, he who was rector here thus for himself had a fitting name. R. de Wotton lies here, to whom may the pious and most beautiful virgin grant heavenly gifts.—Be thou to me O pious virgin, holy Mary, my guide and light."

MODERN BRASSES.

The fashion of erecting brasses as memorials to the departed appears to have died out in the seventeenth century but has now revived. Haines records that brasses have been placed in the following churches:—

Bristol: S. S. Leonard & Nicholas. Rev. John Eden, 1840 (Waller).

Mitcheldean (Waller).

Newent . . . Onslow.

Upper Slaughter. Rev. Francis Edw. Witts (Waller).

In trying to render this a more complete list, I wrote to the leading engravers of memorial brasses in the country, but regret to say that the list has not been much amplified.

Messrs. John Hardman & Co., of Birmingham, have executed the following:—

Barnwood. Mrs. Alice Mary Blathwayt.

Bristol Cathedral. Captain John Sanderson, R.N.

Bristol, Queen Elizabeth's Hospital. Rev. John Hawkesworth, LL.D.

Clifton, All Saints. Rev. R. Randall.

Clifton College. Rev John Guthrie, M.A., and wife Caroline.

In Gloucester Cathedral is a brass—a fitting memorial—to the Rev. H. Haines, M.A., whose exhaustive "Manual," issued in 1861, is still the standard work on Monumental Brasses; to the list in Part II, the writer is indebted for the headlines of each notice. He is represented robed as a priest of the Church of England, in cassock, surplice, stole, and hood, beneath a canopy, and the following inscription is round the margin:—

HERBERTUS HAINES, A.M., SCHOLÆ HUJUS | CATHREDALIS PER XXIII ANNOS HYPODIDASCULUS, OBIIT A.D. XIV. KAL. OCT. A.S. MDCCCLXXII ANNOS XLVI NATUS, CUJUS CORPUS IN | CŒMETERIO JUXTA HANC URBEM SEPULTUM | JACET. HOC MONUMENTUM PAUCI EX DISCIPULIS ET AMICIS, BENEFICIORUM AB ILLO ACCEPTORUM MEMORES, PONENDUM CURAVERUNT."

This may be translated thus:—Herbert Haines, M.A., for twenty-three years second master of this Cathedral School, died September 18th, 1872, aged 46 years, whose body lies buried in the cemetery near this city. A few of his pupils and friends mindful of benefits received from him have caused this memorial to be erected.

CORRIGENDA ET ADDENDA.

P. 3. Line 2 from base, for *carings* read *earrings*.
P. 15. Fig 151 represents the second shield on the Cassy Brass.
P. 17. Line 5 for 𝔗 (T) read 𝔊 (G).
P. 18. *Inscription:* On examining rubbings of this brass taken many years ago, the words added in brackets have been deciphered.
    . Margeria coniux sua femina [dia]
    . . Mihi [succurit"] tempore [vili] *(scroll work)*.
P. 28. Fig. 24, for 1141 read 1411.
P. 29. Fig. 25, for c. 1141 read 1411.
P. 30. Line 12, for p. 176 read p. 116.
P. 37. Line 2, add "also in the Publications of the Early English Text Society, Vol. 78."

Fig. 151.
Shield 1400, Deerhurst.
Should have been on page 15.

P. 42. Line 12, "The Inscription," add "except the first line which is preserved on a step in the Lady Chapel."
P. 44. Line 7 from base for 1444 read 1445.
P. 51. Add the following translation:
By death o'erthrown beneath your feet see Thomas Fortey lie,
A noble merchant, just and true, well known his kindly life
Dame Agnes too his spouse full sweet in like extremity,
Which found no joy in others woe, no gain in baleful strife,
Churches and roads his bounty felt in wise and full repair,
Christ, let Thy soul with pity melt before his humble prayer,
From Thy blest birth a thousand years, four hundred more also
And forty-seven eke had passed ere he Thy bliss did know.
P. 51. *Illustrations:* Add *Reliquary* N.S. Vol. III., p. 175 (Inscription).
P. 55. Line 9, "Initial" on a rubbing kindly lent by Mr. Mill Stephenson, this is shewn to be a very small reproduction of his merchant's mark; see Fig. 53, p. 56.
P. 65. Line 2. *Portions lost*, add "and ends of scroll under figure."
P. 71. Line 26, for *sable*, Burke gives *gules*.
P. 72. Line 4 from base, for 1476 read 1471.

CORRIGENDA ET ADDENDA.

P. 78. *Illustrations:* add Weare (G. E.) Life of Cabot.
P. 78. Line 29, "This Joan," add ("wife of John Jay, senr.")
P. 91. *Illustrations:* Add *Reliquary* N. S. Vol. III., p. 173.
P. 91. Line 10, for *Taylour* read *Tayliour*.
P. 93. For Fig. 7 read Fig. 78.
P. 108. *Heraldry:* Read "Quarterly (1) Gules, a bend engrailed [azure] between three leopards' faces jessant de lis [or] DENYS. (2) [Argent] on a chief [gules] three bezants [RUSSELL]. (3) Lozengy [argent and azure] a chevron [gules, GORGES]. (4) [Azure] a cross moline [or, BRUYN]."
P. 117. Fig. 85, for *Easllinglon* read *Eastlington*.
P. 119. Her younger brother Charles was steward to his cousin Edward Stafford, Duke of Buckingham, at Thornbury.
P. 122. Will of William Henshawe, P.C.C. F. 12 Maynwaring.
P. 124. Line 23, for *i* read *is*.
        Line 24, add "of."
P. 134. Fig. 152, Head of William Freme, 1526, from a rubbing kindly sent in February, 1884, by the late Mr. J. H. Cooke, F.S.A. Mr. T. Wareing reports under date June, 1898, that the head is now replaced.

Fig. 152.
Head 1526. Berkeley.

P. 142. Fig. 103, for 1554 read 1534.
P. 144. *Illustrations:* Add *Reliquary* N. S., Vol. III., p. 173 (end of inscription).
P. 150. Fig. 109, for 1450 read 1540.
P. 163. In the P.C.C. are these wills:—
1561, Grevell, Sir Edward, Knight, Mylcote, Warwick, Seasingcote, Gloucester. . . . . 26 Loftes.
1574, Grevell, Dame Margaret, widow of Sir Edward Grevell, Knight, Milcote, Warwick. . . . . 45 Martin
P. 175. Line 12, 1581, add "P.C.C. 8 Darcy."
P. 180. Fig. 133, for 1890 read 1590.
P. 181. For *Norwood* read *Norwoodd*.
P. 187. Fig. 137, "Shield, 1601 Clifford Chambers." This is on wrong page, it should have appeared on p. 175.
Line 11, for "*Argent, a fesse engrailed sable between 3 boars' heads couped proper for Marrowe,*" read "*Argent, a fess engrailed sable, between three maids' heads couped proper for* MARROWE, *impaling, Argent a cross sable for* RAINSFORD." The shield is not quite complete.
P. 194. Line 1, for *Marg* read *Mary*.

P. 207. ## Bristol Cathedral.

MATRIX OF THE BRASS OF AN AUSTIN CANON IN BRISTOL CATHEDRAL.

Mr. Alfred E. Hudd, F.S.A., Hon. Sec. of the Clifton Antiquarian Society, has kindly forwarded me the following description of a matrix of a brass of an Austin Canon in Bristol Cathedral :—

"During the recent restoration of the Choir of Bristol Cathedral, formerly the Church of the Abbey of Canons Regular of St. Augustine, founded in 1142, a large slab of Purbeck marble was found in the South Choir Aisle, where it had been partially covered by the wooden foundation supporting the Stalls. This slab was found to contain the matrix of what must have been a very fine Monumental Brass of a Priest, probably one of the officials of the Abbey. The matrix is in good condition, and it is evident from it that the deceased Austin Canon was represented in a cope, his head covered by a flat cap similar to those worn by the Austin Canons represented on the mural paintings on the walls of Bishop Carpenter's vault at Westbury-on-Trym now used as the Coal-hole of that Church.

"The figure stands under a very handsome triple canopy, covered with no less than seven late Gothic pinnacles; below the feet was a long inscription on an oblong plate. Size of slab—7 ft. 10 in. x 3 ft. 8 in. Figure of Priest—4 ft. x 1 ft. 5 in. Date about 1500."

INDEX

ABBENHALL, brass at . . 190
Agnus Dei . . . 14, 156, 220
Albany, arms of . . . 130
Albe 60, 75
Almuce 58, 124
Altar Tombs 2, 30, 98, 171, 172, 216
Amerike, Joan 127
Amice . . . 60, 75, 140
Anelace . . . 19, 21, 28
Arabic Numerals . . . 50
Arderburg, arms of . . . 174
Arnold, arms of . . . 130
Atte Barugh, Peter . . . 10
Awmarle, Thomas . . . 81
Avenyng, John—Alice . . 208
Ayleway, Joan 190

BADMINTON, lost brass at . 206
Baldrick 3, 25
Barbe 14, 155
Barnwood, modern brass at . 221
Barons of Exchequer, see Judges
Barstaple, John—Isabella . 28
Barstaple Chapel, Bristol . 28
Bascinet 2, 25, 33
Basilard, see Anelace, Miséricorde
Bazely, Rev. W. . . . 212
Baynham, arms of . . 86, 212
  ,,   Alice . . . 85
  ,,   Margaret . . . 84
  ,,   Thomas . . . 83
Beard 2, 13, 19, 21, 28, 45, 158, 172,
  177, 179, 182, 190, 192, 194,
  196, 197
Beauchamp, Richard . . 9
  ,,   Thomas . . 9
Beaufort, Edmond . . . 9
Beaupyne, Thomas . . . 18
Bedstead 187
Bell-founder 119
Bells, collar of . 5, 13, 20, 26, 64
Belt, *passim*
Belt, *see also* Baldrick
Benett, John and wives . . 94
Berkeley, arms of . . . 5, 6
  ,,   Elizabeth . . 9
  ,,   Margaret . . 2
  ,,   Maurice . . 7, 72
  ,,   Thomas . . 2, 16
  ,,   William . . 72
  ,,   of Coberley, arms of 132, 212

Berkeley, brass at . . . 132
Berwicke, arms of . . . 174
Besford, arms of . . . 32
Bishop's Cleeve, lost brass at . 206
Bisley, brass at . . . 115
Blathwayt, Mrs. A. M. . . 221
Book, 14, 145, 156, 166, 176, 182,
  192, 197, 208
Botiler, arms of . . . 206
Boyffield, John . . . 214
Bradestone, arms of . . 2
  ,,   Agnes . . . 2
  ,,   Blanch . . . 2
  ,,   Robert . . . 2
  ,,   Sir Thos. . . 2
Brassart . 2, 34, 141, 160, 172
Brasses, Duplicate . 141, 144, 196
  ,,   Eccentric . . . 204
  ,,   heraldry of . . 204
  ,,   lost . . . 206
  ,,   modern . . . 221
  ,,   of Children . . 203
  ,, ,, Civilians . . 201
  ,, ,, Ecclesiastics . 200
  ,, ,, Judges . . . 201
  ,, ,, Ladies . . . 202
  ,, ,, Men in armour . 200
Braybrook, arms of . . . 128
Briggs, John—Agnes . . 215
Bristol, brasses at
  Barstaple Chapel . . 28
  Cathedral, matrix . . 223
  ,,   modern . . 221
  Grammar School . . 165
  Queen Elizabeth's Hospital,
    modern . . . 221
  St. James . . . 197
  St. John . . . 73
  St. Leonard & St. Nicholas,
    modern . . . 221
  St. Mary Redcliff 37, 69, 76, 127
  St. Peter . . . 58
  St. Werburgh . 165, 176
  Temple Church . 9, 58
  Trinity . . . 28
Bristol, city of, arms of . . 17
Brook, arms of . . . 128
  ,,   John—Joan . . 127
Brown, John . . . 213
Bruges, arms of . . 132, 212
  ,,   Elizabeth . . 131
  ,,   Sir Giles—Isabel . 211

INDEX

Bruyn, arms of . . 108, 223
Butterfly headdress 83, 84, 88, 90, 216

CALAIS, staple of, arms of . 137
Camail 2, 25
Camber, John 95
Campden, Chipping, *see* Chipping Campden
Canopies, ... 204
Canting Arms 74
Cap . . . 40, 61, 77, 94, 96
Cape 14, 61, 133
Carles, Rev. Thos. . . 210, 211
Cassock . . 58, 81, 124, 139
Cassy, arms of 15
 ,, Elizabeth . . . 131
 ,, Sir John—Alice . 9, 222
 ,, Richard . . . 15
 ,, William . . . 16
Ceysyll, John 91
Chalice 60, 75
Chamfer Inscription . 100, 216
Chape 3, 20
Chasuble 60, 75
Cheltenham, brass at . . 113
Children 203
Chipping Campden, brasses at 21, 51, 66, 82
Churcham, lost brass at . 207
Churchdown, lost brass at . 207
Cirencester, brasses at 16, 33, 39, 42, 62, 68, 75, 81, 94, 103, 138, 177, 195, 222
Cirencester, lost brasses at . 207
Civilians 201
Clare, Maude de . . . 219
Clifford Chambers, brasses at 172, 223
Clifton, arms of . . . 117
Clifton, modern brasses at . 221
Clopton, arms of . . . 32
 ,, Joan 30
 ,, Sir William . . 33
Cobham, arms of . . . 128
Cobyndon, arms of . . 64
Coif 11, 114, 127
Collars 2, 5, 13, 20, 26, 39, 42, 48, 52, 53, 55, 64, 73, 76, 77, 82, 87, 89, 92, 96, 104, 126, 138, 149, 154, 190
Cooke, arms of . . . 158
 ,, John—Joan . . 154
Cooke, J. H. . . 6, 134, 223
Cope 58, 124
Cote-hardie 1
Coton, Richard—Margaret . 163
Cotton, John 185
Crespine headdress . . 3, 45
Crest 6, 47, 141, 158, 162, 174, 195
Cromwell, arms of . . . 117
Cross 64, 142, 143, 146, 220 (*bis*)
Crucifixion 146
Cubberly, lost brass at . . 211
Cushion . 25, 106, 192, 197

DAGGER, *see* Miséricorde
Darby, Isabella . . . 30
Daston, arms of . . . 187
 ,, Anne . . . 187
 ,, Anthony . . 190
 ,, William . . 213
De Bohun, arms of . . 119
De Cailly, arms of . . . 117
De Chandos, arms of . 132, 212
De Clare, Maud . . . 219
Deerhurst, brasses at 10, 124, 131
De la Pole, Anne . . . 9
 ,, Michael . . 9
Demi-figure 8
Denys, arms of . . 108, 223
 ,, Morys . . . 106
 ,, Sir Walter . . 106
De Rous, Thomas—Matilda . 217
De Woodstock, arms of . 117
De Wotton, Richard . . 220
Dixton, arms of . . . 36
 ,, Richard . . . 33
Dogs 5, 13, 20, 26, 35, 64, 159, 162, 178, 215
Dominical Letter . . . 29
Dowdeswell, brass at . . 124
Dumbleton, arms of . . 190
Dumbleton, lost brass at . 213
Duplicate brasses . 141, 144, 196
Dyrham, brass at . . . 25

EASTINGTON, brass at . 117
Eccentric Brasses . . . 204
Ecclesiastical brasses . . 200
Eden, Rev. John . . . 221
Edward, Prince of Wales . 218
Edward, John 60
Enamel 32
England, arms of . . 15, 72
Evangelistic Symbols 32, 51, 89, 90, 110, 125, 126, 137

FAIRFORD, brasses at 98, 141, 144
Farthingale 185
Fermailes . . 5, 20, 31, 117
Fitton, arms of . . . 27
Fitz-Haimon, Robert . . 218
Fortey, John 54
 ,, Thomas—Agnes . 48, 221
Founder of Church . 103, 220
France 72
Franks, Sir A. W. . . 10, 220
"Free-Miner" crest . . 47
Freme, arms of . . . 134
 ,, William . . 132, 223
French, Elizabeth . . . 115
 ,, Margarett . . . 115
 ,, William . . . 115
Fret 12
Froucester, Walter . . 213, 214
Fuller, Rev. E. A. . . 18, 69

GADLINGS . . . 3, 25
Gayner, arms 30
 ,, Isabella . . . 28

INDEX.

Gibbes, Henry—Anne	197
Giffard, arms of	15
Glanville, arms of	174
Gloucester, brasses at	
St. John Baptist	149
St. Mary de Crypt	159
St. Michael	119
Gloucester, lost brasses at	
Cathedral	213
St. John Baptist	215
St. Mary de Crypt	215
Gloucester Cathedral, modern brass at	221
Goold, Thomas	213
Gorges, arms of	108, 223
Gotorest	18
Greene, arms of	174
Grevel, arms of	23
,, William—Marion	21
Greville, arms of	144, 146, 160, 162
,, Agnes	141
,, Sir Edward	162, 223
,, Sir John	158
,, Dame Margaret	223
,, Sir William	113
Greyndour, arms of	86, 212
,, Robert—Joan	47
Groining	16, 76, 154
Guarded spurs	35, 63
Gunter, arms of	197
,, John—Alice	195
Guthrie, Rev. John—Caroline	221
Gybbys, William and wives	82
Gypcière	73, 76, 90, 92, 94, 96, 104, 105, 114, 120
Gyttyns, William—Mary	176
HADOW, Rev. W. E.	16, 18, 40, 44, 64, 68, 81, 82, 95, 103, 139, 195
Haigh, D. H.	15
Haines, Rev. H.	221
Hall, arms of	174
,, Rev. J. M.	97
Halyday, Edward—Margery	122
Hampton, Alice	112
,, John—Elyn	110
Hardman, Messrs.	221
Hawkesbury, lost brass at	215
Hawkesworth, Rev. John	221
Hayward, arms of	130
Heart	133
Hempstead, brass at	130
Henshawe, arms of	121
,, William and wives	119
Heraldry *	
Albany	130
Arderburg	174
Arnold	130
Baynham	86, 212
Berkeley	5
,, of Coberley	132, 212
Berwicke	174
Besford	32
Botiler	206

Heraldry (continued)	
Bradeston	2
Braybrook	128
Bridges	212
Bristol City	17
Brook	128
Bruges	132, 212
Bruyn	108, 223
Calais, Staple of	137
Cassy	15
Clifton	117
Clopton	32
Cobham	128
Cobyndon	64
Cooke	158
Cromwell	117
Daslou	189
De Bohun	118
De Cailly	117
De Chandos	132, 212
De Woodstock	117
Denys	108, 223
Dixton	30
Dumbleton	190
England	15, 72
Fitton	27
France	72
Freme	134
Gavner	30
Giffard	15
Glanville	174
[Gorges]	108, 223
Greene	174
Grevel	23, 142, 146, 160, 163
Greyndour	86, 212
Gunter	196, 197
Hall	174
Hayward	130
Henshawe	121
Hodye	86
Hungerford	195
Juyn	38
Kingston	27, 217
Knevet	117
Lions	174
Lygon	182
Madoc-ap-ryn	130
Marrowe	187
Mede	71
Mollins	174
Molton	193
Norwood	182, 184
Parry	175
Parsons	76
Porter	130
Powlett	194
Prattell	174
Prelatte	64
Purscell	174
Ravnsford	174, 187
Rowlev	74
Russel	27, [108, 223]
Savage	189
Scocathe	174

* The arms of names in italics are blazoned in text.

INDEX

Heraldry (continued)
- Shershal 174
- Spencer 193
- Stafford 117
- Tame . . . 101, 144, 146
- Tatshail 117
- Thorne 167
- Twyniho 102
- Tyndall 171
- Tyringham . . . 143, 146
- Wakested 174
- Walwyn 212
- Warwick, Earl of . . 23
- Wylcotes 174
- Wyllycotes 174

Heraldry, see also p. 204
Hichman, Walter—Cristyan . 126
Hodges, William . . . 179
Hodye, arms of . . . 86
Honeysuckle 15
Hood, Civilian . 9, 20, 28, 37, 127
  ,, Ecclesiastical . . 110
  ,, Paris 166
Hooper, Margaret . . . 211
Hungerford, arms of . . 155
  ,, Margaret . . 194

IRON ACTON, lost brass at . 215

JAY, John—Joan . . . 76
Jewels 3, 4, 5, 20, 28, 31, 71, 155
Judges 201
Juyn, arms of 38
  ,, Alice 39
  ,, Sir John . . . 37

KALENDS 29
Kempsford, brass at . . 126
Kennel headdress 85, 100, 104, 105, 114, 116, 117, 121, 123, 124, 127, 131, 135, 142, 150, 164
Kingston, arms of . . 27, 217
  ,, Sir William—Elizabeth 216
Knevet, arms of . . . 117
  ,, Elizabeth . . 117

LADIES 202
Lance-rest 99
Latimer, Lord 9
Lawnder, William . . . 139
Lechlade, brasses at . 52, 109
Leckhampton, brass at . . 181
Lethenard, John—Joan . . 66
Lilies 208
Lingen, T. 32, 33
Lion at feet . 3, 11, 11a, 12, 26
Lions, arms of 174
Liripipe 96
Lisle, Lord 2, 9
Lombardic Letters . . . 220
Lond, Robert 58
Loose brasses . 58, 83, 153, 185
Lost brasses 206
Lukis, Rev. W. C. . . . 120
Lygon, arms of 182

MACLEAN, Sir J. . . 32, 87
Madoc-ap-Ryn, arms of . . 130
Maniple 60, 75
Mantle, men 11, 20, 37, 73, 149, 154
  ,, women 5, 20, 25, 31, 58, 71, 81, 117, 143, 145
Marks, see Merchant's Marks
Marner, Philip 177
Marrowe, arms of . . . 187
  ,, Elizabeth . . 185
Martyn, Agnes 64
Matrices 206
Mede, arms of 71
  ,, Philip and wives . . 69
Merchant's Marks 22, 29, 41, 44, 56, 74, 77, 88, 90, 95, 110, 123, 126, 136, 205
Mermaids 2, 6
Micheldean, brass at . . 83
  ,, modern brass at . 221
Military brasses . . . 200
Minchinhampton, brasses at 103, 110, 122, 215
Minety, brass at . . . 194
Minever 11
Miséricorde, or dagger 25, 36, 45, 64, 100, 129, 142, 160, 173, 194
Modern brasses . . . 221
Mollins, arms of . . . 174
Molton, arms of . . . 193
  ,, William—Millicent . 192
Monk 112
Monograms . . 44, 106, 176
Mourton, Sir H. . . . 18
Moustache 2, 19, 21, 28, 45, 158, 172, 177, 179, 182, 190, 192, 194, 196, 197
Moys, A. 10
Mural brasses 69, 110, 119, 122, 144, 149, 154, 165, 172, 176, 177, 179, 181, 185, 187, 192, 194, 197

NEELE, Thomas . . . 139
Neville, George . . . 9
  ,, Ralph 9
Newent, brass at . . . 129
  ,, modern brass at . 221
Newland, brass at . . . 44
  ,, lost brass at . . 216
Niblett, J. D. T. . 13, 130, 217
Nicholls, Thomas . . . 95
Nicolas's Ordinances . . 16
Northleach, brasses at, 19, 48, 54, 87, 89, 105, 135, 139
  ,, lost brass at . 216
Norwoodd, arms of . 182, 184
  ,, William—Elizabeth 181
Norys, Hughe—Johan . . 210
Notyngham, Sir William . 69
  ,, William—Christina 68
Nun 112

OLVESTON, brass at . . 106
Onslow 221

INDEX

PAGGE, Robert—Margaret . . 39
Painswick, lost brass at . . 216
Palimpsest brass . . . 58
Paris, headdress . . . 166
Parsons, arms of . . . 76
„ Ralph . . . 75
Parry, arms of . . . 175
„ Elizabeth . . . 172
Porter, arms of . . . 130
„ Arthur—Alys . . 130
„ Fredeswid and Mary . 130
„ Roger . . . 129
Powlett, arms of . . . 194
„ Nicholas—Margaret . 194
Prattell, arms of . . . 174
Prelatte, arms of . . . 64
„ William and wives . 62
Processional vestments . 58, 124
Purscell, arms of . . . 174
Pyrke, Rich.—Joan . . . 190

QUEDGELEY, brass at . . 130
Quinton, brass at . . . 30
„ lost brass at . . 217

RANDALL, Rev. R. . . 221
Raynsford, arms of . 174, 187,
„ Elizabeth . . 185
„ Hercules—Elizabeth 172
Relaid brasses 9, 28, 58, 103, 110,
119, 122, 124, 131, 149, 154,
165, 169, 172, 176, 179, 185
Removal of brasses . 165, 176
Restoration of brasses . . 149
Reticulated headdress . . 12
Rings . . 20, 31, 59, 92, 136
Rivière, Sir John de la . . 219
Robert, Duke of Gloucester . 214
Rodmarton, brass at . . 60
Roos, Ellenor . . . 9
„ Lord . . . 9
Rosary 73, 76, 82 (bis), 90, 92, 94,
96, 104, 120
Rous, Thomas—Margaret . 217
Rowdon, Elizabeth . . . 131
Rowley, arms of . . . 74
„ Thomas—Margaret . 73
Rudyn, John . . . 17
Russel, arms of . . . 27
„ Sir Morys—Isabel . 25
Russell, arms of . . 108, 109

SACRED LAMB . . 13, 157
Saint Anne . . . 14
Saint John Baptist . . 13, 157
Saint, see also Evangelistic Symbols, and Virgin
Sanderson, Captain J. . . 221
Savage, arms of . . . 189
„ Anne . . . 187
„ Richard . . . 196
Scocathe, arms of . . . 174
Scors, William—Agnes . . 48
Seals . . . 5, 6, 71, 72
Seman, Simon . . . 17

Semys, John—Margaret . . 149
Serche, Robert—Anne . . 105
Sevenhampton, brass at . . 95
Sewell, Katherine . . . 115
Shershal, arms of . . . 174
Shrewsbury, Earl of . . 9
Shroud brass . . . 111
Siddington St. Peter, lost brass 218
Sir, title of priests . . 75, 125
Skull . . . 140, 198
Somerset, Duke of . . . 9
Spencer, arms of . . . 193
„ Millicent . . 192
Spycer, Reginald and wives . 42
Stafford, arms of . . . 117
Staple of Calais, arms of 137, 138
Staples, Alexander and wives 180
Stole 60, 75
Surplice . . . 58, 124, 139
Symbols, see Evangelistic Symbols
Sword 3, 25, 34, 45, 62, 69, 100,
106, 129, 141, 160, 162, 172,
194

TABARD . 69, 108, 141, 158, 162
Taces 34, 45, 63, 69, 99, 106, 129,
160, 162,
Tame, arms of . 101, 144, 146
„ Sir Edmund and wives 141, 144
„ John—Alice . . 98
Tassels . . . 173, 194
Tatshall, arms of . . . 117
Tau-Crosses . 110, 126, 142
Taylour, John—Joan . . 89
Temple, W. . . . 10
"Terri" 13
Tewkesbury, lost brasses at . 218
Thornborough, Marion . . 21
Thornbury, brass at . . 169
Thorne, arms of . . . 167
„ Nicholas and wives . 165
Todenham, brass at . . 192
Tomkins, H. B. . . . 109
Tormarton, brass at . . 91
„ lost brass at . . 219
Townsend, arms of . . 54
Townsend, John . . . 52
Trinity, Holy, Symbol of 140, 141, 145
Twinyhoe, John . . . 109
Twynihoe, arms of . . . 102
Twynihow, Alice . . . 98
Twynyho, Joan . . . 64
Tyndall, arms of . . . 171
„ Thomas—Avice . 166
Tyringham, arms of . 144, 146
„ Elizabeth . . 141

UPPER SLAUGHTER, modern
brass at . . . 221

VASE 211
Virgin Mary . 14, 140, 220
Vowess 30

INDEX.

WADLEY, Rev. T. P. 10, 18, 24, 38, 75, 125, 177
Wakested, arms of . . . 174
Wallers, Messrs. . . . 221
Walwyn, arms of . . . 212
Wareing, T. . . . 223
Warren, Ann . . . 199
„ Gerard . . . 9
„ Margaret . . . 2
Warwick, arms of . . . 23
„ Earl of . . . 9
Welley, William—Alice . . 51
Westmoreland, Earl of . . 9
Wills
  Barstaple, Isabel . . 30
  „ John . . 30
  Beaupyne, Thomas . . 18
  Bennett, Agnes . . . 95
  „ John . . 95
  Brugge, Sir Gyles . . 212
  Busche, Johane . . 138
  Busshe, Thomas . . 138

  Combre, John . 97

  Denys, Sir Walter . 109
  Dixton, Richard . 37

  Fortey, John 57

  Gibbs, Henry . . . 198
  Gittins, William . . 176
  Grevell, Sir Edward . . 223
  Grevyll, Sir John . . 161
  Grevell, William . 23, 115
  Grevell, Dame Margaret . 223
  Greyndor, Dame Jane . 48

  Haliday, Edwarde . . 124
  „ Margery . 124
  Henshawe, William . . 223
  Hicheman, Water . . 127

  Jay, Joan . . 78
  Jaye, John . . 78

  Kingeston, Sir William . 217
  Knyvet, Sir William . 119
  Kyngston, Dame Mary . 217

  Langley, Edmond . . 218
  „ John . . 218
  „ Walter . . 218

Wills (continued)
  Marner, Philip . 178
  Mede, Philip . 72

  Nele, Thomas . 139

  Pagge, Robert . 42
  Porter, Roger . 130

  Raynsford, Charles . . 175
  Rouudon, Walter . 132
  Rowley, Thomas . 75
  Rowse, Thomas . 217

  Serche, Robert . . . 106
  Spycer, Joan . . . 44

  Tame, Sir Edmounde . 147
  „ Sir Edmunde . . 149
  „ Dame Elizabeth . 149
  „ John . . 103
  Tayliour, Johane . . 91
  Thorne, Nicholas . . 169
  „ Robert . . 168
  Townesend, John . . 54
  Twynyho, John . . 110
  Tyndall, Thomas . . 172

Weston-upon-Avon, brasses at 158, 162
Whittington, brass at . . 163
Widow 14, 27, 29, 31, 44, 48, 68, 91, 126, 131, 148, 154, 168, 175, 195
Wine Merchant . . 18, 222
Winterbourne, brass at . . 1
Witts, Rev. F. E. . . . 221
Woodstock, arms of . . . 117
Woolmen 20, 21, 39, 48, 52, 54, 87, 89, 135
Wormington, brass at . . 187
Wotton, Richard de . . 220
Wotton-under-Edge, brass at . 2
  „ lost brass at 220
Wylcotes, arms of . . . 174
Wyllycotes, arms of . . 174

Yate, brass at . . . 180

PRINTED AT
W. J. SOUTHWOOD AND CO.'S "DYNAMO" WORKS.
11, 12, 13, CATHERINE ST.,
EXETER.

www.ingramcontent.com/pod-product-compliance
Lightning Source LLC
Chambersburg PA
CBHW020807230426
43666CB00007B/894